T0339946

The Violence-Free
Workplace

The Violence-Free Workplace

A Blueprint for Utilizing Professional Security Officers to Prevent and Respond to Workplace Violence

Andrew Tufano

Taylor & Francis Group

A PRODUCTIVITY PRESS BOOK

First published 2021
by Routledge
600 Broken Sound Parkway #300, Boca Raton FL, 33487

and by Routledge
2 Park Square, Milton Park, Abingdon, Oxon, OX14 4RN

Routledge is an imprint of the Taylor & Francis Group, an informa business
© 2021 Andrew Tufano

The right of Andrew Tufano to be identified as the author of this work has been asserted by him in accordance with sections 77 and 78 of the Copyright, Designs and Patents Act 1988.

All rights reserved. No part of this book may be reprinted or reproduced or utilized in any form or by any electronic, mechanical, or other means, now known or hereafter invented, including photocopying and recording, or in any information storage or retrieval system, without permission in writing from the publishers.

Trademark notice: Product or corporate names may be trademarks or registered trademarks, and are used only for identification and explanation without intent to infringe.

Library of Congress Cataloging-in-Publication Data

A catalog record for this title has been requested

ISBN: 9780367613211 (hbk)
ISBN: 9780367559458 (pbk)
ISBN: 9781003105190 (ebk)

Typeset in ITC Garamond Std
by Cenveo® Publisher Services

Contents

Introduction

Inspiration

I've always been fascinated by the way people dealt with interpersonal conflict in a workplace setting. As I grew up in a law enforcement family, my father, brother (both now retired law enforcement officers), and I had many conversations about violence and how first responders dealt with conflict (I now continue these conversations with my law enforcement officer son). Our early conversations focused on law enforcement officers who seemingly used excessive physical force to subdue resistant suspects and came under scrutiny, whereas other talks involved law enforcement officers who used inadequate levels of force and paid for it with their lives.[1] (The murder of Deputy Dinkheller in 1998 motivated me to investigate the social processes that cause some to believe that violent behaviors can be neutralized using nonviolent means.)

Often the officers involved in these conflicts were harshly criticized by the public and their agencies; some were disciplined, fired, and others prosecuted. These discussions made it clear that first responders have an extremely difficult job deciding the best strategy for managing and resolving interpersonal conflict when facing highly fluid and intense circumstances. Later in our lives, as the three of us transitioned into the private security market (while my son transitioned from the security field to

---

[1] On January 16, 1998, Deputy Kyle Dinkheller of the Laurens County Sheriff's Office was shot and killed after conducting a traffic stop on a rural road about six miles north of Dublin, Georgia. Dinkheller attempted to gain control of a violent, mentally deranged suspect using verbal tactics. But when he finally transitioned to lethal force, it failed to stop the suspect, and he was killed. The incident was captured on Deputy Dinkheller's patrol car video system. Fifteen years after his death the suspect was put to death on January 13, 2015.

law enforcement), all of us continued to discuss our own unique workplace conflict challenges.

Although there are great distinctions between the law enforcement community and the private security industry, these two sectors have at least one thing in common: Their personal and corporate success depends on their ability to safely process interpersonal conflict and violence.

Solving the Problem

Statistics about workplace violence are often confusing and difficult to reconcile due to the different criteria and sampling methodologies used by the various investigating agencies. Workplace violence impacts an organization's two most valuable human assets: its employees and its consumers. According to the Bureau of Labor Statistics in 2017, 18,400 workers in the private industry experienced trauma from nonfatal workplace violence, requiring time off from work. Of those victims who experienced trauma from workplace violence:

- 70% were female,
- 67% were aged 25–54,
- 71% worked in the healthcare and social assistance industries[2]
- 18% required 31 or more days away from work to recover, and
- 25% involved 3–5 days away from work.

Additionally, in 2017, 458 U.S. workers died as a result of workplace homicides. Of those victims who died from workplace violence[3]:

- 82% were male,
- 48% were white,
- 64% were aged 25–54,
- 21% were murdered working in sales and related occupations, and
- 19% were murdered performing protective services.[4]

---

[2] RNs/LPNs make up majority of injured personnel.

[3] https://www.cdc.gov/niosh/topics/violence/fastfacts.html.

[4] According to the 2017 BLS "Fatal Occupational Injuries by Occupations" report, 44 law enforcement officers were killed in 2017 during "assault and violent acts" (down from the previous year of 66 fatalities), whereas 74 security officers were killed in the same category. This is the most current BLS data. According to "Officer Down Memorial Page," 131 law enforcement officers died in 2019.

Workplace violence statistics reveal stark gender distinctions; although rare, men are much more likely to be murdered at work than women, while women represent most of the thousands of nonfatal workplace assaults that take place every year. Physical assaults occurring in a healthcare setting make up the majority of nonfatal physical assaults, and nurses experience work-related violence at the highest rate of all types of healthcare workers (22 per 1000 workers).[5] Women are more likely to be employed in professions where they are face-to-face with consumers, and when consumers act out, these frontline employees are most often the victims of verbal attacks, bullying, taunting, and physical violence.

I'm driven by my passion for people who simply want to go to work, shop, study, seek care, and socialize with others, without having to worry about their safety. To ensure that these environments are safe and no one else is injured or killed, organizations need a responsible workplace violence prevention plan that involves employing professional security officers who are capable of managing interpersonal workplace conflict, and when necessary, neutralizing violent behaviors.[6] My 30 years of experience at various professional levels of organizational safety has convinced me that it's impossible to provide the level of protection that most organization's need (and the law requires) without employing a team of visually obvious, specially trained and equipped, professional security officers.[7]

When discussing workplace violence, the concepts, conflict, and violence are often conflated, making it difficult to clearly identify the problem and then apply the most effective solution. This is partially the result of government agencies and professional organizations defining (or redefining) these two concepts and through natural evolutionary, social processes that affect how words and ideas are understood over time.[8] However, for our discussion, we delineate workplace conflict from workplace violence and the different strategies required to process them. Workplace conflict involves passive–aggressive, nonviolent behaviors and is typically easy to manage

---

[5] The 2018 National Crime Victimization Survey, Bureau of Justice Statistics Special Report, U.S. Department of Justice, Office of Justice Program. www.bjs.gov.

[6] Safety is both a subject feeling and a quantifiable concept. An effective workplace violence prevention plan must respond to both aspects to create a safe workplace.

[7] Involving plain clothes security personnel in this team effort provides an additional layer of protection.

[8] There are various motivations, and possible advantages/disadvantages for defining (or redefining) a concept broadly or narrowly.

and deescalate, while workplace violence involves directly aggressive and/ or violent behaviors and requires different strategies to resolve. Typically, there is a *bridge* between these two types of behaviors; workplace violence is often the result of interpersonal conflict escalating, but not always. Sometimes deviant individuals go to a place of business with the intent of hurting or killing people. Therefore, organizations need contingencies to process both workplace conflict and violence.

It's true that workplace conflict and violence can occur when employees and consumers interact or between two employees, and organizations need to address both concerns. Each unique setting, such as education, healthcare, or retail, has a set of related interactants that fall under the heading of workplace violence. But the focus of our book is on face-to-face customer service, employee/consumer conflict. As an example, the National Institute for Occupational Safety and Health, or NIOSH, delineates four types of violence based on relationship type that occur in a *healthcare* setting:

Type I: The perpetrator has criminal intent and has no relationship to the business or its employees.

Type II: A customer, client, or patient becomes violent when receiving care or services.

Type III: Employee-to-employee violence.

Type IV: Personal relationship violence.

Using the NIOSH designation, our focus would be on type II interactions. Although workplace behaviors such as bullying, harassment, and intimidation, involving only employees, are serious organizational concerns and often thought of as workplace violence, the greater organizational concern is protecting employees and consumers from physical harm. No matter the setting, whenever and wherever people meet to work or to conduct commerce there's the potential that violence will harm people and disrupt an organization's ability to deliver their products or services and maintain financial viability.

Assumptions about Safety

I continue to be perplexed by senior corporate managers who believe it's possible to maintain high levels of organizational safety without employing professional, uniformed security officers who are highly competent and have access to a full range of protective tactics and tools. Unfortunately, many organizations employ untrained security *guards* whose primary job is observing and reporting potential criminal activity or safety concerns but are not trained or authorized to physically intervene to protect people.

History, experience, and behavioral science can attest to the fact that to safely process workplace conflict and violence and protect employees, consumers, visitors, and others from harm that security officers need access to an array of personal and professional resources beyond simply observing and reporting unsafe or unlawful behavior.[9]

Communicative Solutions

My personal frustrations of trying to find the optimum approach for processing interpersonal workplace conflict and violence led me to earn a graduate degree in communication. I was assured by many intelligent people that *talk* was the solution, and a useful substitution, for physical strategies. This theory suggested that with the right quantity and quality of communication, uncooperative or dangerous individuals could be persuaded, without the need to use physical force, to correct their behavior. The underlying premise of this communicative solution posits that if security officers (the communicators) were just more patient, empathetic, understanding, and also said the right things, uncooperative subjects would peacefully submit to those in authority. Critical field conflict outcomes, they argue, are primarily the result of misapplied communication tactics and a lack of impulse control on the security officer's part, which in turn exacerbates (or creates) interpersonal resistance leading to physical altercations. There is some truth to this perspective, but communicative solutions only work up to a point.

Some believe that security officer self-discipline is a key to helping uncooperative or dangerous subjects understand the error of their ways, thus creating in them the requisite motivation for a change in behavior. True, communication is a useful strategy for managing conflict. However, as

---

[9] Throughout the book we use the term *consumer* as a general term to account for any non-employee who's involved in face-to-face commerce with an organization. Additionally, we use the term *others* to include persons who also frequent the organization but may or may not have any legitimate business purpose for being on an owner's property.

interpersonal conflict escalates, communication tactics become less effective, or inappropriate, and their continued use may exacerbate interpersonal tension, enable violent behaviors, and create a false sense of security and safety for employees, consumers, or visitors.

History has taught us that some individuals cannot be reasoned with and need to be physically restrained to keep from harming people. There is and always will be a percentage of interpersonal workplace conflict that can't be peacefully resolved with just talk. Unfortunately, some senior corporate managers don't see the *business* value of requiring their security officers to physically intervene to resolve workplace conflict but instead rely on law enforcement officers.

The Reality of Violence

> The bravest are surely those who have the clearest vision of what is before them, glory and danger alike, and yet notwithstanding, go out to meet it.—Thucydides

The good news is that most people don't have a lot of experience with violence. But for senior corporate managers who only know violence as an abstract concept and try to create an effective workplace violence protection plan involving uniformed security officers, their plan and response are often incompatible. It takes a unique personality type that can be emphatic and understanding when dealing with people in crisis, be forthright, strong, and brave when needing to neutralize life-threatening behaviors, and also help their organization sell or provide its products and services. The truth is that we need people who *choose* to stand between victims and the *strong men*. Since law enforcement officers can't be there when dangerous individuals decide to take advantage of employees, consumers, and those who frequent an organization's place of business, we need capable security officers to be our protectors. This is not a criticism of law enforcement officers—they can't be everywhere. One of the primary advantages of employing professional security officers to protect people is, "they're here—the police aren't!" Law enforcement officers typically respond *after* the problem escalates, while security officers are *on-site* to intervene to keep dangerous behaviors from escalating to violence.

Conflict and Protection

Over the years of studying the ongoing battles between dangerous and violent individuals and private security officers, I've learned the *ugly truth* that many are still uncomfortable acknowledging: No risk-free or forceless policies can protect people from workplace violence. If an organization wants to create the safest workplace possible, they *must* employ uniformed security officers as a *part* of their overall workplace violence prevention plan and accept that to protect people security personnel will *need to* intervene and sometimes initiate physical contact with dangerous behaviors, and they will get hurt, and, unfortunately, the good guys may, too.

Today, every business is faced with the inevitability, unavoidability, and unpredictability of workplace conflict, and occasionally, violence. Unfortunately, when interpersonal conflict is not properly managed, it creates unsafe environments, physical injuries, property loss and damage, increased legal and civil liabilities, and it tarnishes an organization's reputation. The essential point is that failure to effectively manage workplace conflict and resolve violence impedes an organization's ability to do the two most important things it does: Serve its consumers and maintain financial stability. Although a significant quantity of workplace violence results from a poorly managed conflict that escalates to violence, we also realize that occasionally people will simply show up at an organization with the intent to steal property and/or hurt people, and one method for stopping them (or limiting their impact) is to involve the organization's security officers to provide *limited* personal protection until law enforcement officers respond. However, our focus will not be on these kinds of violence.[10]

Invention

My diverse life experiences as both an operator and intellect have allowed me to test and prove many of the protective principles and solutions to workplace violence that I share in this book. As the owner/operator of a security and consulting organization, who's employed uniformed security

---

[10] Most organizations don't employ armed private security officers to provide protection from armed attacks such as robberies or active shooters; more should. However, professionally trained security personnel are a huge asset in the event of a random act of lethal violence.

officers that were assigned to our clients in various educational, healthcare, and retail settings; from high crime ("you'd be scared to shop there") retail environments, to low crime, extremely pleasant ("I want to live there") college campuses, and many other settings in between, I live these ideas. On the one hand, as an intellect/professor, I've learned important lessons from dialoguing with students, business professionals, and security leaders, and analyzing and testing their various perspectives on organizational safety. The totality of my formal education and experiences over the past 30 years has helped me to develop a useful blueprint for organizations who need to employ private security officers as part of their overall workplace violence prevention plan.

There are several driving forces behind my need to write this book. First, it's plainly obvious that workplace conflict and violence is more prevalent today than ever, and if it's not managed and resolved effectively using security personnel, it creates a myriad of personal and business problems. Moreover, failure to create a safe workplace has an *exponential* or force multiplier effect on a business's bottom line: people who are afraid to work or consume products or services, also tell other people, who then tell other people, so on and so forth.[11]

First, most of the workplace violence prevention literature published today doesn't approach organizational safety from a business perspective. I've spent a great deal of my life as an entrepreneur, business owner, protection specialist, and employed in the retail sector, where I've learned the two *big things* that successful private organizations must do to create safe workplaces: (1) sell their products and/or provide services, while competing in their unique market *and* (2) protect their employees and consumers without interfering with their ability to sell their products and/or provide services, while competing in their unique market. It's much easier to do one (or one, better) of these. But doing both well takes juggling multiple business priorities to find the proper balance between protection, service, freedom, and control, while remaining flexible enough to make *minor* adjustments when circumstances demand it. For instance, military bases have retail spaces where they sell products and services and are *extremely* safe because they emphasize control and

---

[11] Nextiva.com cites a Harris Interactive Poll that determined report that 89% of consumers have switched to doing business with a competitor following a poor customer experience. https://www.nextiva.com/blog/customer-service-statistics.html.

protection. However, most private, free-market organizations succeed by emphasizing freedom and service. Similarly, the use of public law enforcement principles to protect people in a private, free-market context *can't* produce the proper balance of service, freedom, and control. Success in law enforcement and military context can be achieved *without* focusing on freedom and service, but not in a private business context.[12] Control and protection are easy. Service and freedom are easy. But aligning these four values successfully in private, free-market commerce is a complex undertaking.

Second, the failure to prevent and respond to workplace violence can result in an organization getting sued civilly, which not only creates expenses due to punitive and compensatory costs but also increases liability for insurance protection and workers' compensation costs and impacts financial viability and reputation. Failure to prevent and respond to workplace violence can result in an organization being perceived as unsafe by consumers (even by people who don't witness it but are told about an incident!), which results in a loss in sales and revenue and impacts financial viability and reputations, and by employees, which makes it more difficult to hire and retain workers. Failure to prevent and respond to workplace violence can result in OSHA violations and possible civil and criminal charges, effect regulatory accreditations and certifications, and impact financial viability and reputation. Failure to prevent and respond to workplace violence can result in victims of violence having to endure long-lasting physical and emotional injuries which also impacts the employee's families, friends and their way of life, and impacts financial viability and reputation. There's a lot riding on the line to not get it right.

Third, I noticed there were no unifying principles on how to best utilize uniformed security personnel to prevent workplace violence. In fact, some organizations use contract security personnel, while others employ their own proprietary security officers. Some security personnel resemble customer service agents, while others resemble law

---

[12] We're not making an argument that in these contexts service and freedom is not important. Rather, the key point is about the focus and degree of attention given to these values in those contexts. For instance, if a citizen interacts with a law enforcement officer and doesn't like the way they are being talked to, they can't decide to "take their business elsewhere." Likewise, if it takes two hours to get on one word to a military base (or off it!) to shop at the PX, no one is going to apologize for the delay.

enforcement officers. Additionally, there is a wide range of duties and responsibilities assigned to these security officers that may or may not create real value. On the one hand, most organizations know that they need uniformed security officers, but on the other hand, they're not sure how best to utilize them. This has led to many failed experiments in organizational safety. There are clearly no unifying principles, processes, or standards that are uniformly used by organizations that employ uniformed security personnel to prevent or respond to workplace conflict and violence.

Finally, I noticed that many of the proposed solutions to workplace violence don't address the *business* realities of processing violence in a free market. As a long-term entrepreneur, I've had to wrestle with these principles and how to integrate them into a realistic *business-focused* workplace violence prevention plan. Currently, most organizational safety programs are influenced by former, retired, and current law enforcement officers, with little or no business experience, who use public law enforcement philosophies and methods that are often incompatible with private, free-market business principles. In short, since private non-sworn security officers aren't police officers and the organization's security department isn't a *police* department, a law enforcement approach to organizational safety naturally impedes sales and customer service, even if it provides a high degree of organizational safety.

The Intended Message of Our Book

The truth is, we spend a significant amount of time discussing public law enforcement principles, practices, and personnel and contrasting them with private, free-market principles, practices, and personnel. A key to understanding (and appreciating!) these distinctions is our focus on the *context* and not the individuals. To be clear, we admire and appreciate law enforcement officers and military personnel (former and current). Our society depends on these public heroes to keep us safe. Some of my family, my best friends, and my employees have worked, or work, in both law enforcement and military contexts. However, one of the reasons that private organizations continue to struggle to create both safe *and* financially viable workplaces is because they hire former law enforcement personnel, who over the years, have attempted to apply public law enforcement community safety philosophies and practices (what they know) to a private, free-market, competitive business market that are incompatible (what they don't know). This is *not* a criticism of the former law enforcement individuals; it's really a criticism of senior organizational managers who've conflated these distinct vocations based on superficial similarities. Over time, they've been convinced that individuals who had success in creating safe *public* neighborhoods would be able to transfer their success to a *private* organizational context. Before dismissing my thesis, consider the inverse. Would a public law enforcement agency create the kinds of generalized community safety they currently achieve if they used private, free-market, competitive business principles and hired people who have never actually worked in it to lead and run their agency?[13] To be clear, law enforcement experience is not a disqualifying characteristic for security leadership. However, organizations should not hire anyone to head their security department without prior private, free-market, organizational safety leadership experience.[14]

Our goal is to improve the ability of private, free-market organizations to create the safest and best places to work while engaged in commerce and employing professional security officers plays an important role in that success. This master plan involves the efforts of both experts, the private security officers on the ground, who are (or should be) experts at developing and maintain relationships and *talking with* people to keep interpersonal workplace conflict from escalating,[15] and if/when conflict escalates to violence, the responding law enforcement officers, who are experts at processing violent behaviors. Law enforcement personnel are experts at processing criminal behaviors and private security personnel are experts (or should be!) at processing noncriminal behaviors; they don't necessarily share both expertise. To really make a difference in these organizations, preventing and responding to workplace violence, we need to synchronize our efforts and work together which requires being honest about how these vastly different contexts, the free market and publicly financed enterprises, impact the

---

[13] Civilian police oversight boards often suffer the same problem when they try to apply free market protective principles to law enforcement tactics.

[14] Ideally, they should also have experience in the same industry they're being hired for, such as education, healthcare, or retail.

[15] I realize they're not experts yet. Keep reading!

ability of these respective experts to succeed at their jobs and protect people. The flaw here is clearly not the people, these are some of the finest individuals who protect our neighborhoods and the organization's we frequent.

Our Approach

The Violence-Free Workplace: A Blueprint for Utilizing Professional Security Officers to Prevent and Respond to Workplace Violence is both a persuasive essay and a practical guide for helping organizations that utilize uniformed security officers (or need to) as a part of their workplace violence prevention plan, to map out the necessary organizational safety principles, processes, personnel, and standards needed to prevent and respond to workplace violence, maintain safe workplaces, protect people, and remain financially viable. To be clear, this text is *not* a security operations manual and won't delve into many important security topics and procedures. For organizations seeking guidance on security operations, there are many excellent resources available through ASIS International, International Association for Healthcare Security and Safety (IAHSS), International Foundation for Protective Officers (IFPO), and The National Retail Federation (NRF).

I wrote this book to support organizations that employ private uniformed security officers or for those who recognize the benefit of utilizing professional security personnel to improve workplace safety. However, the principles, processes, personnel, and standards we recommend will strengthen any organizational safety program, such as ad hoc security programs, and those using contract security personnel.

Each chapter starts by identifying a problem that impacts an organization's ability to effectively employ private, uniformed, security officers to prevent and respond to workplace violence. We detail possible causes and then end each chapter with recommendations to address the problem. Most of my readers will easily identify with the problems. However, some may not agree with the causes that we identify and link to those problems. One possibility is that poor organizational leadership is responsible for many of the deficiencies we've noted; it's hard to discuss solutions without people taking the criticisms personally. However, we hope that our readers will appreciate our directness because we think there should be (or is) an urgency to disseminate these ideas, and discuss, debate, digest, and implement them. These ideas have a direct effect on the lives and livelihoods of real people.

The Trust Tautology

After deciding to write this book, I had a difficult time deciding in what order to present my ideas. A phrase that I've heard many times by nonsecurity senior corporate managers, and unfortunately even from some security directors/managers, "I don't trust them," kept popping into my mind and was interfering with my ability to organize my thoughts. So, should we begin this journey on how to improve workplace safety starting with trust or by discussing principles, processes, personnel, and standards? The nagging and recurring lack of trust theme, or as I call it, "The Trust Tautology," gets right to the heart of the matter. Here's how it works: Security personnel do something or fail to do something that seems obvious to everyone as being wrong.[16] Senior corporate managers use the incident to generalize about their security personnel as being *untrustworthy*. Too often judgment ends there, and no additional critical processing or organizational self-reflection takes place, assumptions harden, and *lack of trust* (or value) becomes an embedded organizational axiom. However, another way to determine if an organization's security personnel are *trustworthy* is to ask a few questions about the *organization's* trustworthiness with questions such as:

- Do they have effective leadership and appropriate supervisory controls in place?
- Is the officer's supervisor competently trained to lead and manage?
- Did the officer have to meet and maintain professional standards and competencies before/after being hired?
- Is there an ongoing and continuous security officer training program to maintain proficiencies?
- Are effective written processes, policies, and procedures in place?
- Are the officer's job duties clearly detailed and up-to-date?

---

[16] Failed expectations, regardless of whether they're very clearly articulated, are responsible for assumptions about behavior.

- Was the officer hired without having to demonstrate they can meet reliable competency standards?
- Does the organization adequately pay and benefit the officer?
- Does the organizagtion demonstrate through practical methods of *care and concern* that they appreciate the officer?
- Do employees generally demonstrate respect for the officer?

They Can't Be Trusted

Organizations that can answer these questions in the affirmative typically trust their security personnel. I'm convinced that when organizations focus on principles, processes, personnel, and standards that *trust* (and many other positive attributes) is a natural byproduct.

Organizational Safety: New and Improved

The solution to these organizational safety challenges involves significant culture change and a paradigm shift from a 20th century *security* mindset to a 21st century *protective* mindset. Security strategies that may have worked in the past are not applicable in today's highly competitive information and service economy. Consumers have lots of options, including purchasing products and services online, and completely avoiding face-to-face interaction with an organization's employees. Similarity, consumers can form opinions about service personnel, products, and even safety without ever setting foot on an organization's property. Consumers who choose to interact in person with an organization seek an *experience* not just a transaction and need to be cherished and protected.

This improved approach to organizational safety will require a serious commitment from top-level nonsecurity organizational leadership who hold power and the purse. Organizations that decide to follow our recommendations will face some initial resistance and practical challenges; change is never easy. In fact, the main reason that very few organizations have started down this path is not necessarily because they haven't thought about these ideas; rather, it's because of the very nature of diagnosing and solving a problem that never sleeps. It's like the effort required to repair a merry-go-round that never stops turning; the fixes are much more challenging because they need to be applied while it's in motion![17] (In some organizational contexts commerce never stops. But even in environments that close during nonbusiness hours, although they may not have to worry about protecting their employees around the clock, they still need systems in place to protect their assets.)

It's true that many of the ideas presented here may at first glance seem counterintuitive because "they've always been done that way" and they haven't been exposed to *scrutiny* outside of the law enforcement community.[18] We are making a persuasive (and somewhat controversial) case that to build an effective workplace violence prevention program, the underlying organizational safety principles used and the personnel employed for the task of managing conflict and resolving violence must operate using private, free-market business principles, processes, and standards. Likewise, personnel hired need to have the right personality and temperament to process the power inequities and ambiguities that naturally occur when delivering or selling services or products in a competitive free market. The typical security officer profile that *may* have had success in the past has become obsolete for meeting today's organizational safety challenges.

The Benefits of Employing Professional Security Officers as a Component of an Organization's Workplace Violence Prevention Plan

In short, professional security officers through their presence and protective duties help create a safer place for employees to work and ensure a positive customer service experience. Since safety is both perceptual and quantifiable, an environment that *feels* safe may not be quantifiably safe; a *quantifiably* safe environment may not feel safe. In fact, if consumers *feel* an environment is unsafe, it's virtually impossible to convince them otherwise with safety stats alone. Professional security officers provide a visible assurance to employees and customers, on both an emotional and physical

---

[17] One possible method is finding "place holders" to temporarily take over the department's leadership responsibilities while the "repairs" are being completed. This can be accomplished by contracting with a reliable security vender. See our recommendations and implementation systems.

[18] In fact, many of the leading security consultants used by organizations to conduct risk and vulnerability assessments and recommend ways to improve workplace safety are former law enforcement officers who have little or no business or private market organizational safety experience.

level, "that it's safe here." The key for successful organizations is creating an environment that is both perceptually and quantifiably safe and uniformed security officers play an important role in the creation of both.

COVID-19 Challenges

Moreover, although I started writing this book long before the COVID-19 pandemic and isolation, the implications of these ideas are now understood in a different light. A confluence of law enforcement being less available due to officers being sick and some possibly being furloughed due to budget cuts, reductions in police patrols, more prisoners being released from jail and no bail requirements, coupled with a generalized sense of personal despair and desperation, due to skyrocketing unemployment, increases in homelessness, and the emotional and psychological implications of people being isolated from their social safety nets, naturally will lead to dysfunctional relationships, increased interpersonal conflict, and a greater likelihood that people will resort to physical means to solve interpersonal problems, which creates additional pressures for an organization and will require organizations to rely more than ever on professional security personnel.[19]

Our Audience

Any organization that employs private uniformed security officers (or needs to) as a component of their overall workplace violence prevention strategy will benefit from our recommendations. But since hospitals, schools, and retail organizations have a long history of conflict and violence, and employing security officers in public spaces, these industries may benefit most from our recommendations. Each of these industries has vulnerable populations: Hospitals need to protect their employees and patients, schools need to protect their administrators, teachers, and students, and retail stores need to protect their employees and consumers. However, since the money

---

[19] Although the effects of COVID-19 pandemic are dynamic and evolving, and no one can predict with great certainty how it will affect organizations, it seems reasonable to conclude that disruptions in people's lives will impact employees and consumers and create unprecedented levels of interpersonal conflict to be worked out at the organizational level.

needed to fund an organization's security department, and the authority to perform the duties necessary for preventing and responding to workplace violence protection, come from the top of the organizational pyramid, and since the people who lead these efforts are in senior management, we write to two primary audiences:

1. Senior nonsecurity management who are directly or indirectly responsible for, or have direct influence or oversight over, their organization's security posture, security department, and workplace violence prevention programs.
2. The dedicated, honorable, and frustrated security managers/directors who are on the front lines, managing their security departments and leading their security officers, who regularly interact with uncooperative, dangerous, and violent individuals to protect their organizations, employees, consumers, and visitors and who are not always appreciated. Thank you!

Acknowledgments

No one works alone or accomplishes anything of real value without the significant support of others. I would like to thank several people who directly or indirectly assisted in this work.

First, I want to thank my wife Cindy, who has continued to reassure me that the ideas that I was writing about were important and needed to be heard.

Next, I need to thank three friends, Scott Martin, Charles Chase, and Henrie Watkins. They have spent hundreds of hours brainstorming with me about the challenges that the security industry faces and ways to help improve it. Scott is a pioneer in the healthcare security industry (now retired) and has contributed more to this project and my life than he could ever know. Charles, a U.S. Marine Officer (Retired), and current healthcare Security Director, is a technical expert *par none*. Henrie, an entrepreneur, and emergency management executive, is an expert at spotting unrealized talent in people and coaxing it out.

Additionally, I am grateful to countless other unnamed security professionals, law enforcement officers, and friends who have been sounding boards for many of my ideas and have challenged me to think more deeply about them.

Finally, I would like to thank my father for paving the way. As a retired law enforcement officer, he eventually became a V.P. of Loss Prevention and Security for a Fortune 500 organization before his final, final retirement. In this case the apple fell close to the tree!

Either write something worth reading or do something worth writing.

—Ben Franklin
My attempt!

About the Author

Andrew Tufano has worked in the security industry since 1990. He holds a master's degree in Communication from California State University at Fullerton. Over the past 30 years, Andrew has been employed in various senior security positions, including as a regional manager and director. He operates a contract security company and trains and consults with clients in the healthcare, education, and retail sectors. Andrew has created several businesses including Goldstar Security LLC, Goldstar Training, and is the Executive Director and founding member of the "Consortium for Professional Security Officer Standards and Training" (PSOST). He is an industry-recognized subject matter expert in private person use-force and workplace conflict and is a prolific writer and speaker on security-related issues. Andrew has written articles for security publications and has also been a keynote speaker at IAHSS and ASIS events. He is currently an adjunct professor and experienced college educator at a public southern California college.

He is available to present these materials for in-person or remote seminars, training sessions, or conferences. He can be reached at andy@goldstartraining.org.

About the Author

Chapter 1

Introduction

Problem

Organizations build their workplace violence prevention programs on incompatible public safety principles.

Introduction

Successful organizations perform many important tasks, but few are more important than "serving and protecting" their employees, consumers, and visitors. An organization's ability to successfully manage workplace conflict and resolve violence is a key to an organization's success. The truth is, regardless of how great an organization's product or service, it's impossible to compete in any *face-to-face* market if employees, consumers, and visitors are at risk.

Process

Even though the protection of employees, consumers, and others is the most important security-related task that organizations perform, it's not the only risk they need to prepare, plan, and respond to. The challenges facing today's businesses are much different than they were 30, 20, or even 10 years ago and require a proactive and nimble security/safety posture to address a myriad of contemporary issues like access control, active shooters, bomb threats, contraband, cyber-security, espionage, homelessness, internal theft, labor strikes, medical/health epidemics, mental health, natural disasters, public relations, reputation protection, and substance abuse, to name just a few. To minimize risks associated with these vulnerabilities, security personnel may or may not need to be directly involved; however, all *experts* should be. But to protect employees, consumers, and others from physical harm, organizations need to assign *protection specialists*, or professional security officers, to the task.

Organizations continue to experiment with various organizational safety philosophies and workplace violence prevention strategies. Many businesses have created reasonably safe workplaces but are still plagued with nagging and recurring safety concerns and are one violent incident away from organizational disaster. Poorly managed violent encounters create unsafe conditions and compromise an organization's goodwill and reputation. Even organizations that have successfully performed many of these required safety tasks have overlooked, perhaps, their most important and necessary organizational concern:

> How to best utilize professionally trained security officers to minimize organizational risk associated with preventing people from harming employees, consumers, and others who frequent their business.

Workplace Violence Prevention Plans

To reduce violence in the workplace, organizations need to have a plan to address workplace conflict and violence. People play the biggest role in managing interpersonal conflict and keeping conflict from escalating to workplace violence. A reliable Workplace Violence Prevention Plan includes:

1. Policies that require all workers who interact with consumers to receive education, training, and the opportunity to discuss questions and answers with a person knowledgeable about an organization's workplace violence prevention plan.
2. Training on how to recognize potential for violence and when and how to seek assistance to prevent or respond to violence.
3. Advanced verbal de-escalation and protective training for officers who regularly deal with workplace conflict.

4. Employee resources for coping with incidents of violence, including but not limited to critical incident stress debriefing and an employee assistance program (debriefing).
5. Information on how to report violent incidents to law enforcement (documentation).
6. A process for responding to and investigating violent incidents.
7. A system for documenting and reporting acts of violence.
8. Complete and total support from senior leadership.

The Occupational Safety and Health Administration, better known by its acronym OSHA, provides a good overview of workplace violence that could be used as a guide to develop a reliable workplace violence prevention plan for any organization.[1]

Workplace Violence Prevention and Security Officers

Although there are many other important safety/security-related questions that should be asked and solutions proposed, this book focuses on the role and responsibilities that security officers play in managing and resolving interpersonal conflict, protecting people, and maintaining violence-free workplaces.

Organizations—or more rightly, senior corporate managers—have legal, ethical, and pragmatic reasons for creating violence-free environments for the people who frequent their organizations' physical boundaries. However, they don't often focus on them until their position or status in the organization is threatened, or a critical incident occurs. Although there are various organizational processes and activities that influence the formation of violence-free environments, security officers play a powerful role in deterring conflict and responding to behaviors that endanger employees, consumers, visitors, or others. However, even organizations that employ uniformed security officers still struggle to integrate their activities into their workplace violence prevention plan. Unfortunately, security officers are rarely used to their fullest potential because they're usually untrained, constrained, poorly led, and not mission focused.

The truth is that it's impossible to mitigate the effects of workplace violence unless trained, professional security officers are mission focused

---

[1] https://www.osha.gov/SLTC/workplaceviolence/

and *required* to intervene during conflicted consumer/employee interactions. Although some argue that intervention may increase organizational risk, the total liabilities associated with "doing nothing" are greater than acting. When security officers take deliberate action to protect individuals from harm, it's ethically, legally, and socially easier to defend their actions than their inaction.

Even organizations that allow their security officers the option of using protective action[2] to mitigate the effects of workplace violence often fail to provide supervisory oversight and personal accountability. When attempts to resolve workplace violence go badly, organizations often use these incidents as proof that the risks associated with intervention are too high. In fact, senior corporate managers often cite "elevated risk" as the reason for prohibiting their security officers to intervene or use certain protective tactics and tools. However, when protective action is used within a comprehensive workplace, violence prevention program risk is mitigated to acceptable levels.

Evaluating Risk

It's easy for corporate human resource managers, risk managers, and corporate attorneys to use negative field conflict outcomes as representative examples to affirm their worst suspicions for allowing security officers to be proactive. For years, a myth has existed (an unexamined assumption) that giving security officers broad authority, including the use of protective force to intervene during intense interpersonal conflict, is always too great an organizational risk. (These conclusions may be true for basic, untrained security guards but not for professionally trained security officers.) In fact, sometimes senior corporate managers use these perceived (or hypothetical) risks to justify outright prohibitions for the use of protective action, restrictive protective force limits, and restrictions on the type or kind of protective tools that security officers are authorized to carry. However, when professional security officers meet reliable standards, are supervised, trained, and authorized to use a full spectrum of conflict resolution strategies, the results of

---

[2] We use the term protective force throughout our text as a substitute phrase for the law enforcement term, "use-of-force."

their interactions, although imperfect,[3] significantly minimize injuries to personnel and resistant combatants.

Since organizations are legally and socially required to maintain violence-free environments that provide a reasonable level of *due care* for anyone that frequents their organization, including employees, consumers, visitors, and others, the consequences for failing to successfully process workplace conflict are potential legal, financial, and social catastrophes.

The Los Angeles Dodgers found out the hard way. Attorneys for Brian Stow, a fan who was severely beaten at Dodger Stadium in April 2011, report that Stow's medical bills would exceed $50 million! Stow's attorneys filed a lawsuit asking for "punitive damages on top of compensation for the family's losses, contending that … a lack of security constitutes malice, oppression and/or a conscious disregard of the rights and security of Stow" (Kim, 2011). Failing to provide a responsible level of due care may end up costing the LA Dodgers more than $100 million.

Incomprehensibly, on March 30, 2019, another baseball fan, Rafel Reyna, was assaulted in the parking lot of the LA Dodgers stadium and was seriously injured. He filed a lawsuit against the LA Dodgers for failing to provide adequate security, claiming negligence, premises liability, and intentional infliction of emotional distress, which led to a traumatic brain injury (Fenno, 2020).[4]

A comprehensive workplace violence prevention system should support an organization's core organizational safety priorities, such as:

1. Establishing organizational standards for acceptable behavior.[5]
2. Enacting legal, administrative, and social processes to process safety violators.
3. Maintaining consistency in the application of consequences for safety violators.
4. Utilizing trained professional security officers who uphold the organization's safety standards and restrain violators from causing harm.

---

[3] Any time security personnel are involved in attempts to protect people from violence, it's impossible to guarantee that no one will be injured. Likewise, when people are being assaulted and security personnel are not involved there's a greater likelihood that victims of violence *will be* injured.

[4] Feno LA Times. 4.25.20. "Man beaten in Dodger Stadium parking lot files lawsuit against team."

[5] Known as the *code of conduct*.

People generally don't like being told that their behavior is potentially harmful or contrary to an established community standard, so organizations need professionally trained security officers who are *excellent* communicators. Whether contrarian behavior is inappropriate or criminal, organizations need personnel who can identify escalating behaviors and intervene to keep minor interpersonal conflict from escalating to violence.

Every organization has a "built-in" or default response to workplace conflict and violence that may or may not be effective at reducing interpersonal conflict or maintaining violence-free workplaces. This *default strategy* may involve simply ignoring or placating conflict or conflict makers until the disruption finally becomes so intolerable that someone calls the police. This *reactive* approach is ineffective and unreliable and ultimately creates serious safety concerns for organizational members.[6] There's too much at stake for employees, consumers, and visitors for organizations to not have a well-thought-out and systematic workplace violence prevention program in place.

Juxtapositions: Comparing and Contrasting

Throughout our book we juxtapose and compare various organizational and community safety principles, processes, and personnel types to help explain our preferences and recommendations for improving organizational safety. When people think about safety, they can't help but to think about the obvious subject matter experts, law enforcement officers. Similarly, it's impossible to discuss organizational or community safety without talking about law enforcement principles; or talk about policies on personal safety without talking about law enforcement tactics or tools; or even talk about security officers without talking about law enforcement officers. It's true that the local law enforcement department and its officers are an organization's most important external stakeholder because they are *experts* at processing criminal behaviors. But over time its philosophies and former officers have become embedded organizational *stakeholders*. But are law enforcement principles, processes, personnel, and standards best suited for the everyday

---

[6] The key to processing conflict is identifying escalating verbal and nonverbal tension before (proactively) it escalates to dysfunctional behaviors and nonphysical conflict management tactics become ineffective or inappropriate.

job of managing workplace conflict, resolving violence, and protecting people in private, free-market, business environment?

Definitions and Distinctions

Moreover, throughout our writings we use certain words and phrases and try to explain and describe our reasoning; some of these ideas may be new to our readers. Early on we identify these terminologies and provide some background and context for our deliberate language choices. Finally, we think a change in verbiage is an important component of culture change which is necessary to empower the paradigm shift we're proposing.

There are several reasons we use these specific words and phrases to describe our ideas. First, they are more precise and accurate for describing these organizational safety processes and the individuals that perform them. Second, we want to use language that clearly distinguishes *private*, free-market organizational safety principles from *public* law enforcement community safety philosophies and *private* security officers from *public* law enforcement officers, and untrained *basic* security guards/officers from *professionally* trained security officers.

Contract security guards/officers operate in a limited capacity based on their employee profile, background and training, and involve *observe and report* activities (noninterventionist) and are often hired to protect property.[7] A more recent trend is replacing proprietary (in-house) security personnel with contract security personnel. Depending on the contractor, the new personnel may or may not demonstrate a higher level of professionalism as the personnel they replace. But the primary reason organizations opt to replace their own employees with contract personnel is usually not to improve *performance*, it's to reduce their labor costs, which are significantly lower for contracted security services.[8] However, others argue that the *total costs* of replacing proprietary security personnel with contract security personnel are higher. It's true, in a free market responsible organization should always seek to find ways to reduce their costs. But organizations

---

[7] In California, the B.S.I.S. licenses contract security *guards* not security *officers*. Although most private organizations that employ proprietary security personnel use the title *Security Officer*. *Guard* is often used pejoratively.

[8] There's no business principle that supports the premise that lowering wages improves employee performance. However, there is one that says, "You get what you pay for!" These principles apply to all employees, not just security personnel.

need to be cautious that the reductions in cost don't negatively impact organizational safety, and in the long run, increase liabilities. Contract security companies and their security personnel play an important role in creating additional layers of protection for organizations, mainly protecting assets or supplementing in-house security personnel. However, based on the needs and expectations of today's organization's and the current configuration of the contract security industry, they're not equipped to provide the level of protection that's legally, socially, and pragmatically required to prevent and respond to workplace violence, and protect people in today's competitive business environment.[9]

The following are characteristics that define a *professional* (uniformed) security officer:

1. Managed and led by a security director/manager, or a senior nonsecurity manager with experience leading security personnel.
2. Professionally trained.
3. Obligated to protect employees and consumers.
4. Authorized to use protective tactics and tools.
5. Their job responsibilities are organized within a security architecture.
6. Their activities are integrated with other organizational departments.
7. They operate within a quasi-military chain of command/hierarchy.
8. They wear a uniform that best suited for their environment and effect.

Another important distinction we make is among security and law enforcement processes, behaviors, and personnel. One of these distinctions is how the phrase "use of force" is used and understood in these different vocations. It's true that *force* is sometimes used to resolve conflict and protect people in both security and law enforcement contexts. However, there are, or should be, distinctions in *why* force is applied in these two contexts. For instance, law enforcement officers use force to control, detain, and arrest subjects who are suspected of, or who have violated the law, whereas private security officers use (or should use) *force* solely

---

[9] I've owned and operated a contract security company that provided armed protection for high-level former government personnel and never experienced an injury to my security personnel or our protectees. It's not the type of contractual relationship that exists between an employee and employer that determines a security officer's capabilities. We proved that it's possible to provide high levels of protection from violence using contract security personnel. But many organizations are not willing to pay the prevailing wages that are required to employ and *keep* highly competent uniformed security officers that are capable of preventing and responding to workplace violence.

for protecting people. In fact, when private security officers attempt to use physical force to enforce laws, rules, or policies, they usually end up exacerbating the interaction. Consequently, when private security officers use force to resolve conflict or to gain control of a resistant subject, we identify those behaviors as "protective force."

We define protective force as:

> Deliberate, non-punitive, personal interaction, whether it's accomplished through the use of a protective tactic or with a protective tool, used for the narrow purpose of protecting the involved individuals (including employees, consumers, or visitors) from immediate or active physical harm; or used to control a subject who is a danger to themselves or others, or has committed an interpersonal crime, and applied in a manner that balances employee safety with the resistant individual's legal/civil rights.

Historical Aspects of Conflict Resolution

Organizations established their preference for hiring law enforcement officers, both active and retired, and in some circumstance's former military personnel (both enlisted and commissioned officers), to manage and lead their organizational safety needs, long ago. There are two basic prevailing thoughts on how this preference became the established hiring pattern for many private organizations. One view suggests that law enforcement officers and military personnel are *de facto* safety/security experts; another view suggests that these individuals provide a level of prestige and influence for the employing organizations.[10] In many instances, these vocations produce individuals with exceptional character and superior leadership skills. However, in some instances these perceived benefits may not actually be benefits for private organizations. We've reached this controversial conclusion not because these individuals are flawed (they're usually some of the finest people we know), but because of the operational limitations inherent in providing protective services in a private, free-market setting. In their past professions, law enforcement personnel were obligated to enforce the law

---

[10] It's often argued that former law enforcement managers, especially those who retire in the same law enforcement jurisdiction (e.g., city, county, or state) as the organization headquarters, will have special access to government resources that nonpolice-oriented personnel wouldn't. However, this type of access can also create public perceptions of an abuse of power.

under statutory requirements (letter of the law), while corporate guidelines (policies, procedures, processes, and rules) require a great deal of flexibility.

The Role of Setting

There are significant differences between public and private settings. The primary reason our law enforcement officers and military personnel are successful in their respective community safety missions is not because of their exemplary personal character, training, or expertise. Although it's true that these individuals typically embody exemplary persona traits, and there's no doubt that they play an important role in their vocational success, it's not the primary reason for it. In these public settings, *task effectiveness* is primarily the result of legal and social authority, not an individual's personal character traits. Military and law enforcement officers' personnel are given broad authority and power under various statutes, State Constitutions and the U.S. Constitution, and they enjoy broad societal support for their unique community safety missions. But these character traits are *contributory* factors, not the primary reason for their success.

When law enforcement officers or military-oriented individuals leave their unique employment context and become employed in the private market, they have no more/less authority or power than individuals who haven't served in the military or have no law enforcement experience. In fact, for some of these individuals, the loss of social power is often a source of frustration. Many former law enforcement officers or military personnel struggle to make the transition from a career characterized by authority, prestige, and power to one with virtually none. There's a significant dropout rate among those who can't adapt to working in a profession with limited (or no) authority, power, and trust. These realities may give individuals with no law enforcement or military experience an advantage over these former public servants. Since private security officers are rarely afforded a high degree of organizational or legal authority with which to influence behavior, they have no other option but to rely on creative, collaborative, accommodated, and negotiated interpersonal solutions to create the necessary social power required to manage passive–aggressive behaviors and protect people. Unlike private security officers, law enforcement officers always have their statutory authority to *fall back on* to influence people.[11]

---

[11] Unfortunately, sometime officers use *fall back* as their primary method to make people comply, which creates unnecessary interpersonal tension and complaints.

Unlike organizations that hire security officers, law enforcement agencies and the military don't place newly hired and untested individuals, who have no actual experience working in their vocation, into field operations without first determining whether these individuals have the proper temperament, character, training, and competencies to perform these unique tasks. For law enforcement officers and the military, potential candidates are tested and qualified by successfully completing a police academy or a military boot camp. Similarly, if law enforcement officers or military personnel were simply placed into field duties without this scrutiny, they will similarly fail to produce the desired community safety outcomes. These processes assure communities that only *qualified* people will take on these roles.

Recommendations

1. Develop workplace violence prevention strategies that are based on private, free-market business principles.
2. Employ security officers who have the personality and temperament to balance principles of personal protection with customer service when processing interpersonal workplace conflict and violence.
3. Don't place newly hired employees into leadership positions until they've proven they can lead private security officers in a free-market environment.

References

Fenno, N., 2020. Man beaten in Dodger Stadium parking lot files lawsuit against team. LA Times, 04 April 2020.

Kim, V., 2011. Medical costs for Bryan Stowe to exceed $50 million, attorneys say. LA Now, Los Angeles Times, 13 September 2011; Web: <www.latimesblogs.com> 10.06.12.

Chapter 2

Business-Focused Organizational Safety

Problem

The strategies that organizations use to prevent and respond to workplace violence interfere with their ability to remain financially viable, competitive, and socially relevant in their unique market.

Introduction

Organizational safety is a business problem, not a security problem! The strategies that businesses use to create and maintain violence-free workplaces need to be natural extensions of their underlying business principles. Unfortunately, safety/security is often thought of and processed as a separate, standalone, and disintegrated business function that operates outside normative business principles.[1] Moreover, organizations continue to rely on community safety philosophies that are meant for *public* law enforcement and when used in a *private* free-market setting, end up exacerbating interpersonal conflict.

---

[1] Since a security department also processes internal (employee based) safety and security threats, it must operate with a certain level of confidentiality and autonomy so complete integration may not be possible.

To effectively manage workplace conflict and resolve violence, organizations need to utilize business-focused organizational safety strategies that integrate principles of service with protection.

Although many organizations employ uniformed security officers for the purpose of preventing and responding to workplace violence, security officers don't have the requisite authority, power, expertise, or training alone to accomplish this task. To create violence-free workplaces requires every vested stakeholder to use their unique expertise to minimize interpersonal tension and keep interpersonal conflict from escalating to violence.

Process

The main reason private organizations exist is to create revenue and profit to remain financially viable so that they can meet the needs of their consumers and, if possible, increase their market share or influence. The success of private organizations depends on their ability to remain competitive, financially viable, and socially relevant in their unique market.[2] Since security officers play an important role in preventing and responding to workplace violence, their activities need to be integrated into businesses' broad organizational processes. When security officers understand basic business principles, and how their activities add value to the organization, they're more likely to act in ways that support their organization's primary business mission. Since private organizations exist for vastly different reasons than law enforcement agencies, it's important that security officers understand and act according to these respective differences and these distinctions need to be reflected in an organization's plan for managing and resolving workplace conflict and violence.

Critical Decision-Making

Security officers, like other senior corporate managers, regularly make multimillion-dollar *business* decisions. But their decisions aren't made in the boardroom; they're made in the field every time they interact with people in crisis. The decision to physically interact with a violent subject to protect

---

[2] Every private organization, including non-profits, need to be focused on achieving and maintaining financial viability.

people is one of the most complicated and important business decisions that any stakeholder can make. To effectively process workplace conflict and violence and act in an organization's best interests, security officers need to interact with uncooperative, dangerous, and violent individuals *more like* corporate business managers and *less like* law enforcement officers.

Too often organizations are so concerned with mitigating civil liabilities associated with using force to protect people that they enact risk aversive policies that end up ignoring other, more potentially devastating liabilities, such as negligence associated with a failure to protect their employees, consumers, or visitors. To be effective, and to minimize risk, security officers need a comprehensive understanding of how the use of, or the failure to use, certain conflict management or conflict resolution strategies impacts their organization's financial standing. When security officers use excessive force or they fail to intervene to protect victims, not only are people's lives impacted, but it also impacts an organization's ability to retain a valuable workforce, and remain competitive, financially viable, and socially relevant.

Duty, Ethics, and the Law

Organizations have a legal duty to create a safe environment for everyone that frequents their jurisdictional boundaries under the *general duty clause* of State and Federal OSHA guidelines. This *due care* responsibility involves creating a safe environment for consumers, employees, visitors, or others (including those who have no legitimate reason for being present on an organization's property!). However, the challenges associated with carrying out this *first duty* are complicated because of an organization's *concurrent duty* to act reasonably when carrying out its first duty! These concurrent legal and civil duties often cause some senior corporate managers to believe that it's better to do nothing rather than act.

To further complicate these organizational obligations, organizations don't have an option to not act proactively or reactively to *foreseeable* safety concerns. Organizations that fail to meet any of these duties create potential civil and criminal negligence. Organizations often interpret these responsibilities as a double-bind dilemma: damned if they do (their duty to act), damned if they don't (their failure to act).

There's no need here to list the thousands of examples in which organizations were sued for negligence. However, one recent example stands out: A female college student sued Southwestern Oregon Community

College and their campus security department for $5 million alleging that a lack of adequate security led to her kidnapping and rape (Denson, 2011). Their lawsuit alleges that on the day of the incident, a campus safety officer who was assigned to the areas where the student was assaulted failed to report to work that day. A seemingly basic organizational safety principle of having security officers patrol an assigned area to deter crime may have led to this young woman's injuries and the corresponding lawsuit.

The Right Principles—The Right Mission

There continues to be a high degree of confusion among various senior corporate managers on the distinctions between public law enforcement philosophies of community safety and private organizational safety principles. One of the greatest mistakes organizations make is misapplying *public* community safety philosophies that were created for *public* law enforcement officers to *private* organizations and *private* security personnel. To help reinforce and explain these benefits, we'll juxtapose private free-market organizational safety principles with public law enforcement safety philosophies and private security officers with *public* law enforcement officers.

Whose Needs?

First, *public* community safety principles focus on the *generalized* needs of *all organizations* and *all people* located within a law enforcement agency's city, county, state, or federal jurisdictional boundaries. On the other hand, in a *private* setting, the organizational safety focus is on meeting the particular and varying needs of *one organization*, and one subset of people, namely the shareholders, and the people who work and consume services and products there. Although a local law enforcement agency and its law enforcement officers are one of an organization's most important external stakeholder groups, especially when it comes to suppressing crime and responding when individuals are behaving violently, especially armed violence, they don't have the resources to respond to the unique needs of every organization, much less the needs of all the residents within their jurisdiction. As an example, many cities or counties have areas that are considered the "bad part of town" or less desirable, where crime occurs at higher rates.[3] But responsible organizations can't successfully operate if a part of their facilities or grounds (their area of jurisdiction) is the *bad part of town*. The reality is that private organizations have very little influence on creating *generalized* community safety outside of their business's geography, and law enforcement officers can't focus all their attention on *one* organization's needs. Unlike a local law enforcement agency that has a multitude of competing needs and public agendas within its jurisdiction, a private organization must prioritize the unique needs of *their* own consumers, employees, and shareholders.

Relationships and Influence

Second, there are great distinctions in how law enforcement officers and private security officers interact and communicate with uncooperative people in their respective contexts. Security officers represent the organization's interest, and protect their reputation, much like an ambassador, and they use (again, they should use) *relational* communication to meet the social needs of consumers and attempt to maintain the organization's goodwill, even when trying to influence resistant behaviors.[4] Relational communication is established and maintained through mutual respect, open dialogue, active listening, emphatic responses, compromise, accommodation, and negotiation. For instance, when security officers interact with difficult consumer behaviors, the relational goal may be influencing safe behaviors, whereas when interacting with employees, the goal may be creating productive teams and information sharing. Therefore, when security officers become engaged with uncooperative consumers, they must communicate in ways that demonstrate and uphold these relational characteristics.

When private security officers interact with uncooperative individuals in their workplace, they typically use (or should use!) collaborative communication such as active listening, dialoguing, responding, accommodating, compromising, and negotiating to influence a consumer's behavior. One model we use and recommend is the LEARNS de-escalation system. The first three steps are: listen, explain, and ask. Conversely, in a law enforcement model, "ask" is typically the first step, whereas "ask" is

---

[3] Some important industries are based in these areas.
[4] Communication is discussed in greater detail in Chapter 11.

the third step in the consumer model, demonstrating the different uses of communication.[5] Listening is a key to developing relationships and creating and maintaining good will, and often reveals the motivations (or reasons) that drive an individual's behavior.

Law enforcement officers, unlike private security officers, respond to interpersonal conflict with a greater reliance on statutory authority, enforcing laws and arresting lawbreakers to resolve conflict. Law enforcement-based communication training uses *instrumental* communication and social power to effect behavior change.[6] They often use a condensed, short-hand, communication technique known as A.T.M., or Ask, Tell, Make, when attempting to convince uncooperative individuals to cooperate. Generally, law enforcement officers don't have the *time* or the *need* to develop or maintain relationships with uncooperative individuals. Their goal is to get the individual to correct their potentially criminal behavior quickly, they can threaten to arrest them, or arrest them to *solve* the problem.[7] In many jurisdictions, failing to cooperate with a law enforcement officer is grounds for an arrest. This is one reason (or the primary reason) that very few individuals argue with or resist a law enforcement officer's verbal commands[8] (unlike resistant individuals who often mock, bully, and intimidate private security officers knowing there are no legal, or other, consequences for actively resisting them). Law enforcement officers often operate under significant time constraints and only have a short window of opportunity to solve a problem before they need to move on to their next *call*.

When an individual interacts with a law enforcement officer and doesn't like *the way* the officer treats them, there isn't much recourse. (It may seem counterintuitive to some, but when individuals fail to cooperate or actively resist the authority of law enforcement officers, there are broad societal

---

[5] See Chapter 11 for more information on communication and the LEARNS de-escalation system.

[6] A metaphor that may help to explain the difference between the use of instrumental and relational communication is, *talking to* versus *talking with*, an individual. Influencing behavior often requires both types of communication but communicators should always begin a conflicted interaction using relational communication.

[7] In many jurisdictions, failing to cooperate with a law enforcement officer is ground for arrest. This is one reason the very few individuals resist a law enforcement officer's verbal commands. Unlike, private security officers who are often mocked, bullied, and intimidated when they interact with resistant behaviors.

[8] However, it may also create an incentive for officers to rely more on their *legal* authority, instead of using a more *personal* approach to influence behavior change and solve interpersonal problems.

implications. This reality often justifies a more verbally forceful response, and less personable, or a physical response for failing to cooperate with them.) Conversely, in a private, free-market commerce setting, when a consumer feels offended by the way an employee treats them, they have lots of recourse!

Who's Responsible

Third, private, free-market organizations have a legal obligation to protect their *employees* from violence; law enforcement agencies don't, nor are they even legally obligated to protect their citizens! In the 2005 Supreme Court case *Castle Rock v. Gonzales* (No. 04-278), the court ruled that law enforcement personnel have no legal duty to protect people. This legal doctrine has been upheld by federal judges over the past 15 years including in a recent lawsuit against the Sheriff's Department in Parkland, Florida, alleging that deputies had a legal responsibility to protect the students who were killed and injured at Marjory Stoneman Douglas High School in Parkland, Florida, in 2018. Unlike law enforcement officers who had no affirmative legal requirement to protect people at this school, organizations are on notice that if an active shooter were to come on their property, as in Parkland, Florida, and start shooting people, it would now be considered a *foreseeable act* and organizations need to have contingencies in place to protect employees, consumers, and others.

Or consider the case of Rebecca J. Phebus, who was murdered at work in 2019. She asked her local law enforcement agency to protect her from a violent ex-partner, who was prohibited from any contact with her based on a lawful court restraining order against him because of previous physical abuse. They weren't able to protect her, and she was subsequently murdered. Although the law enforcement agency may not be liable for this victim's death, the organization she worked for may be (Fields, 2019).[9] Moreover, besides the personal anguish, this incident would severely disrupt the business's ability to serve its consumers and create a massive negative media response impacting their reputation.

The bottom line is that organizations, and their security personnel, *not* law enforcement personnel, are responsible for protecting the

---

[9] https://www.seattletimes.com/seattle-news/crime/woman-allegedly-killed-by-ex-husband-at-everett-business-identified/.

immediate physical needs of their employees and consumers. Moreover, I am writing this book during the COVID-19 pandemic and isolation and hundreds of law enforcement officers are getting ill from the virus and not reporting to work. In response, law enforcement agencies are limiting calls for service and arrests or where they'll respond and letting criminals out of prison early. These circumstances require businesses to become more self-sufficient and rely on their professional security personnel more than ever.

Competition and Motivation

Fourth, unlike private organizations, law enforcement agencies aren't motivated by profit, nor do they have to compete for market share. These business principles not only improve products and processes; they also improve the way that people interact with one another. Although law enforcement agencies need to be responsive to community needs, they don't lose market share like private organizations if *their* community is offended by their approach to violence prevention. (In fact, offending the right segment of the public community, *the lawbreakers*, may be a useful community safety tactic!) However, in a private, free market, organizations always operate under a double bind. If their consumers perceive their approach to organizational safety as being too harsh, or if they perceive the organization as unsafe, they may respond by taking their business elsewhere. To succeed, private organizations must compete for market share in their unique market, which emphasizes customer service, positive consumer feedback, and a high regard for positive public perceptions.

Generally, you get treated better at Starbucks than at the DMV, treated better at UPS than at the US Post Office, treated better from private organizations than government agencies, but why? To succeed in a competitive, free market, organizations *must* treat their consumers (or potential consumers) in a way that makes them *feel good* about their choice to spend their time and money with them; consumers have choices. In short, successful organizations sell and offer great products and services, but in a competitive market, it's not enough; to succeed, they also must create an *experience*. When the *need* to compete to succeed is removed from interpersonal processes, it also removes extrinsic motivations (the costs or benefits) and accountability that's *necessary* to keep communicators focused on the needs and expectations of *the other*, and off themselves.[10] The truth is, when people can *get away with* treating people poorly, some will be rude, while others will be downright mean! Although it would be unfair to evaluate law enforcement officers, and to a lesser degree, security officers, based on how the people they interact with *feel* when trying to deescalate violent behaviors, it's not unreasonable to expect them to adhere to high interpersonal standards regardless of the circumstances.[11]

Resources

Fifth, although law enforcement officers and private security officers are responsible for maintaining safe communities, one public and the other private, they use different resources to achieve their respective goals. Unlike private security officers, the public law enforcement community has a myriad of physical methods and resources available only to them. They include additional officers, mutual aid from other agencies, special response teams, K9 units, helicopters, and various weapon options, to name a few advantages. Unlike law enforcement officers, most private security officers don't carry protective tools, nor are they trained in the use of protective tactics, and if they have access to them, their use is limited by policy or unsafe use. Moreover, law enforcement officers have statutory protections and are immune from certain liabilities arising from using force to resolve conflict that private security personnel don't have.

Disintegrated

Finally, whether *senior managers* are completely conscious of its effects, the social-psychological inertia that's created when organizations rely on public law enforcement principles and processes and staff their security department with former law enforcement personnel and police academy graduates, and wear police-type uniforms, especially when the department and its personnel are isolated from the broad organizational community,

---

[10] Again, many negative communication behaviors are unconscious; over time they become naturalized without the communicators being consciously aware of them. Many law enforcement officer spouses and family members have told their law enforcement officer partner's to "Stop treating me like a suspect!" as a way of identifying these embedded interpersonal characteristics.

[11] Some law enforcement officers are excellent communicators, no doubt. But an officer's demeanor and actions are crucial to perceptions of police legitimacy. If officers communicate well, listen and treat citizens with respect, citizens will respond in kind. National Institute of Justice, "Perceptions of Treatment by Police: Impacts of Personal Interactions and the Media," March 17, 2014, nij.ojp.gov: https://nij.ojp.gov/topics/articles/perceptions-treatment-police-impacts-personal-interactions-and-media.

their security departments, and their security posture often morph into and begins to resemble a law enforcement agency, complete with all the ritual artifacts.[12] I've heard from more than one senior manager who proudly referred to the security department as their own "mini-police department."[13]

But unlike a contract security guard vendor that's a separate and distinct entity with its own mission and motivations, when an organization employs its own security personnel as a component of their workplace violence prevention plan, it doesn't transform into a *security company* replete with competing missions and motivations; it remains a private, free-market enterprise, with the primary mission of selling or providing services or products in a competitive business market.[14] To be effective, an organization's security personnel and their activities must be integrated into and aligned with an organization's primary mission, *in addition to* upholding its respective (and complementary) protective mission: "you serve-we protect." When an organization's security personnel are perceived as acting like *law enforcement officers* (negative attributes) and the security department is thought of as "our police department (a disintegrated business unit)," it may create *positive feelings* among security personnel, but in reality it creates barriers to relationships and team building among other non-security employees that's necessary for creating an organizational safety net and violence-free workplaces.

Unfortunately, the use of law enforcement principles, processes, and personnel can create the false belief, even if its inadvertent, that the best way to manage conflict, resolve violence, and prevent workplace violence is for security officers to focus a significant amount of their worktime on enforcing rules, policies, and arresting lawbreakers; in the short term, this may be effective. But forced compliance will ultimately backfire because the employees (revenue facilitators) who produce or deliver the products or services and the people who consume them (revenue generators) fund organizational safety and the security department (the expenses) and have

---

[12] In some instances, walking into the lobby of a security department *looks and feels* just like walking into a police department lobby.

[13] Conversely, I've not heard a Mayor or a County Supervisor brag about their law enforcement agencies being their own "mini-corporation."

[14] This, in a nutshell, is the glaring weakness of using contracted security services in lieu of an organization employing their own proprietary security personnel. Some organizations believe contracting out their security and safety responsibilities will reduce their total security expenses and liabilities. Even if that were possible, it's impossible to integrate competing missions, goals and objectives into one unified response.

greater organizational influence than the security officers. Too often, security personnel are unaware of how the thoughts, opinions, and feelings of the revenue generators, revenue facilitators, and revenue influencers impact their ability to effectively solve problems.

College police departments find themselves in a similar dilemma when law enforcement officers try to create safe college campuses using traditional public policing theories because college students (the revenue generators) and college professors (revenue facilitators and influencers) are much less likely to consent to being *policed* than many other personality types. The often-heard lament of, "I pay your salary," in a private setting, and to a lesser degree on college campuses, is an accurate statement of funding and related influence. (Interestingly, the statement "I pay your salary" may not apply to a traditional law enforcement agency when making arrests. The person being arrested may not create any revenue used by the policing agency and becomes an additional expense when arrested!) In fact, college law enforcement officers interact much differently with college students *on campus* than their city police officer *compadres* do when interacting with same college students *off campus*. Public community members are much more open to using enforcement and arrests to create safe public neighborhoods than private organizational members. To be clear, we are not making a case for never enforcing laws on a private business's property; under the right circumstance and when used by the right expert stakeholder, it can be effective (e.g., writing parking tickets or towing vehicles). However, the bottom line is, it's impossible to *enforce* one's way to a violence-free workplace.

Serving and Protecting: Getting the Balance Right

Herein lies the organization safety dilemma: "How to provide high levels of personal protection without creating the feelings of a police state?"[15] Although there's no perfect workplace violence prevention program, successful organizations need to find the delicate balance between serving and protecting their employees and consumers. To accomplish this, security personnel must have a broad understanding of an organization's basic business operating principles and how unmet needs and failed expectations

---

[15] This question may nicely summarize the complexities of providing security services in a private, free market environment.

impact interpersonal tension, workplace conflict, and violence.[16] Additionally, security officers need access to a full spectrum of conflict resolution strategies, including the option of using physical protective force to resolve workplace conflict and violence.

Too often, organizations don't see the *business value* in requiring their security officers to intervene to protect employees and consumers from dangerous (unarmed) individuals. These organizations simply don't believe it's worth the risk to allow their security personnel to intervene to resolve interpersonal conflict, so they rely on law enforcement. As a security consultant, I've had many conversations with senior corporate managers who are sincerely convinced that any physical contact between security officers and uncooperative subjects creates an unacceptable organizational risk. However, when harm to employees, consumers, visitors, or others is imminent, it's never a good idea to wait for help to arrive, especially when security officers are already present and able.

Mission Focused

Every organization operates based on a mission or purpose, regardless of its well-articulated, communicated orally and/or in writing and organizational safety should also be a mission-focused activity. An organization's corporate mission statement is simply a formal summary of its aims and values. But a reliable corporate mission statement should detail the specific behaviors required of all individuals who frequent an organization for serving its consumers, enhancing financial viability, and maintaining safe and secure environments for employees, consumers, visitors, and others. However, the activities required to accomplish those aims and uphold those stated values are often ill defined and vague.

Organizations employ people who sell or provide their products and services to consumers and people who support those activities; one group generates *revenue* while the other is an *expense*.[17] The combined

---

[16] The ideas presented in this section should be mandatory for all security personnel to learn. We discuss them in greater detail in Chapter 10.

[17] Later in the book we discuss the challenges of funding the security department and financing security officer training. Organization always find it challenging to spend money on support services because the ROI is not always easy to quantify, and the results may not be realized until the distant future, unlike, spending that is meant to improves the sales or delivery their products of services, which is easy to track and gauge its influence.

activities and efforts of these individuals are guided by one overriding and unifying organizational mission. However, each separate department within the organization has a unique mission that only it performs (or it's their primary mission) in support of an organization's overall mission. The security department's *support* mission, in a nutshell, is protecting the sales and service people, and the organization's consumers and visitors. In other words, it's not the salespeople's job to protect people and it's not the security officers' job to sell or provide the services or products; these are mutually supporting and beneficial responsibilities. Therefore, to be effective at preventing and responding to workplace violence, the security officers' activities need to be missioned focused on protecting people, *without* interfering with the organizations overall mission, a delicate balancing act.

A key to effectively utilizing security officers to protect people is for organizations to first define their officer's mission. Unfortunately, since most organizations don't define their security officer's mission, it's not unusual for them to be involved in all sorts of (non-mission focused) activities that may or may not have any impact on minimizing workplace conflict or mitigating violence. We argue that a security officer's (or a professional security officer's) activities should be *primarily* focused on activities that protect people who frequent an organization's facilities, such as employees, consumers, visitors, and others and *secondarily* on protecting physical assets.

Below is an example of a healthcare organization's corporate mission statement that we can use to illustrate and diagram mission-focused security officer activities and responsibilities.

> Our mission is to help people keep well in body, mind and spirit by providing quality health care services in a compassionate environment.

There are two components of this mission statement: protection and service. Security officers play an important role "helping people keep well in body and mind," while waiting for the healthcare practitioners (non-security employees) to "provide quality health care services in a compassionate environment." To successfully and safely meet the above organizational mission, both employee groups perform separate but complimentary duties. A key to utilizing uniformed security officers to maintain violence-free workplaces and protect people is keeping them *mission focused* on protective duties, so the service personnel are safe to perform their jobs and consumers are safe to browse, purchase, receive services, and enjoy their *experience.* We realize that security officers also play a role in protecting an organization's physical assets, but protective duties should encompass 80% of their total efforts. The use of technological solutions (e.g., access control and video surveillance, to few name activities) to support asset protection in lieu of labor is a much more efficient method for protecting property and allowing security officers to focus on doing what technology can't do, solve interpersonal problems and protect people.[18]

Nonessential Duties and Distractions

Security officers should not be involved in everything. They are (or should be) experts at protecting people. Unfortunately, there are various activities that are often assigned (directly or indirectly) that distract them from upholding their essential mission by being overly involved in non-protective or asset protection duties. Too often, organizations assign non-protective duties to security officers without critically examining the justification for doing so. Sometimes duties are assigned just because "security has always done them," or because no one else wants to do them and they have no sociopolitical organizational power to resist them.[19]

Many of the duties that security officers currently perform (and their "other assigned duties" …) that are not protection-focused could be (or should be) reassigned to other stakeholders. To be clear, we are not making an argument that there are some activities that are undignified or beneath security officers to perform (e.g., cleaning a bathroom). We recognize there are times when any employee may be called on to perform duties outside their normal scope of duty to *temporarily* support their organization. But few other departmental employees outside of security are asked (or required) to perform duties *clearly* outside their scope of duty (even when their duties are well defined) that distract them from their primary mission of protecting people.

The primary reason that security officers are easily redirected from their primary duties is due to a lack of leadership on the part of the security director/manager and other senior corporate managers. Effective leadership

---

[18] Standing guard posts are labor intensive and require constant managing and supervising around the clock.

[19] Alternatively, it's argued that because they're the only employees who work 24/7 and the task needs to be completed when other employees aren't working.

would delineate tasks to various departments based on their job duties, expertise, and importance. Although most employees are capable of cleaning toilets, the reason they're not assigned to clean them is because their assigned duties and expertise are more valuable to the organization than toilet cleaning (and they weren't hired for that job). To be clear, all duties, including cleaning duties, play a role in the success of an organization.[20] A doctor or college professor doesn't clean toilets, not because it's beneath them, but because its "not their job." Additionally, security officers are often required to perform non-protective duties due to their duties not being well defined, their activities don't generate revenue, a lack of standards, and other corporate managers believing their own duties create *greater* organizational value.[21] Protecting employees and consumers from workplace conflict and violence is a valuable and challenging duty for security officers to perform, and they shouldn't be distracted with other non-protective duties.[22]

Below are *some* of those regularly assigned security officer duties:

1. Cleaning restrooms,
2. Escorting people,
3. Feeding animals,
4. Gathering shopping carts,
5. Issuing visitor badges,
6. Locking and unlocking doors,
7. Manning information booths,
8. Picking up and distributing inter-departmental mail,
9. Raising and lowing flags, and
10. Taking out garbage.

This is obviously a short list of *irregular* duties and anyone who's spent more than a few minutes employed in the security field can come up with more (outrageous) examples. Clarifying and redefining the duties assigned to security officers, reassigning the *non-protective* duties to other (expert)

---

[20] In fact, the people that clean are perhaps the second most looked down upon job assignment in many organizations.

[21] Or, other senior corporate managers don't understand how the security officer's duties *save* the organization money. See Chapter 10 for more detail on ROI.

[22] I once had a client that required my security officers to feed the feral cats on the property we were contacted to protect. No matter what types of incentives I tried, they universally resisted this part of their assignment. My officers felt that feeding cats was not a legitimate task for a security officer; we eventually lost the account!

stakeholders, and implementing technological asset protection solutions will free up security officers to stay mission focused on protecting people.[23]

Structural Impediments and Effectiveness of Security Officers

Corporate sociopolitical organizational power plays an important role in organizational safety, workplace violence prevention, and security officer effectiveness. Corporate power struggles are common in every organization, and in every stakeholder group, not just in security departments, and there are personal, professional, and social costs to those who point out its influence. Many organizations assign the direct oversight of their security function to another non-security department (e.g., support services, human resources, accounting, operations, or facilities) that's situated low in the sociopolitical organizational power structure, which naturally inhibits their security personnel's organizational influence. This structure situates the senior security employee, typically the security director or security manager, several rungs down the corporate ladder compared to other departmental heads.[24] Unfortunately, this alignment also positions the security function, and the processes for adjudicating workplace conflict, at the lowest levels of the organization's power structure. To further exacerbate these sociopolitical dynamics, the security director or security manager's non-security direct report may have limited, if any, security expertise or experience.[25] This positioning, although popular, creates additional impediments for the security director/manager, and their officers for developing cooperative interdepartmental relationships.

---

[23] Some may resist this reclassification because it may lead to a reduction in payroll for some security departments as nonessential duties are passed on to other senior corporate managers or departments.

[24] This may be true even when the security director or manager is on the same level as other departmental heads since historically "security" has not had a *seat at the table* and some senior corporate managers are still not comfortable with the seating arrangement!

[25] Moreover, sometimes organizations complicate these processes even further when they hire a former law enforcement officer as their security director or manager with no private, free market experience leading and managing private security personnel. In short, this arrangement places two executives between the line personnel and the top of the organizational pyramid that have no practical experience processing workplace violence.

When the most senior security manager/director doesn't report to the top of the organizational hierarchy, it forces their non-security, direct report to juggle a multitude of organizational priorities and agendas, including personal, professional, and social alliances. Although it's true that some non-security managers may act on their subordinates' expert advice, some may use (or abuse) these power inequities to their own organizational advantage. These additional layers of socio-political organizational hierarchies and personal agendas interfere with timely critical decision-making, decisive leadership, and effective conflict resolution, which in the end may decrease safety and increase potential civil or criminal liabilities.

Where a business function is socially, politically, and organizationally situated within the corporate hierarchy impacts its effectiveness and communicates its relative value (or a lack thereof) to the organization and community. Locating an organization's security function at the lowest sociopolitical organizational level limits mission effectiveness, creates additional obstacles for security officers, and exacerbates workplace conflict. Unfortunately, this *power-down* arrangement is the norm in many organizations. When organizations fail to clearly communicate (and demonstrate)—across all internal and external stakeholder groups—the importance of adhering to the organization's code of conduct, cooperating with and supporting their security officers and the consequences for these failures, these sociopolitical organizational inequalities are exacerbated. In fact, all too often security officers are the only departmental members who are fair game to berate, mock, or bully, and this often happens with tacit approval of senior corporate managers!

Tracy Wallach, who conducts research in Peace and Conflict studies, argues that these kinds of attitudes may influence other stakeholders. Although Wallach is not writing about security officers, her conclusions are relative to the formation of stakeholder attitudes. She writes, "In an organization, the process of a particular group within it tends to reflect the larger organizational culture, the assumptions, values, and beliefs associated with a particular business or profession, which is, in turn, influenced by the culture of the larger community and nation" (Wallach, 2004 p. 87). These underlying dysfunctional organizational cultural attitudes (whether they're deliberate or inadvertent) may lead to uncooperative attitudes that influence relationships between security officers and organizational members.

These organizational structures may also create impressions among other employees that the security function and the security officers have a *lower value* than other organizational functions or personnel. In some organizations, this social dynamic has created an environment in which every employee feels comfortable telling security *what to do*.[26] Security officers often perceive this organizational positioning as a lack of value that influences the often-heard complaint of "not being appreciated." Sociopolitical organizational power plays an important role in creating the type of authority necessary for influencing behavior and protecting people. The truth is, *powerless* security officers can't effectively prevent workplace conflict and protect people.

Unfortunately, these sociopolitical organizational power inequalities also influence security officer training. Since the security director or security manager may have to rely on other non-security stakeholders to articulate their security officer's needs, including the need for training and funding, up the corporate ladder, other sociopolitical and personal agendas may take priority over the needs of the security department.[27] These barriers may make it difficult for non-security senior corporate managers to communicate the importance of security officer training, and to argue forcefully for financing security officer training.[28]

Summary

The organizational safety strategies implemented to create violence-free workplaces, prevent and respond to workplace violence, and protect people need to be based on free-market principles and integrated into the organization's underlying business operating principles. An effective organizational safety program needs to both "serve and protect" its employees, consumers, visitors, and the organization's business interests.

---

[26] This includes asking/requiring security officers to perform activities outside of their scope of duty or expertise.

[27] A senior security leader once told me that their direct report resisted approving security training because it affected their potential bonus. On the one hand, training was necessary, on the other hand spending on training impacted the individual's ability to meet their *performance indicators* and obtain a financial bonus. Paradoxically, the person that related this to me also had a bonus program that was based partially on training their officers!

[28] Security officer training is discussed in greater detail in Chapter 10.

Recommendations

1. Align the organizational safety processes with the organization's basic business operating architecture.
2. Assign the security director/manager's direct report to a senior manager who has direct experience managing and leading private security personnel.
3. Communicate across all internal and external stakeholder groups the importance of supporting the organization's security officers and the consequences for failing to support them.
4. Integrate the security department and its personnel into the broad stakeholder community.
5. Replace law enforcement community safety philosophies and law enforcement type behaviors with business-focused organizational safety principles and business-minded security officers.
6. Reposition/move the security function and the security director/ manager position higher up in the organization's socio-political hierarchy. Ideally, the senior most security leader should report directly to senior corporate managers at the top of the organizational pyramid.

References

Denson, Bryan. 2011. Student accuses Community College in Coos Bay of failing to protect her from kidnap, rape. The Oregonian.

Fields, Asia. 2019. Woman allegedly killed by ex-husband at Everett business identified. The Seattle Times, 28 May 2019. <https://www.seattletimes.com/seattle-news/crime/woman-allegedly-killed-by-ex-husband-at-everett-business-identified/>

Tracey, Wallach, 2004. Transforming conflict: a group relations perspective. Peace Conflict Stud. 11-1. 81–92.

Chapter 3

Operational Deployment Modes (ODM)

Problem

Organizations deploy uniformed security officers using deployment modes that don't prioritize the protection of people.

Introduction

To prevent and respond to workplace violence, organizations must use a deployment model that focuses on protecting employees and consumers and supports the business functions that facilitate the sale or delivery of their products or services. There's a direct line between sales and safety; consumers will not frequent an organization if they believe it's unsafe to do so, no matter the price or quality of the product or service. Likewise, employees will not choose to work in an unsafe environment, or if they do, they won't thrive. Some of the most popular deployment models involve observing and reporting violations, deterring unsafe and unlawful behaviors, advising violators, and protecting people and attempts to force people to adhere to an organization's the code of conduct. The two most popular operational deployment modes (ODMs) are the observe and report (OAR) and the forced compliance (FC). The OAR is the most often used mode, but it doesn't provide physical protection for potential victims, while the FC mode often exacerbates interpersonal tensions. Although all operational deployment modes borrow from these two perspectives, they're really remnants of a bygone era, inapplicable to the 21st century workplace violence prevention challenges organizations face. In a competitive, private, free market setting, security officers should be deployed using the SAP mode that focuses on service, advisement, and protection.

Process

Unfortunately, the observe and report ODM, a noninterventionist mode, has become the current national security industry standard. The OAR mode is often used when security personnel are inexperienced, unsupervised, unfit, and not professionally trained.[1] In fact, this mode is recommended by most state security licensing agencies. For instance, in California, the Bureau of Security and Investigative Services (B.S.I.S.), the state agency that licenses private security guards, promotes this mode.[2] Many organizations believe that deploying uniformed security officers using an OAR operational deployment mode is the best option because it limits liabilities associated with security officers engaging with uncooperative individuals. It may minimize the liability associated with allowing untrained security officers to use physical force. However, even if it were true that using force to protect a victim created greater liability to inaction, acting to protect people satisfied an organization's legal responsibility and is morally superior to inaction.

The observe and report operational deployment mode has become embedded in the security industry for two reasons. First, many state security guard licensing bureaus advocate for these types of behavioral limits primarily based on the safety concerns of the security officer, not on efficiency, effectiveness, or a concern for an employee's safety. Since most basic security officers are hired with little or no prior experience, receive just the basic levels of state-mandated training, are low paid, often work alone, and are rarely closely supervised, the risk to both the security officer and the organization is naturally high if security personnel become physically involved with dangerous subjects.

---

[1] See Chapter 9 on health, wellness, fitness and obesity.

[2] The B.S.I.S. *Powers to Arrest* Manual (p. 22) suggests that security (guards) officers be consigned to observing and reporting problems. Some have interpreted this admonishment as the law, but private security personnel are not legally prohibited from intervening. They don't intervene because they're typically untrained, inexperienced, unsupervised and unfit.

Another reason an OAR mode remains popular is that it is supported by a majority of senior non-security managers who sponsor and fund security operations. A noncontact, noninterventionist approach to conflict is a philosophical fit for many senior corporate managers who have concluded (I would argue, uncritically and primarily anecdotally) that security officers create more problems than they solve when they become physically engaged with dangerous subjects. The prevailing wisdom among many professional risk managers posits that when security officers physically engage with resistant subjects, risk elevates to unacceptable levels. This risk/benefit assessment is accurate when organizations employ inexperienced, unsupervised, and untrained security officers, but not for professionally trained security officers.

The obvious weakness of an observational mode is that it prohibits security officers from intervening to physically protect victims from violence. However, proponents of this noncontact mode argue that even though officers are prohibited from intervening, their visual presence provides value by deterring potential criminal activity. However, when attempts to prevent criminal activity through visual presence fail, security officers can only report safety violations or criminal activity to other responsible stakeholders, such as supervisors or law enforcement. Security officers deployed using an observe and report mode become the "eyes and ears," not the hands, of the community. Moreover, because of the improvements in digital video recorders, cameras, monitors, and access control (to name a few useful new advancements), there's very little need to employ people just to be the *eyes and ears*. The truth is, if a security officer is not able or not required to intervene to protect people, those payroll costs may be better spent on technological solutions.

Forced Compliance (FC)

Some organizations deploy security officers using a forced compliance (FC) mode. Forced compliance is an ineffective method for preventing and responding to workplace violence. In a private, competitive, free market context, attempts to enforce laws, policies, or guidelines often exacerbate interpersonal tensions and escalate harmful behaviors and distract security officers from their protective duties. Forced compliance may be an effective strategy for resolving conflict in some contexts, and when used by other non-security senior corporate managers, but when used by private security officers, it's usually an ineffective strategy.[3]

Unlike security officers, when law enforcement officers use enforcement as a *public* community safety strategy, it discourages unsafe behaviors, removes criminals from the community, and deters violence. However, unlike law enforcement officers, private security officers don't possess the enabling statutory authority, extensive training, or additional back up personnel needed to empower forced compliance. (It's one thing to ask someone to leave the property; it's quite another to *force* them to.) Since private security officers don't have the requisite enabling attributes and authority to safely resolve interpersonal conflict through forced compliance, it's rarely a good idea for private security officers to try to force people to comply.[4] Moreover, unlike law enforcement officers who can enforce laws and then leave, security officers who are involved in forced compliance activities have to deal with the sociopolitical ramifications of their actions, remain at the location (since they're employed there), and continue to interact with the violators, and their friends and associates, day in and day out![5]

Adversaries or Advisors?

Involving private security officers in forced compliance activities naturally creates adversarial relationships with employees, and to a lesser degree with consumers. When employees perceive security officers as partners, not adversaries, they're more likely to become *willing* participants and support the organization's community safety mission, including being more likely to share information with security personnel. Involving security officers in forced compliance activities creates the impression that their main interest is catching employees doing something wrong, rather than supporting and protecting them. Once these impressions become imbedded in organizational culture, even the *mere presence* of a security officer could create hostility. The truth is, employees don't like being *hassled* at work, especially by uniformed security officers who

---

[3] Forced compliance is also known as enforcement. But we think forced compliance is a better way to describe these types of organizational activities.

[4] One exception could be parking enforcement duties. But ideally, even if this duty is assigned to the security department, the department should develop a separate division to distinguish its protective duties from its enforcement duties.

[5] Law Enforcement officers know a moving target is easier to avoid than a stationary one.

often focus their attention on identifying bad behaviors. Alternatively, when employees perceive security officers as advisors, whose primary motivation is looking out for their best interest, they're much more likely to cooperate when being confronted about their potentially unsafe behavior.

The death of Kelly Thomas may be a representative example of the challenges of using an enforcement mode. In July 2011, a violent field incident occurred in the city of Fullerton, California, between Fullerton law enforcement officers and Kelly Thomas. After a physical altercation with the police, Thomas died. This field conflict led to the death of a young man and the arrest of three law enforcement officers for murder!

Tony Rackauckas, the Orange County, California, District Attorney, pushed to prosecute the involved law enforcement officers for murder based on an allegation that the officers "created the environment" that led to Thomas's death. At a press conference on September 21, 2011, Rackauckas stated, "The biggest shame about this case is the fact that it could have been avoided." Rackauckas went on to say, "[Fullerton Police Officers] Ramos set in motion the events that led to the death of Kelly Thomas …" (2011, Orange County, California, District Attorney's Office Press Release). Two Officers, Manual Ramos and Jay Cicinelli, were eventually fired, charged with murder and later exonerated in the criminal trial. However, in 2015, the City of Fullerton, California, settled a wrongful death lawsuit brought by Thomas's father for 4.9 million dollars (Ponsi et al., 2015).

This case highlights a new organizational safety reality for first-responder personnel. When assessing the negative outcomes of physical interactions between uniformed officers and resistant subjects, more corporate managers, risk managers, and lawyers are now thinking along these lines. The claim of "setting events into motion" could be made against any private security officer (or any uniformed authority figure), especially when involved in forced compliance activities. If organizations can't find other methods for modifying unacceptable behavior, and they require forced compliance activities, they should assign other internal or external *experts*, who have the requisite authority, not security officers, to process violators. Often, senior corporate managers assign their security department-forced compliance duties without fully understanding the unintended consequences of involving them. We are not proposing that organizations abdicate all enforcement activities; under the right circumstances, forced compliance is an important and necessary operational task. However, when security officers become involved in forced compliance (or quasi-enforcement) activities, there's a greater chance that the interactions will escalate conflict.

Paradoxically, security officers often end up being assigned forced compliance duties because they argued for it or because they didn't forcefully resist it being assigned to them by other non-security senior corporate managers. The truth is, there are abundant opportunities in every organization to be involved in pointing out poor behavior and enforcing policy compliance. Security departments sometimes assume forced compliance activities are a simple way to create relevance or to increase or maintain their operating budgets. (To a lesser extent, some senior corporate managers may think forced compliance activities mitigate workplace violence.) Additionally, because of an overrepresentation of police-oriented security officers in the private security industry, forced compliance activities feel like a good fit for many officers. Over time, these self-assigned (or unresisted) forced compliance duties have become embedded in organizational culture (and codified in policy), and now community members expect security officers to enforce certain guidelines, policies, or rules. This approach to creating relevance often backfires, since enforcement activities don't always improve organizational safety.

A key to using forced compliance to resolve conflict is assigning the right expert *enforcer* to the corresponding type of conflict that enforcement is best equipped to solve. Some appropriate examples are calling a law enforcement officer to ticket or tow an unlawfully parked vehicle or having a dean of students suspend a dangerous student and require them to leave the campus. However, when personnel who don't have the requisite authority and ability (e.g., *not* experts) try to force employees or consumers to modify their unacceptable behavior, attempts to intervene often escalate interpersonal tension and may lead to violence. However, in both the above-listed examples, if the violators became aggressive, security officers should be utilized as *peacekeepers* (e.g., experts), whereas the other senior corporate managers would still function as the *enforcers*.

Serve, Advise, and Protect (SAP): Operational Deployment Modes

To prevent and respond to workplace violence and protect people, uniformed security officers should be deployed using the serve, advise, and protect (SAP) mode. The SAP operational deployment mode keeps security officers focused on activities that prioritize the protection of people and reputations, and an organization's ability to serve its consumers and financially compete in their unique market. Unlike other operational deployment modes, the SAP accounts for the natural limitations of all personnel, including security officers, and maximizes the collective synergy of every expert stakeholder to minimize interpersonal workplace conflict. Moreover, the SAP operational deployment mode helps establish clear role, responsibility, and jurisdictional boundaries for security personnel, senior corporate managers, and law enforcement officers, who all share in the responsibility of protecting employees, consumers, and others.[6]

Social-Psychological Influence

Deploying visually available, professional, uniformed security officers addresses both the perceptual and quantifiable components of safety and has a social-psychological effect on everyone who frequents an organization. The presence of security officers helps create positive feelings of personal safety and security for employees, consumers, and visitors. But for individuals who may be tempted to steal property or to act violently, it discourages those behaviors because criminals know they'll be confronted.[7] Second, when security officers interact with people and demonstrate effective customer service skills and professionalism, low-level interpersonal conflict is easily managed and de-escalated. The saying "an ounce of prevention is worth a pound of cure" may be old, but it's still a useful workplace violence prevention technique; an incident prevented is one that doesn't require a response or resources.

Service

A key to success in a competitive free market environment is meeting the needs and expectations of the people who purchase your products and services or use them. Security officers play an important role in supporting their organizations by maintaining a safe place for their employees to work and their consumers to engage in commerce. Professional security officers

---

[6] Jurisdictional boundaries allow experts to operate in the area of responsibility. When people operate outside of their area of responsibility and expertise it often creates power struggles and exacerbates workplace conflict and violence.

[7] Using plain clothes (non-uniformed) security personnel to complement a uniformed staff can be an effective method for improving safety.

are often the first employees that consumers see and interact with when they visit an organization's property. Often, when consumers arrive, security officers are available to provide information that helps reduce uncertainties and anxieties by directing visitors where to park, or where to go, or how to find certain personnel. Or, if employees or consumers need more personal assistance, like unlocking a car door after accidently locking the keys in the car, security officers are available to assist them. In short, when security officers continually find ways to serve employees and enhance the *customer experience*, they're operating in *service mode*.

Advisement

When security officers interact with consumers and employees and identify potential interpersonal violations of an organization's *code of conduct* or the law that could harm others, they're operating in *advisement mode*.[8] When officers observe behaviors that could harm others, they contact the individual and advise them of the violation and request that they change their behavior. If an individual offers verbal resistance, security officers use collaborative communication, such as active listening, dialoguing, responding, accommodating, compromising, and negotiating, to influence the individual's behavior and keep it from escalating. In advisement mode, security officers don't use physical protective force on nonviolent resistors to correct their inappropriate behavior. Instead, they involve other expert internal or external stakeholders who have the requisite authority to de-escalate unsafe behavior or remove the individual from the premise, temporarily or permanently. The advisory function is one of the most important and overlooked functions of an effective workplace violence prevention program because it proactively heads off potential escalation of harmful behaviors.

Protection

Perhaps the most important benefit of deploying security officers utilizing an SAP operational deployment mode is providing physical protection for employees and consumers. If an individual's behavior escalates to direct aggressiveness, and they refuse to correct their *unsafe* behavior, security

---

[8] Some violations may not involve potential harm.

officers are *required* to intervene to keep potentially harmful behavior *from escalating* to violence. As behavior escalates, communicative solutions become less appropriate or inappropriate, and security officers may need to use protective tactics and tools to de-escalate an individual's unsafe behavior. However, once an individual's behavior *creates* active physical harm, security officers are authorized and *required* to physically intervene to *stop* the individual from harming others. I argue that professional security officers are morally and ethically obligated (or they should be) as a condition of employment (and as a condition of continued employment) to physically protect employees, consumers, visitors, or others from unarmed physical assaults.[9] For some, this may be a controversial position, and this is due in large part to a culture of low expectations that is rampant in many organizations; it requires a paradigm shift. It should be a *reasonable expectation* that trained professional security officers *ought to be* required to provide tangible and quantifiable benefits to their organizations; prime among them is protecting employees and consumers from violent individuals and protecting an organization's most tangible asset, its reputation.

Conflict Resolution Misalignment: Staying in Your Lane

A key reason that an SAP deployment mode is effective is because it synthesizes each employee's unique power, authority, and training and expertise, not just the security officer's, to maximize their *collective efforts* to prevent and respond to workplace violence; each expert operates within their assigned lane. Processing workplace conflict involves interacting with many different conflicted scenarios, various violator relationships, complicated interpersonal dynamics, and numerous organizational safety violations. Moreover, some types of conflict are better resolved by internal stakeholders and managers, whereas others are better dealt with by external stakeholders. Many interpersonal problems are easily resolved by involving the *right* employee with the *right* authority and expertise, who can create the necessary motivations for a *voluntary* de-escalation in behavior. Conversely, when the *wrong* employee is involved, without the requisite authority (operating outside of their lane), they're unable to create the necessary motivations for voluntary behavior change and they exacerbate

---

[9] Unarmed and untrained security personnel should not confront armed attackers and should rely on the police.

the interaction. However, security officers who are trained and equipped to process interpersonal conflict need to intervene early in the interaction and act proactively to prevent behaviors from escalating.

The two most common conflict process failures occur when security personnel try to *resolve* highly volatile conflict, such as armed violence, themselves (nonexperts) instead of calling on law enforcement officers (the experts), or conversely, when security personnel (the experts) call law enforcement officers to help them *manage* conflict that they could have easily processed themselves. Similarly, conflict process misalignment wastes the time, energy, and resources of other busy experts (e.g., corporate administrators or law enforcement officers) and decreases personal and organizational safety.

Moreover, during a conflicted incident, especially involving injuries, senior corporate managers often scramble to determine departmental and organizational jurisdictional boundaries and allow personal and corporate agendas to interfere with critical decision-making and the coordination of an ethical and timely response. To overcome these natural interpersonal processes, organizations should create a conflict response matrix that includes a comprehensive list of senior corporate managers correlated to the various jurisdictions and expertises.

Advisory Mode

There are three types of behaviors that security officers will interact with: passive–aggressive, directly aggressive, and violent.[10] (The vast majority of interactions will be with passive–aggressive behaviors.) However, when security officers interact with passive–aggressive behaviors that violate an organization's code of conduct but *don't* involve immediate or active physical harm, security officers function in *advisory mode* and utilize effective communication to influence behavior change. Their noninterventionist options include:

1. Advise the violator of their inappropriate behavior and request they correct it.
2. If the violator fails to comply with the request, officers should attempt to identify the violator's affiliation status and the specific organizational safety violation to determine if they are the right (expert) stakeholder

---

[10] There are four behaviors. But we assume that *cooperative behavior* is easy to identify and it doesn't require an interaction.

to process the interaction themselves or if it needs to be assigned to another (expert) stakeholder who has the requisite power, authority, and training to process it (e.g., Dean of Students, Human Resources Manager, or Law Enforcement Officers, to name a few options).

Affiliation status is important because it defines the social, legal, or pragmatic type of relationship an organization enters into with a person who frequents their property, such as a patient, family member, visitor, student, professor, client, associate, employee, contractor, or consumer, to name a few types of relationships. Affiliation status influences the range of solutions available to employees. For instance, if a disruptive person is asked to leave the owner's property and refused, their refusal would be treated much differently if the person was an employee of the organization or a housing challenged (non-employee) On the other hand, in a health care setting if a mentally ill person wanted to leave the owner's property (hospital), the organization may be legally required to keep the person from leaving. (In fact, the healthcare organization may be in violation of regulatory or statutory requirements if it allows the person to leave.)

Consider how the advisory mode would be applied if the security officer observed an individual smoking a cigarette on campus when the organization has a non-smoking policy. The security officer would advise the smoker of the policy and then ask the individual to cease smoking (ask for policy compliance). However, if the smoker refused to cooperate, the security officer would contact another non-security stakeholder (expert) who has the requisite authority to process the violation, and if necessary, *force* compliance.

Protective Mode

Conversely, when processing directly aggressive or violent behaviors that involve the potential for immediate or active physical harm, the security officer functions in *protective mode* and has access to an array of protective tactics and tools to effect behavior change. The security officer's interventionist options include:

1. Physically intervene if it's safe and appropriate to do so.
2. Apply a protective force option that's appropriate to the violator's affiliation status, type code of conduct violation, the subject's resistance level, as authorized by the organization's policy.

3. Contact additional responsible stakeholders (experts) as needed for support and processing (e.g., additional security officers, law enforcement officers, or medical aid).

As in the previous non-smoking policy violation example, if an administrator were to advise a subject to stop smoking and the smoker became verbally abusive toward the administrator, it would be appropriate for security officers to become involved—but only to keep the peace and ensure that the interaction doesn't escalate to violence. However, if the interaction escalated, security officers would transition to protective mode and be authorized to intervene to protect people.

Summary

Security officers, including all other internal and external stakeholders, should use their unique authority, power, expertise, and training to collectively support an organization's ability to prevent and respond to workplace violence without interfering with their ability to remain financially viable. Focusing security officers' duties using an SAP operational deployment mode is the ideal for preventing and responding to workplace violence. First, employees from all departments and jurisdictions use their requisite authority, power, expertise, and training to best manage and resolve the unique conflicted interaction. Second, personal protection for employees, consumers, visitors, or others is prioritized. Third, if individuals are in physical danger, security officers are trained, authorized, and required to intervene. Finally, security officers are not assigned to forced compliance (or enforcement) tasks, allowing them to stay focused on their primary organizational safety mission: protecting and serving.

Recommendations

1. Assign non-security corporate managers to forced compliance activities.
2. Clearly articulate each stakeholder's roles and responsibilities for managing and resolving workplace conflict.
3. Implement an SAP operational deployment mode (ODM).

4. Maximize conflict resolution efficiency by establishing a conflict resolution matrix for all stakeholders.
5. Require security officers to intervene to keep conflict from escalating.

References

Rackauckas, T., 2011. Remarks by district attorney Tony Rackauckas investigation results and filing decision regarding the death of Kelly Thomas. Office of the District Attorney, Orange County CA, 21 September 2011; Web: <www.orangecountyda.com> 21.09.11.

Ponsi, L, Emery S, and Walker, T. $4.9 million settlement reached in Kelly Thomas wrongful-death case. Orange County Register. November 24, 2015.

Chapter 4

Presenting a Professional Image

Problem

The security industry as a whole and individual organizations that employ uniformed security officers have failed to create a unique, distinct, and effective professional security officer identity.

Introduction

Organizations that employ uniformed security officers, and to a lesser extent, the individual security officers themselves, have an identify disorder! They can't decide if they want to be associated with the law enforcement industry, the private security industry, or both. The lack of a consistent and stable identity creates many challenges for the organizations that rely on security officers, the security industry, and its personnel. Some of those challenges include vocational insignificance, low wages, poor working conditions, and a lack of organizational influence and trust. However, perhaps the greatest problem associated with this dissonance is an inability to develop working partnerships with the people they're tasked to protect.

A security officer's uniform or attire plays an important role in impression management, identity formation, and conflict. Unfortunately, many organizations overlook how something as basic as a uniform can help or hinder how security officers are perceived and how it impacts processing workplace conflict. Organizations err when they allow their security officers to wear uniforms that create public impressions that they're law enforcement officers. Public impressions created by uniform choices impact both employees' and consumers' perceptions. Wearing a law enforcement-style uniform creates the impression among employees that their organizations' security officers are mimicking law enforcement and not protectors and creates barriers to cooperation. Similarly, when consumers and visitors perceive security officers as law enforcement officers, unreasonable expectations of service arise. The change to a distinctive non-law enforcement-style security officer uniform will mitigate the internal and external barriers to developing cooperative partnerships.

Process

Organizational members don't want to be *policed* at work, but they do expect their organization to maintain a safe work environment without creating a police state. If security officers are perceived like law enforcement officers because of their uniforms, duty gear, and personal demeanor, organizational members may unconsciously project negative and uncooperative public *policing* attitudes onto their organization's security officers, making it more difficult to gain their cooperation and process interpersonal conflict.

Uniforms and Duty Gear

Choosing the right color, type, or style of security uniform and duty equipment that private security officers carry plays a powerful role in creating a reliable security officer identity and aids the conflict management process. Simply put, a uniform is a statement of an organization's purpose. Private organizations should create mission statements that focus on the protection of people, so their security officer's uniform should reflect that mission. Since most organizations that employ uniformed security officers don't (or shouldn't) require them to enforce rules or policies, or even most laws, law enforcement or military-type uniforms and duty equipment may be counterproductive to an organization's published or implied mission.

The selection of uniforms and duty equipment should be determined by a detailed risk and vulnerability assessment based on the tasks that security officers perform and their operating environment. Unfortunately, many security departments make seemingly pragmatic but counterproductive and unwise uniform choices that purposefully mimic the law enforcement community. Some continue to argue that wearing law enforcement-type uniforms helps create "perceptions of authority" that aid in processing interpersonal conflict. (This is an assumption that's carried over from the law enforcement community.)

Uniform Attributes

Positive public perceptions of authority are important for establishing and maintaining social control necessary for influencing behavior. However, the color or type of uniform worn by a security officer is not the primary reason for positive public perceptions of authority. Some security stakeholders argue that wearing law enforcement-colored and law enforcement-style uniforms creates public perceptions of authority, but they make the mistake of conflating uniform attributes with personal attributes. How an individual wears a uniform or an individual's personal attributes (e.g., height, body type, physical fitness level, age, or demeanor) play a much bigger role in the creation of positive public perceptions of authority than uniform attributes (e.g., color, color combinations, fabric, or style). Overweight or unfit law enforcement officers may not have positive personal attributes, but they still enjoy high levels of social control because of statutory authority, extensive training, availability of backup officers, and access to other protective resources. Private security officers don't have statutory authority, extensive training, or access to additional resources and must rely on their personal attributes to gain and maintain social control needed to influence behavior. Being obese or unfit creates a serious impediment to security officer effectiveness and personal safety.

Conflation

It's easy to conflate uniform and personal attributes and wrongly conclude that the uniform is a primary reason that people cooperate with an officer. Consider how the public may respond differently to an obese or unfit security officer wearing a dark blue law enforcement-style uniform with a physically fit security officer wearing a non-law enforcement-style uniform.

Public perceptions of competency and effectiveness are often directly linked to positive personal attributes. Physical fitness, the most obvious personal attribute, plays a greater role in establishing positive public perceptions than uniform attributes. Unfortunately, since there are typically no health, wellness, or fitness standards required for employment in the private security industry or by organizations, security officers are rarely perceived as having positive personal attributes, which creates negative perceptions of competency and effectiveness, and influences how the public interacts with them.[1]

The mistaken belief that certain law enforcement-colored uniforms (e.g., dark navy-blue shirts and pants) create public perceptions of authority is refuted simply by surveying the various uniform colors and styles worn by the global law enforcement community. Shirt and pants colors and combinations range among white, light blue, green, khaki, dark blue, tan, brown, black, and yellow. Similarly, uniform styles range from causal to military style. Since law enforcement officers throughout the United States wear various colors and types of uniforms, it seems implausible that a specific color or uniform style alone would be responsible for creating universal perceptions of authority and respect among the general public.

You Are What You Wear

Everyone—not just the uniformed security officer—is a poser. Not much has changed since Shakespeare said, "All the world's a stage." What one wears is part of the public pose of creating and managing public impressions. All professions, from the UPS driver to an airline pilot, use attire, manner, and setting to create specific public impressions that set themselves apart from other people and other professions and help improve their productivity. It's obvious that there's a social-psychological relationship between the way a person dresses, the way the wearer is perceived by others, the way the wearer processes those impressions, and the way the wearer acts. The right security uniform should create and maintain a unique security identify that helps, not hinders, its personnel's ability to create positive perceptions and gain people's cooperation.

Everyone has experienced the feeling of "acting like how they felt" because of what they were wearing, whether it's because of a suit or dress

---

[1] See Chapter 9 for more detail on physical fitness.

that fits just right or a feeling that's created when we're getting dressed for a special event. There's an abundance of scientific research in the area of clothing, perceptions, and behavior. Adam Galinsky and Hajo Adam of Northwestern University have recently extended a new area of clothing research and are credited with coining the term "enclothed cognition." The theory suggests that we think with both our brains and our bodies. What one wears creates perceptions of the wearer, and in turn these perceptions affect the wearer's behavior. Prior to this new research, little attention was paid to the social-psychological processes that activate the wearer's behavior based on the wearer's interpretations of how others perceived the wearer. The researchers note, "The current research provides initial support for the enclothed cognition perspective that clothes can have profound and systematic psychological and behavior consequence of the wearer." The researchers go on to say, "… the effects of wearing a piece of clothing cannot be reduced to the wearer simply feeling identified with the clothing. Instead, there seems to be something special about the physical experience of wearing a piece of clothing, and this experience constitutes a critical component of enclothed cognition" (Adam and Galinsky, 2012 p. 5).

The sociopsychological connection between attire and behavior is well established. In fact, it's not limited to the UPS driver, the airline pilot, or the security officer. This sociopsychological effect is like the one that affects the way trick-or-treating children feel and act when they wear a Spider-Man costume.

All organizations use attire as a pose or a way to create certain public impressions of their employees and their organization. Some organizations or industries prefer professional business attire, such as suits and dresses; others prefer a distinctive uniform. Doctors wear white jackets, nurses wear scrubs, college professors wear sports jackets with elbow patches. These clothing choices are often made to visually distinguish an organization's employees from one another, to distinguish employees from their competition, or to create a professional image. However, when private security officers pose like they're law enforcement officers, they add an undesirable dimension—deception—to the legitimate reasons for wearing a distinctive uniform. Unfortunately, this kind of deception has the potential to back-fire, since the public doesn't like being deceived. Attempting to gain the cooperation of community members by manipulating them into believing that private security officers have law enforcement power or authority they don't possess creates barriers to organizational and community partnerships and interferes with the conflict resolution process.

S.A.I.D.: Security Attire Identity Dissonance

Through our research and experience with private security officers and the security industry, we've noticed a unique social-psychological relationship between the type of security uniform officers wear and the way officers act while wearing it. We've tentatively identified the social-psychological processes that are activated when security officers wear law enforcement-type uniforms as security attire identity dissonance or S.A.I.D. Security attire identity dissonance effects non-sworn, private security officers who wear law enforcement-type uniforms, carry law enforcement-type duty gear, drive in law enforcement-type vehicles, and operate in a quasi-military chain of command, especially while using law enforcement titles such as Chief, Captain, Lieutenant, or Sergeant. To assuage this social-psychological tension, known as cognitive dissonance, security officers often exhibit-law enforcement-type behaviors and exert authority and social power they don't legitimately possess.

Even though uniformed private security officers intellectually know they're not law enforcement officers, when they dress like them and interact with other law enforcement trappings such as law enforcement gear, law enforcement radios, and law enforcement codes, security officers often find themselves in a constant state of emotional-psychological dissonance. In fact, cognitive dissonance theory suggests that all humans have a real physical need to resolve their psychological discomfort (Festinger, 1957 p. 20). One typical way is to simply "act the way you feel." Private security officers often relieve their dissonance by acting in ways that make them feel like law enforcement officers.

Unfortunately, the emotional-psychological tension created when private security officers wear law enforcement-type uniforms may enable behaviors that decrease personal safety and increase potential liabilities. Additionally, since the security industry is overrepresented by police-oriented individuals, wearing law enforcement-type uniforms tends to recreate the familiar feelings of "police authority."

One way to relieve the tension stirred up by Security Attire Identity Dissonance is to deliberately (or subconsciously) insert oneself into intense conflicted interactions that necessitate the use of authority, power, or physical force. Since private security officers don't typically have the training, statutory authority, or social power to safely resolve conflicts by asserting authority, these "dissonance-relieving" behaviors often create or exacerbate interpersonal tension, rather than diffuse it.

Although S.A.I.D. is influenced by various social-psychological experiences, the wearing of a law enforcement-style uniform has the greatest influence. Our tentative findings indicate that security officers who wear distinctively "non-law enforcement-style" uniforms, experience lower levels of emotional-psychological dissonance than security officers who wear "law enforcement-style" uniforms. Lower levels of dissonance may minimize a security officer's propensity for using inappropriate, inadequate, or excessive physical force, thus reducing potential civil and criminal liabilities.

Presenting a False Image

Security officers often waste their valuable and limited resources trying to convince organizational and community members they have authority and social power they don't possess. Unfortunately, some private security departments deliberately adopt "law enforcement-type" uniforms with the stated (or implied) purpose of attempting to create the public impression that security officers have quasi-law enforcement powers. Some believe this incidental deception creates added protections, such as perceptions of authority that deter criminal behaviors. Some argue that criminals may be dissuaded from assaulting security officers if they are initially convinced that security officers are law enforcement officers; there's some truth to this. Unfortunately, this theory cuts both ways. Criminals are known to assault law enforcement officers simply based on being easily identified by their law enforcement uniforms. (We don't think criminals who target law enforcement officers will be dissuaded by the fact that the individuals they plan on attacking aren't really a law enforcement officer.)

Dressing like a law enforcement officer may provide other benefits for security officers. For private security officers, especially those who have regular contact with law enforcement officers in the course of their duties, they often feel belittled, disrespected, mistreated, and *talked down to*, by law enforcement officers when they call them for help, and one way to improve this social inequity is to *model* a law enforcement officer.[2] Modeling, from a psychology perspective, is the process of observing the behavior of another

---

[2] Modeling, by definition the process of observing the behavior of another and imitating it, may also be used to describe the art of presenting oneself; both may explain the processes that impact a security officer's feelings and behaviors.

and imitating it. Moreover, the desirability or attractiveness of *the model* is partially influenced by the prestige the model has to the observer. (But the word model may also be used to describe *the art of presenting oneself* and may also be apropos!) But again, this approach may create the opposite effect. Law enforcement officers often think of a security uniform as a costume; the person wearing it is playing "dress up." From their perspective, they had to *earn the right to wear it*, but anyone can simply put on a security officer uniform. To be clear, this does not excuse law enforcement officers from being dismissive or rude to private security officers in the scope of their employment. Sometimes, law enforcement officers don't understand (or forget!) how our culture venerates them and how people admire and look up to them.

As an example, I was recently at an event with my 4-year-old grandson and there were uniformed law enforcement officers walking around. An officer walked up to us and introduced himself. He then knelt to be *eye to eye* with my grandson and offered him a police badge sticker. My grandson was extremely excited because this *prestigious* officer acknowledged him and gave him a police badge sticker (gift). However, before the officer walked away, I said, "Hey, where's my sticker?"[3] We both laughed. But there are some invaluable lessons embedded in this inconsequential interaction. Like my grandson, security officers look up to and admire law enforcement officers and many dream about becoming one; some will, but most won't. But in the meantime, they can take a job where they can dress, act and feel like one, and interact with the "real deal."

Again, dressing like law enforcement officers may create temporary feelings of *power equity* ("see we're on the same team") for security officers, but these feelings are short lived, and these efforts are counterproductive. A professional security officer, even a police-oriented one, must use other representative ideas or people to compare themselves to, and for setting an appropriate standard for determining their personal value and worth. Private security officers represent, serve, and protect their organization's employees and consumers and have a different, not a lower, value than the law enforcement officers.

In the private free market, an organization's jurisdiction or area of responsibility is limited to the property it owns or controls. Private security officers function as agents of the owner; therefore, they have the same

---

[3] There's a little *Walter Mitty* in all of us! I too admire and have expectations about how law enforcement officers should interact with me.

behavioral limits as the owner or the party responsible for the property where officers are assigned. In short, if it's legal for the owner to act, it's legal for security officers to act. The owner's range of protective activities that can be assigned to its security officers is limited by the laws that govern the owner's specific jurisdiction. Organizations limit their security officer's influence through written policies, and socially through practical demonstrations of their organizational safety mission. However, organizations don't typically allow security officers to operate at their full legal and operational limits; they draw narrower behavioral boundaries that are thought to protect their organization from certain liabilities. Security officers often use these restrictive behavioral limits and their organization's perceived lack of social, political, or organizational support to justify their own creative attempts to manufacture authority. Although security officers don't have power to create legal authority themselves, their individual and collective behavior does influence the way the organizational and community members perceive them; positive perceptions of security officers create social influence. But the security officer's personal attributes, demeanor, and communicative expertise, not the law, are the primary ways they gain social control and influence behavior within the organization's behavior limits.

Since authority and social power play an important role in preventing workplace violence, maintaining safe workplaces, and protecting people, it's understandable that security officers would want high levels of authority to help influence social control and influence uncooperative, dangerous, or violent behaviors. To get what most organizations and some legal statutes withhold, private security officers often try to create their own *quasi-legal* authority that they believe will help protect themselves.

Paradoxically, the deliberate withholding of organizational authority is often a motivating factor for deciding to clothe security officers in law enforcement-type uniforms and the choice of various law enforcement-type gear as compensation for organizational constraints. Unfortunately, these choices may create the inverse effect and further alienate organizational and community members, creating additional barriers for positive community interactions.

They include:

1. Unrealistic community expectations,
2. Psychological projection,
3. Dysfunctional social groupings, and
4. Public perceptions of impersonating law enforcement officers.

When security officers dress like law enforcement officers, the community's expectations of service are elevated. Law enforcement officers, unlike security officers, have a wide array of resources and training to help support their jurisdiction's public safety needs. Dressing like law enforcement officers creates an expectation that a uniformed security officer should be able to perform many of the same community safety tasks as law enforcement officers, including coming to a community member's aid under very complicated and potentially dangerous circumstances. This is especially problematic when organizations allow their security officers to dress like law enforcement officers while prohibiting or limiting physical contact with uncooperative or dangerous subjects.

From the community's perspective, not providing them with the same level of service as law enforcement officers ("Especially since you look like them ...") may be perceived by the community as a cruel joke. The failure to meet the community's expectations of service, especially after tricking them, creates negative community attitudes and barriers to cooperation.

Another consequence of security officers dressing like law enforcement officers is the likelihood that community members will project their own negative feelings and attitudes about law enforcement officers onto their private security officer. The public often perceive law enforcement officers as unfriendly, aggressive, and rude. Even law-abiding citizens develop negative attitudes toward law enforcement officers based on negative interpersonal experiences, such as getting a speeding ticket. In the context of creating safe public communities, these negative perceptions of behavior may create some benefit for law enforcement officers, but for organizations and private security officers, they're counterproductive. In the free market, there's an expectation of customer service that's characterized by being accommodating, flexible, friendly, and cooperative. Negative perceptions of an organization's "law enforcement officers" create uncooperative community attitudes that ultimately interfere (consciously or unconsciously) with an organization's community safety mission.

Barriers to Relationship Building

Another consequence of security officers being perceived as law enforcement officers is the unintended consequence of creating an "us versus them" social dynamic. When security officers are socially isolated from the community members they serve, it creates an impediment to the free flow of information and could decrease corporate and officer safety. When private security officers dress (and sometimes act) like law enforcement officers, especially when officers are involved in forced compliance activities, community members may perceive them as spoil sports, or worse, not one of us! Feelings of distrust may lead to increases in conflict and increase the possibility that simple interpersonal workplace conflict will escalate to violence.

When security officers are perceived as part of "them," community members are less likely to talk to them and share strategic information about potential community safety issues, which are necessary for mitigating conflict and maintaining safe communities. Information is an important and necessary commodity for formulating proactive organizational safety strategies. Security officers need to be perceived by community members as being part of "us" in order to maintain open lines of communication with the community members.

Physical and social protection from outsiders is one of the many benefits of being perceived by a community as a member of an in-group (Tajfel and Turner, 1992 p. 126). When security officers are isolated from community members, they become "them." If a security officer becomes involved in a physical altercation and they're perceived as a member of the out-group, it may create an unwillingness for community members to come to their aid or to publicly defend their actions after a critical field interaction. Although most communities have unsophisticated ways of defining in-groups and out-groups, law enforcement officers (and other authority figures) are generally not thought of as members of the in-group, especially when they're responsible for enforcing policies, rules, or laws.

However, when security officers are socially integrated into the broad organizational stakeholder community, they're more likely to be considered part of the in-group, and community members are more likely to physically and philosophically defend them from outsiders.

Impersonating Police Officers

Besides the pragmatic reasons for not allowing private security officers to wear uniforms that look like those of law enforcement officers, there may also be legal considerations.

Most states have laws that specifically forbid non-sworn security officers from looking like or being confused with law enforcement officers. Although private security officers are required to wear a distinctive uniform, their uniform should not create public impressions that a security officer is a law enforcement officer. In California, the Bureau of Security and Investigative Service (BSIS) and the California Business and Professions (B&P) Code forbid security officers from wearing a uniform "with the intent to give an impression that he/she is connected in any way with a government … [law enforcement] agency …." California B&P Code section 7583.38 also states that local law enforcement agencies may regulate the wearing of a private security officer's uniform to make sure it's clearly distinguishable from their officer. Additionally, most states make it a violation of law to impersonate a law enforcement officer.

Practically, even if it wasn't a violation of the law to wear law enforcement-type uniforms, it may still be a poor business decision. Law enforcement-type uniforms interfere with the projection of a unique professional security image because they create high levels of confusion among security officers and the public. Allowing private security officers to wear law enforcement-type uniforms and carry law enforcement-type duty gear is a remnant of an age when enforcement was thought to be the best way to create safe organizations. However, since the primary mission of security officers is to protect people, not enforcing policies and rules, the security officer's uniform should reflect this business imperative.

Perception, Influence, Personnel Titles, and Insignias

Abraham Lincoln is quoted as saying, "Nearly all men can stand adversity, but if you want to test a man's character, give him power." But what may be worse is giving someone the *illusion* of power or allowing them to *act* as if they have it. The use of law enforcement or military titles by private, uniformed security officers *amplifies* the effects of S.A.I.D. and influences public perceptions. "I want to see the manager" is an often-heard expression when a consumer's expectations of service are not met, and they think the person they're interacting with is powerless to *make it right*. However, when the person titled *manager* arrives on scene, there is a sense that they have the *power* to fix what the line (non-manager employee) couldn't. Personnel titles, along with other personal and social influences, impact how consumers will respond to employees and how employees feel about power.[4] Although line customer service personnel occasionally must process low levels of workplace conflict, security personnel (experts) are tasked with processing conflict and violence with emotionally unstable and dangerous individuals and power plays an important role.[5]

When uniformed security officers attempt to resolve conflict with emotionally unstable or dangerous individuals, the impact of S.A.I.D. is activated and referring to themselves or being identified (or called) by law enforcement or military titles may assuage their dissonance. But again, dissonance-relieving behaviors may also lead to law enforcement-type behaviors because it ascribes to officers' feelings of authority they don't possess.

Organizations that employ private, uniformed security officers play a powerful role in crafting public opinions about their security officers, and by extension, the broader security industry. Creating a distinctive non-enforcement security officer-style uniform is an important step to establishing a unique and effective identity. We are not arguing that security officers adopt a nonprofessional uniform; there are obviously certain uniform colors, styles, and the way it can be worn that could create obstacles to social influence that's necessary for managing and resolving workplace conflict and violence. As an example, during "Breast Cancer Awareness," typically in October, many law enforcement agencies create a pink uniform patch, and other law enforcement-related pink items that are worn or used by law enforcement officers. But they don't wear pink uniforms or carry pink law enforcement gear because it would create public impressions and responses that would interfere with their mission.[6] However, one excellent example of a professional, non-enforcement-style uniform that helps create a unique and effective identity is worn by Disneyland security officers in Anaheim, California. And not coincidentally, it's both the "Happiest Place on Earth" and one of the safest![7]

---

[4] It's obvious that there's a social-psychological relationship between: (1) the way a person dresses, (2) the way the wearer is perceived by others, (3) the way the wearer processes those impressions, and (4) the way the wearer acts (see the above discussion). But we think a similar argument can be made substituting personnel titles for attire.

[5] All employees should be trained to process passive–aggressive behaviors, but as conflict escalates only specially trained personnel (the experts) such as supervisors and security personnel should be involved.

[6] The Los Angeles Police Department even painted some of their police vehicles pink! But they only used them to create awareness and not for regular patrol duties.

[7] Disneyland employs approximately 1200 security personnel who interact with approximately 40–50 thousand visitors per day.

To create violence-free workplaces, security officers need to mobilize the efforts of all organizational and community members, and the use of law enforcement or military titles may create the impression that they're more concerned with pointing out *bad behaviors* (enforcement) than *advising* or *protecting* them. Moreover, the use of law enforcement or military titles may cause some to unwittingly transfer their negative perceptions of law enforcement officer interactions onto the organization's security officers and create additional barriers to open communication.

In most organizations, the title of the highest ranking security department member is usually Security Manager or Security Director, business-oriented titles that align perfectly with all other non-security senior management titles.[8] Oddly, some of the same organizations that refer to their *boss* as director or manager then refer to their subordinate supervisors using law enforcement of military titles such as Captain, Lieutenant, and Sergeant. Some even wear various insignias and emblems on their uniform sleeves, chest, and collars to indicate their ranks.[9] The use of law enforcement of military titles and the accompanying *accoutrement*s such as stars on a collar, hash marks on the sleeves, medals, or award pins create impediments to relationship building ("us versus them") with the people security officers need to influence.[10] Likewise, when security personnel interact with employees, they should use their names (we prefer using first names) not their titles or rank. Unfortunately, I've heard security officers interacting with internal stakeholders and refer to themselves using their titles instead of their name, which creates unnecessary interpersonal tension.[11] Conversely, when interacting with resistant consumers or visitors, the use of one's official title may influence an initially resistant person to cooperate.

A more effective method for creating positive perceptions of an organization's security personnel, resisting the disintegration processes, and facilitating integration into the broad organizational social safety net, is to

---

[8] Titles should reflect and emphasize the business not the person.

[9] Many former law enforcement supervisors and former enlisted NCOs and officers I've talked to don't think private security personnel, who didn't *earn* their title in a law enforcement or military setting, should be *given* one.

[10] A metal police-style badge could also create negative attitudes toward security personnel and could be removed from the front of a uniform shirt and replaced with a photo identification card.

[11] Once while employed as supervisor for a law enforcement agency, I needed to talk to a human resources representative during my work shift and went to the HR department in full uniform and carrying full duty gear. When I met with the HR rep, I introduced myself by my first name. She then commented that by using my name and not my title that she felt comfortable (less intimated) talking to me as compared to when she met with other officers who used their titles.

create *business-minded* titles that are consistent with other departmental organizational stakeholders such as associate, lead, or supervisor and title the senior most departmental leader as manager or director.[12]

Internal Challenges

There are significant sociopolitical forces that will resist these necessary perceptual and cultural changes. Since law enforcement officers and security officers continually cross back and forth between the law enforcement and security communities, these two vocations have strong personal and sociopolitical ties that belie some advantages and disadvantages. On the one hand, law enforcement officers are often more attentive and provide better service to organizations when *one of their own* (or several of their own!) is employed there. But on the other hand, it's more difficult to openly discuss the apparent challenges associated with private, free-market enterprises adopting LE philosophies and employing law enforcement-oriented individuals.

Summary

An organization's security officers should not be perceived by organizational members as *enforcers* but rather as *protectors*—partners not adversaries, the good guys; a uniform can influence how security officers are perceived. The truth is, it's difficult to be perceived as one of the good guys (part of *our* team) when security officers dress and act like law enforcement officers and spend a significant portion of their daily duties enforcing policies and rules and pointing out the employees' faults.[13] Security officers should be the stakeholders who come to the employee's and community's aid, 24/7/365, not the group that is perceived as "out to get them."

Something as simple as a uniform or a *look* has the power to create impressions about an organization's security officers who ultimately help or hinder interpersonal relationships and workplace conflict. Uniform and

---

[12] In some organizational settings the title "Chief Security Officer" or "V.P." are appropriate.

[13] Although these changes are necessary and important for building partnership with employees, there will always be a small segment of an organization's population that will interpret security personnel as adversaries no matter how they look. Some simply mistrust people who they perceive as having authority over them, no matter the uniform style that security personnel wear.

equipment selection are an important decision that many organizations and private security departments minimize. Wearing the right security uniform helps create an effective professional security identity that aids in the development of community partnerships and the creation of violent-free communities.

Recommendations

1. Adopt a softer, non-enforcement-style uniform that creates public impressions of approachability and protection.
2. Choose uniform colors and styles that make it difficult for organizational community members (and responding law enforcement officers) to confuse security officers with law enforcement officers.
3. Develop and maintain social influence and authority through interpersonal and social processes.
4. Use business-minded security supervisory titles in lieu of law enforcement or military ones.

References

Adam, H., Galinsky, A.D., 2012. Enclothed cognition. J. Exp. Soc. Psychol. 48. 918–925. http://dx.doi.org/10.1016/j.jesp.2012.02.008.

Festinger, L.A., 1957. Theory of Cognitive Dissonance (fifth ed.). Stanford University Press, Stanford, CA.

Tajfel, H., Turner, J.C., 1992. The social identity theory of intergroup behavior. In: Gudykunst, W.B., Kim, Y.Y. (Eds.), Readings on Communicating With Strangers, McGraw-Hill, New York.

Chapter 5

Protecting Your Reputation

Problem

Organizations are unable to effectively manage workplace conflict and resolve violence without damaging their public reputation.

Introduction

Managing the public's perception of an organization's workplace violence prevention program, including perceptions of the strategies used by their security officers to manage workplace conflict and resolve violence, is necessary to protect people and the organization's reputation. Organizations typically do an effective job of creating positive public impressions of their products or services while simultaneously managing negatives ones, but many of these same organizations fail to include organizational safety as a *service* for which their employees and the public's impressions also need to be managed.

Being competitive and socially relevant in one's marketplace is an important component of an organization's success. Although the use of physical force by security officers may be necessary for resolving workplace conflict and violence, its use has the potential to create negative perceptions of an organization, impacting its social relevance, damaging its reputation, and influencing its ability to stay financially viable.

Process

Negative community perceptions, such as being perceived as too aggressive and feelings of being insensitive to a community's needs, may damage an organization's good reputation. Since people naturally dislike conflict, especially conflict that has the potential to escalate to violence, violent encounters between security officers and resistant subjects have the potential to harm an organization's reputation. No matter how well organizations manage workplace conflict, there will be occasions when it escalates to violence and an organization's response to it has the potential to demonstrate respect or create controversy and impact its reputation.

Reputation as an Intangible Asset

According to George Neufeld, an expert in organizational risk management, a socially acceptable reputation is necessary for maintaining financial viability. In the September 2007 issue of *Risk Management Magazine*, in an article titled, "Managing Reputation Risk," Neufeld argues that an organization's reputation is an intangible asset that accounts for 70% of its value (Neufeld, 2007 p. 70). Neufeld summarizes a 2005 report by the Economist Intelligence Unit (EUI) entitled "Reputation: Risk of Risks." The EUI's report is based on survey input from 269 risk managers in companies of various sizes. The report lists five assumptions about the importance of maintaining a solid business reputation:

1. Corporate reputation is a hugely valuable asset that needs to be protected.
2. Serious reputational damage can occur simply as a result of perceived failures, even if those perceptions are not grounded in fact.
3. Understanding how different aspects of an organization's activities impinge on stakeholder perceptions is a vital aspect of protecting a company's reputation.
4. Many companies feel that their capabilities in managing reputational risk leave much room for improvement, but the high rewards of success should provide strong motivation for progress in this area.
5. Incurring reputational damage can be fatal but establishing a robust reputation can provide a strong competitive advantage.

These five business imperatives demonstrate how valuable an organization's reputation is and how important it is to protect it. Similarly, complaints from the public, both from individuals and through mediated sources, resulting from attempts to protect employees, consumers, and others, also need reputation protection.

Is Perception Reality?

"Perception is reality," as the adage goes. No workplace violence protection program can succeed if a large portion of the community perceives it as ineffective or abusive. Alienating large blocks of organizational stakeholders or community members makes it much more difficult for organizations to meet their organizational safety goals and their state and federally mandated workplace violence programs.[1] A successful strategy should include a strong focus on organizational safety education and interpersonal conflict perception management. Community members that understand the rationale behind their organization's response to workplace violence are more likely to support and defend their choices, especially in the aftermath of a critical incident.

Organizations that fail to implement a comprehensive strategy to manage the public's perception of their workplace violence prevention strategies might not be able to successfully protect their reputation when they're publicly challenged. Absent a comprehensive strategy, organizations could find themselves under the scrutiny of social media without the ability to defend themselves. Unfortunately, once an organization becomes the focus of media attention, it's often too late to manage perceptions; the organization is then forced to shift valuable resources and energy to reputation *damage control.* Many organizations never recover from the social and financial costs resulting from redirecting their limited resources to damage control.

Community Sensitivities

Organizational and community members have varied sensitivities toward using physical force (or failure to use force) to resolve workplace violence and protect people. Generally, there's broad support for *theories* of conflict

---

[1] Such as OSHA 3148 in a healthcare context.

resolution, but not always in their *application* (especially when physical force is used); offended parties may react in a very public manner. Since a large percentage of the public believes in a *forceless* approach to conflict, reinforced by the mass media, society, peers, and even some employers, it's important to educate the community on an organization's rationale and justification for its preferred strategies for keeping them safe. It's not uncommon for community members to voice their disapproval of the strategies used *after* security officers are involved in a critical field incident.

In some communities, security officers are perceived as not assertive enough; in others, even talking to a person with a firm voice could be interpreted as overly aggressive and generate a complaint! It's understandable, but not good policy, when organizations overreact to public challenges of the methods used to protect people and make changes based on public opinions. In many cases, these complaints are the result of poor organizational leadership and a lack of information about an organization's corporate approach to workplace violence, *not* in the actual use of a strategy or technique.

When security officers are observed in critical field interactions with resistant individuals, community members make judgments (uncritical) about the involved participants, known as the *observer bias effect* (Thompson, 2009 p. 1577). These judgments form the basis for how the community members perceive their organization's security officers. There are no neutral perceptions of critical interactions; everyone takes a side! Today when there's a physical altercation between uniformed officers and resistant subjects, community judgments (especially the initial ones) tend to be more critical of the authority figure or uniformed individual.

Historically, when community members witnessed an altercation between a uniformed individual and a resistant subject, there may have been a bias in favor of the uniformed individual (the authority figure) and against the resistant subject. The general assumption used to be that the resistant subject probably deserved the type of treatment he or she was receiving from the uniformed individual. Today, because of the mass media's influence, including social media, and the systemic leadership failures in the criminal justice system, *observer bias effect* seems to be solidly against authority figures (uniformed officers).[2]

---

[2] In 2009, Thompson investigated the impact of observer bias effect resulting from *traditional* broadcast media prior to the advent and easy accessibility of *social* media platforms.

Although observer bias effect is not new, we've recently noticed two quantifiable and associated trends. One trend is a greater willingness of community members (and propagated by the media) to assume that during a critical incident the uniformed individual is probably overstepping their authority; these conclusions are often made without any discernible facts to support them. The other is an overemphasis on cultural, ethnic, racial, and gender-related factors thought to motivate an authority figure's decision to use physical force on a resistant individual.

Protective Strategies for Your Reputation

Every organization needs a systematic approach for evaluating challenges to its security officer's force decisions. Even with a well-crafted public relations campaign, it's difficult for organizations to stand up to community pressure that inevitably comes after a critical field incident between security officers and resistant subjects. Unfortunately, some organizations attempt to assuage the community every time their public image is challenged. Constantly apologizing or kowtowing to community members also makes it more challenging for security officers to resolve future conflict, because it reinforces the perception (or reality) that security officers, or their organizational safety mission, lack organizational authority or value. Successful workplace violence prevention depends on high levels of understanding and tacit agreements among senior stakeholders, organizational members, consumers, and visitors. Establishing and maintaining cooperative partnerships with these various stakeholder groups provides an additional layer of organizational reputation protection.

Education is an important component of reputation protection. Organizations should educate employees and community members on their standards for acceptable behavior and their approved strategies for identifying and processing violators. Organizations should maintain an active public relations campaign that highlights the positive contributions that security officers make every day protecting people and enact a comprehensive crisis communication plan to effectively confront reputation attacks. Moreover, when security officers act appropriately to protect people, even when people are hurt in the process, the organization should publicly advertise and praise their efforts and reinforce its security officer's commitment to safety.

No one who frequents an organization should be surprised to learn that their behavior violates a community's standard, especially when individuals are uncooperative. If security officers are responsible for protecting people from harm, their role and methods for resolving workplace conflict should be clearly articulated to all organizational and community members. If an organization's reputation is challenged after a critical field incident between their security officers and a resistant subject, a lack of clarity on the security officer's role in preventing workplace violence becomes a vulnerable area for a reputation attack.

To protect their organization, stakeholders must be able to document and demonstrate that individual violators were aware of the community standard, the consequences for violating it, and the role their security officers play and the methods they employ to resolve conflict and protect people. There needs to be a clear and defensible pattern demonstrating that uncooperative individuals are treated fairly and consequences for inappropriate behavior have been consistently applied. Finally, the organization needs an internal system for holding security officers accountable for their protective action choices.

Conflict Resolution in Reputation Management

Organizations should communicate their approved conflict resolution methods to all stakeholders in clear and unambiguous ways. In many organizations, there's a mystery surrounding their security officers and the security department's role in resolving workplace violence. (Unfortunately, if a critical field incident becomes public, this mystery may turn into a legal thriller!) Demystifying or personalizing the security department, its role, its methods, and its officers will improve an organization's ability to defend against a reputation attack. Since security officers are often seen as *spoil sports*, the better integrated they are into the organization's broader social networks, the more difficult it will be to develop negative perceptions, especially when security officers are involved in a critical field incident.

An organization's protective force policies and procedures and the acceptable methods for resolving workplace conflict and violence should be communicated to all internal and external stakeholders. (However, the depth and breadth of the details communicated to external stakeholders shouldn't reveal information that creates impediments to organizational safety.) Again, transparency is the best defense against an allegation that security officers acted inappropriately. As an example, if an individual were to complain he was "tased" by security officers and the community was unaware that their security officers carried Tasers, this surprise, not necessarily the fact a person was tased, could be the impetus for creating negative public opinions of the organization.

The Public Relations Campaign: A Key Tool

Many organizations regularly promote aspects of their organization, product, or service to their organizational and community members and the general public, but rarely do they highlight the achievements of their individual stakeholder groups or departmental personnel. Organizations need to expand their current public relations campaign to include an ongoing effort to create, promote, and maintain positive public images of their organization's safety programs, their workplace violence prevention plan, and their security officers. The goal is to create positive perceptions of their organizational safety program and the officers that may be involved in critical field incidents. Since most security officers work 24/7/365, there are numerous and regular opportunities for a public relations campaign to promote and highlight the *good deeds* their security officers regularly perform.

Crisis communication management plays an important role in protecting an organization's reputation. Organizations need a systematic crisis communication strategy to manage crises and respond to public challenges to their reputations. Every organization needs to have trained members of the organization (or the responsibility could be outsourced to a reliable vendor) who are responsible for coordinating the organization's crisis communication plan. In the current social media age, videos filmed, posted, and promoted on the Internet, even by nonaffiliated individuals, could have a devastating impact on an organization's reputation and its ability to remain competitive and profitable, especially if it's unprepared.

The reality is that every organization, especially organizations that take a proactive approach to organizational safety and workplace violence, will be involved in some type of critical field incident that may generate unwanted public attention. Although there are many different types of public attacks to an organization's reputation, including investigations by governmental agencies, allegations of criminal wrongdoing, media inquiries, and civil lawsuits or employee wrongdoing, our primary concern is responding to public challenges to an organization's reputation when force (or protective action) is used by its security officers.

Failure to Manage Perceptions

An organization that fails to manage the public's impressions of its workplace violence prevention program will generate unwanted public attention that will distract from the organization's primary business functions, causing it irreparable harm and negatively impacting its ability to remain financially viable and competitive in its market.

There are thousands of representative examples whereby organizations failed to manage their community's perceptions after a critical field incident between first responder personnel and community members that resulted in irreversible damage to the organization's public reputation.

Examples from Today's Headlines

Headline: "Officers Did Nothing to Help"

On January 28, 2010, two juvenile subjects were videotaped fighting in the Seattle bus terminal while three uniformed security officers stood by and failed to intervene. This video went viral on the Internet and brought worldwide attention to Seattle and to the organization that employed the security officers. The community was outraged because the security officers were perceived as doing nothing while a young girl was being savagely beaten. The video shows one of the combatants being knocked to the ground while a suspect continually kicks a young girl in the face and the security officers stand nearby.

After the video went viral, the security company and the city were sued for failing to act to protect the victim. This interaction ignited a debate about the validity of observe and report policies. The organization was embarrassed because of the worldwide community outrage at the organization's policy that forbade security officers from protecting a person from being attacked. The public's response to this interaction and the organization's poor public response damaged this organization's reputation beyond repair.

Headline: "Officers Pepper-Spray Peaceful Protestors!"

On November 11, 2011, a University of California (UC) Davis campus police officer pepper-sprayed protestors that were blocking a public walkway. The interaction was videotaped and posted online. After the videotape of the interaction went viral, there was an enormous public outcry alleging that the police officers who sprayed the individuals acted in a criminal manner when they pepper-sprayed the nonviolent protestors. This interaction created a public relations battle between the UC Davis administration, the UC Davis Police Department, and the public. The public eventually sided with the UC Davis administration and the protestors. Police Chief Annette M. Spicuzza subsequently resigned and other police officers were suspended (Gordon, 2012b). On September 26, 2012, the university settled a lawsuit for $1 million brought by the affected protestors who alleged the officers used "excessive force," (Caesar, 2012). In the end, this case cost the UC system over $2.5 million: $1 million for legal fees, $500,000 to investigate it, and $1 million to settle with the 30 plaintiffs.

Headline: "Chinese Students Grill USC, LAPD, Raps on Shooting and Security Issues"

On April 9, 2012, two international students were shot and killed while sitting in their car just outside the University of Southern California (USC) campus in Los Angeles. Many in the USC community were not happy with the Los Angeles Police Department (LAPD) and USC campus security department response to these murders. On April 17, 2012, the university community and local law enforcement met to talk about the community's concerns. Several people attending the meeting voiced concerns about security, whereas others said they would transfer to a safer campus (Zheng, 2012). The parents of the two slain students subsequently filed a multimillion-dollar wrongful-death lawsuit against USC (Winton, 2012).

In a Los Angeles Times online article, "USC Hopes Slayings Won't Hurt Foreign Enrollment," Barmak Nassirian, an official at the American Association of Collegiate Registrars and Admissions Officers, stated, "What may have been a very random event may turn into an impression that Southern California is not safe in general, whether that's accurate or not" (Gordon, 2012a).

Whether the USC campus is safe may depend more on how the university manages the community's perception of these senseless killings than on the actual community safety facts!

Headline: "Guards Were Told to Ignore Mayhem"

On January 17 and 18, 2015, a University of Michigan fraternity, Sigma Alpha Mu, rented rooms at the Treetops Resort in Gaylord, Michigan and created approximately $430,000 in damages. At the time, the resort's security staff did nothing to stop the unsafe behaviors that resulted in the damage because they were instructed not to intervene in *damage-causing incidents*. According to the police report, three security officers witnessed a lot of mayhem, but could do nothing about it. Mark Thomas, a security guard at Treetops who thought the college guests "should have been ejected," also felt embarrassed when other resort patrons complained to him about the fraternity, yet "he was unable to do anything." Attorney Paul Dillon, who represented the Treetops said that the security officers didn't intervene in the rowdy behavior because the officers were faced with a "difficult balancing act" in weighing the desires of some visitors to have peace and quiet against those who want to have a good time. He went on to say, "Certainly, at some point, a group of guests may need to be told that their behaviors are out of line." Treetops manager Barry Owens is aware that people will likely criticize their handling of the situation. But he presented an interesting *bright side* of the event. Owens said, "… I already know things we can do to avoid this kind of situation in the future … But based upon the information our people had at the time, I'm proud of how our team responded." In this instance not advising hotel guests that their behavior was unsafe and could create unsafe conditions and damage, and not evicting them from the premise, made the general manager proud.

The Treetops initially estimated damages at $100,000. However, they later adjusted it to more than $430,000, and received nearly $200,000 from its insurance company based on the damage and loss. Ann Arbor attorney John Shea, a prominent Michigan lawyer who has closely monitored the Treetops case, said he was struck by the security guards' claims that they were instructed not to take steps to stop the property damage. If proven, he said, that could be construed as insurance fraud.

"I think Treetops should be concerned about whether its insurer will claim fraud if Treetops failed to disclose that it had specifically instructed their security personnel not to take any action to stop any damage prior to the insurer paying Treetops over $200,000 for that very damage," Shea said. In 2014, the Treetops resort filed for bankruptcy.

This organization's failure to empower security officers to advise people that their behavior is inappropriate, and other leadership failures, including security supervisors and senior management, may have exacerbated the damages and, more importantly, led to unnecessary civil, legal, and social costs, influencing the organization's decision to declare bankruptcy.

Headline: "Hospital Dumps Woman in Wheelchair in the Street"

On September 20, 2019, an incident involving a discharged patient at the Antelope Valley Hospital in Lancaster, California, and its security officers was captured on video and posted to YouTube and Live Leak, where thousands of people viewed it. Although the details of this incident are still disputed, the individuals who filmed the incident are convinced that the hospital and their security officers acted insensitively to the former patient, while the hospital stated that it was "… based on a fabricated situation …" and "The content of their video is both misleading and based on a fabricated situation …" (Gatlin, 2019). In the video posted to YouTube, security officers are seen assisting medical personnel pushing a woman in a wheelchair through the parking lot. Several of the security personnel are seen trying to cover their faces to hide their identity and covering their photo identification badges, as if they were involved in unethical activities. Additionally, some of the security personnel became defensive when aggressively interrogated by the individuals filming and made comments that exacerbated the interaction. Regardless of which perspective is more accurate once the incident became widely known, it affected the ability of the security officers to focus on activities meant to protect people and the organizations ability to serve its patients. This incident created a public relations crisis for the hospital and its security officers.

These are a few examples among thousands in which an organization failed to effectively manage its community's perceptions of workplace violence prevention, leading to a loss in reputation. The experience and wisdom gained from these interactions (and many others) and the public's reaction to these types of interactions needs to influence an organization and its security officer's conflict resolution decision-making processes.

Summary

Responsible organizations need to employ uniformed security officers to prevent and respond to workplace violence and protect people. However, they also must anticipate and manage how the public will respond when their security officers use force in carrying out their duties and are involved in critical field incidents. No matter how perfect an organization's response to workplace violence prevention, there will be occasions when security officers will interact with violent individuals and have no choice but to use protective action to neutralize the threat. These responses have the potential to save lives, but they also have the potential to damage an organization's reputation. Crisis communication plays an important role in helping the community and the general public understand (and appreciate) the processes organizations use to protect its most valuables assets, its employees and consumers.

Recommendations

1. Educate organizational and community members on the strategies used by their security officers to prevent workplace violence.
2. Educate organizational and community members on the security officer's roles and responsibilities in preventing workplace conflict and violence.
3. Highlight the positive contributions that security officers make to organizational safety.
4. Develop a comprehensive crisis communication strategy to manage the community's perceptions to critical field incidents involving the use of protective force by security officers.

References

Caesar, S., 2012. UC reaches pepper spray deal. B2. Los Angeles Times, 26 September 2012.

Gatlin, A., 2019. Video of Patient at AV Hospital was 'fabricated'. Antelope Valley Free Press, 21 September 2019; Web: <https://www.avpress.com/news/video-of-patient-at-av-hospital-was-fabricated/article_8c7d6a2c-dc33-11e9-b73d-efaf191bea76.html>

Gordon, L., 2012a. USC hopes slaying won't hurt foreign enrollment. Los Angeles Times, 14 April 2012; Web: <www.latimes.com> 07 July 2012.

Gordon, L., 2012b. UC Davis police chief quits after critical report on pepper spraying. LA Now, Los Angeles Times; Web: <www.latimesblogs.com> 12.07.12.

Neufeld, G., 2007. Managing reputation risk. Risk Resolution Magazine. 54. 70–79.

Thompson, W.C., 2009. Interpretation: Observer Effects. In: Jamieson, A., Moenssens, A. (Eds.), Wiley Encyclopedia of Forensic Science Wiley, Chichester, UK, pp. 1575–1579.

Winton, R., 2012. Parents of two slain Chinese students sue USC. Los Angeles Times, 18 May 2012; Web: <www.latimes.com> 02.07.12.

Zheng, G., 2012. Chinese students grill USC, LAPD reps on shooting and security issues. USC Annenberg Digital News, 17 May 2012; Web: <www.neontommy.com> 04.07.12.

Chapter 6

Developing Policies on Workplace Conflict and Violence

Problem

Organizations are unable to formulate effective processes that guide their security officer's workplace violence prevention activities.

Introduction

Organizations need to implement processes that guide their security officer's activities for managing workplace conflict and resolving violence, and protecting people, based on a realistic understanding of the nature of conflict and conflict makers.

Workplace conflict is inevitable, unavoidable, and unpredictable, and to effectively address it, security officers need policies that afford them the greatest latitude possible for the use of protective tactics and tools to keep simple interpersonal workplace conflict from escalating to violence. For the sake of our discussion, we'll refer to these policies as *protective force* policies.

Process

Organizations often base their protective force policies on a flawed understanding of conflict, violence, and safety. Workplace safety is not the absence of conflict; rather, it's effectively managed and resolved conflict. Failure to understand this axiom often creates a false belief that violence can be avoided or assuaged without force. Unfortunately, this failure has led to the creation of ineffective protective force policies that increase risk for security officers who engage with dangerous individuals.

Conflict Defined

Strictly defined, interpersonal conflict is an expressed struggle between at least two interdependent parties who perceive incompatible goals, scarce resources, and interference from the other party in achieving their goals (Wilmot and Hocker, 2007 p. 102). However, face-to-face employee/ consumer interpersonal conflict, known as customer service conflict, is a unique type of interpersonal conflict. It involves a clash of failed expectations, unmet needs, and desires, when non-affiliated individuals (consumers) interact with an organization's employees, where products and services are sold or provided, and their behavior violates an organization's code of conduct and it has the potential to harm employees, visitors, or others.[1] In an organizational setting, there are other types of workplace conflicts that don't involve consumers, but our focus is on the effects of failed customer service interactions that have the potential to escalate to workplace conflict or violence.

Processing Workplace Conflict: A Unique Business Task

The task of managing workplace conflict and resolving violence is unlike any other regularly performed business duty. The most obvious reason for this is that it involves *deliberately* placing a small cadre of employees (security personnel) in possible physical danger in order to protect others.

---

[1] We discuss how failed expectations and unmet needs influence interpersonal tension and workplace conflict in Chapter 11.

This fact is often overlooked or minimized in discussions of workplace conflict, violence, and policies for addressing it. Unlike other employees, security officers choose to run toward potentially dangerous situations while many others run from them. Moreover, when interpersonal conflict becomes unbearable (even when other employees instigate it), "security" is often called in to deal with it. Additionally, there are unique challenges associated with managing processes that never sleep. Security officers are typically the only organizational stakeholder group that performs their job duties 24/7/365 and on every major holiday.

Security officers interact with potentially uncooperative, dangerous, and violent individuals under two conflict scenarios, directed or initiated:

1. Security officers are directed to reports of possible violations of policy, safety, or law.
2. Security officers initiate contact with individuals whom they observe in possible violation of policy, safety, or law.

There are many types of unacceptable behavior that may violate an organization's behavioral standards; some violate the law, and some violate policies. However, the primary focus for professional security officers should be on mitigating behaviors that have the potential to create unsafe conditions for employees, consumers, visitors, or others.

Sometimes when individuals are advised by security officers to correct their inappropriate behavior, they respond aggressively and/or become physically assaultive. Passive aggressiveness and direct aggression are the two most common behaviors that security personnel are confronted with. Although most aggressive encounters can be managed using effective communication, some interpersonal workplace conflict can only be resolved safely by physically intervening.

Potentiality and Complacency

The most effective way to minimize conflict's potentiality is for trained security officers to intervene early and disrupt the interpersonal frustration cycle before emotions become unstable and behavior escalates. In fact, even relatively safe organizations are not immune from the potentiality of simple interpersonal conflict escalating to workplace violence. Low-conflict environments have some unique and additional challenges compared to historically high-conflict or less safe environments. In low-conflict environments where conflict is rare and violence is even rarer, complacency can create a false sense of safety for community members and security officers. Unlike low-conflict environments, high-conflict environments provide regular opportunities for security officers to interact with conflict makers and learn how to defuse interpersonal tension. Complacency, created by the infrequency of interpersonal conflict, also creates additional training challenges for organizations and security officers.

At this point in our social evolution, there's no need to make an exhaustive list of the thousands of violent interactions that have already taken place in so-called "safe" communities where there was a low probability of anything bad happening. Every organization, regardless of a lack of previous violent activity, needs to have contingencies in place to process workplace violence and not solely rely on their local law enforcement agency.

Whose Force Is Best?

Even senior corporate managers who have a realistic view of workplace conflict and violence still prefer that their security officers *wait* for law enforcement officers to respond to their facility to interact with dangerous individuals. Moreover, they argue that when security officers are involved, unlike involving law enforcement officers, they often *create* rather than *mitigate* liabilities when they use protective tactics or tools to resolve violent encounters. It's true that law enforcement officers have statutory protections when they use force within the scope of their employment, such as being immune from liability, and private security officers don't.[2] Although law enforcement officers may be personally immune from liability when they use force, when they use it to subdue a violent subject on an organization's property, they're not immune from the public's response! Regardless of whether security officers or law enforcement use force, organizations need to consider their *total* liabilities such as their ability to serve their consumers, maintain financial viability, and protect their reputation.

---

[2] California Penal Codes 148a, 834a, and 836.6a.

The Roles of Response Time and Proximity

Unlike law enforcement officers, security officers have the distinct advantage of *being there* when a conflicted incident occurs. *Response time* plays an important role in protecting people and preventing workplace violence; being in proximity to the conflict and knowing the organizational geography gives security officers a unique advantage over responding law enforcement officers. *Being there* provides victims immediate assistance and a greater level of physical protection, and mitigates potential liabilities associated with negligence. A stark reminder of how important response time is was seen in the Sandy Hook school murders in Newtown, Connecticut. It took Adam Lanza about 11 minutes to kill 20 children and 6 adults![3] In the aftermath of this tragedy, and other school shootings, many schools now employ armed law enforcement officers, school resources officers, and private security personnel to protect students and staff.

Force as a Normative Business Strategy

The simple truth is to prevent workplace violence, maintain violence-free workplaces, and protect people; there will be occasions when it's necessary to force individuals to correct their harmful behavior because it's in the best interest of the entire community and the right thing to do. Ideally, when individuals are confronted about their potentially harmful behavior, they would simply correct it and be grateful that it was brought to their attention. However, today more seemingly simple interpersonal conflict often ends up escalating to violence. Today, individuals are seemingly becoming more resistant to being asked to perform even the simplest tasks, such as adjusting their potentially harmful behavior to conform to an organization's code of conduct standard. Unfortunately, some organizations abdicate their responsibility when they appease conflict makers, which ultimately backfires by emboldening more potentially harmful behavior and in the end creates a greater potential for simple conflict to escalate to violence.

---

[3] The first police officer arrived approximately 3 minutes after the 911 call. The Newtown Police entered the school about 14 minutes after the shooting began.

Forceless Organizational Safety

It's impossible to resolve workplace conflict without occasionally using physical force. There's no perfect forceless strategy that can stop some individuals from being physical threats. The goal is to create an environment where reasonable people are likely to voluntarily submit to an organization's behavioral standards when they're advised by its security officers. However, when they won't, it may be necessary for security personnel to force them to conform to the standard. Although many of these violations should be resolved by law enforcement officers, it's naïve (and dangerous) to think that all violent encounters could (or should) be resolved by waiting for the local law enforcement to save the day.

No sensible person prefers processing workplace conflict using physical means. There are many reasons to prefer talk over physical means; it's safer for personnel, for resistant individuals, and for the community. In fact, when security officers are competent communicators, fewer interpersonal conflicts escalate to the point of needing force to solve. However, when talk isn't effective or there are exigent circumstances, victims of violence can't wait for law enforcement to respond; security officers need to act to protect.

The Role of Security Professionals

The type of people who are drawn to the security industry typically are passionate about helping people. For security officers, it's extremely frustrating to be constrained by policies that forbid them from intervening to protect potential crime victims. It's also unrealistic to expect people with these personality traits, who are drawn to the helping professions, to stand by while people within their reach are being victimized. They know that it may take a simple interaction to dissuade subjects and protect victims from harm.

There's no policy that will stop security officers from protecting themselves from physical harm and, in many cases, from coming to the aid of others who are being victimized. In fact, even when there are explicit policies forbidding security officers from getting involved, ethical individuals will act anyway, placing their ethos in conflict with possible corrective action, because their personal character and integrity dictate it. One practical outcome of restrictive protective force policies is making ethical individuals into lawbreakers! The only way to create ethical and responsible security officer behaviors that will provide high levels of protections is to enact situational protective force policies enabled by reliable training and effective supervisory leadership.

Case Examples: Why Policy Is Important

These following examples are stark reminders of the potential dangers that every organization faces.

October 12, 2011: Salon Meritage, in Seal Beach, California; eight killed.

February 27, 2012: Three students at Chardon High School in rural Ohio were killed when a classmate opened fire.

April 2, 2012: A 43-year-old former student at Oikos University in Oakland, California, walked into his former school and killed seven people, "execution-style." Three people were wounded.

May 29, 2012: A man in Seattle, Washington, opened fire in a coffee shop and killed five people and then himself.

July 9, 2012: Three people were killed at a soccer tournament in Wilmington, Delaware, including a 16-year-old player and the event organizer, when multiple gunmen began firing shots, apparently targeting the organizer.

July 20, 2012: Aurora, Colorado; James Holmes entered a midnight screening of *The Dark Knight Rises* and opened fire with a semiautomatic weapon; 12 people were killed and 58 wounded.

August 5, 2012: A white supremacist and former Army veteran shot six people to death inside a Sikh temple in suburban Milwaukee, Wisconsin, before killing himself.

August 14, 2012: Three people were killed at Texas A&M University when a 35-year-old man went on a shooting rampage; one of the dead was a police officer.

September 27, 2012: A 36-year-old man who had just been laid off from Accent Signage Systems in Minneapolis, Minnesota, entered his former workplace and shot five people to death and wounded three others before killing himself.

December 14, 2012: Adam Lanza murdered 26 people at Sandy Hook Elementary School in Newtown, Connecticut, including 20 children, before killing himself.

March 13, 2013: Herkimer, New York; Kurt Meyers, 64, killed four people at a car wash and barbershop with a shotgun before he was shot and killed by police.

Sept. 16, 2013: Washington, DC; Aaron Alexis, 34, shot and killed 12 people inside the Washington Navy Yard with a 12-gauge shotgun before he was shot and killed by police.

June 7, 2013: Santa Monica, California; John Zawahri, 23, opened fire in a home and later the campus of Santa Monica College, killing five people with a semiautomatic rifle. He was killed during a shootout with police.

July 26, 2013: Hialeah, Florida; Pedro Alberto Vargas, 42, shot and killed six people with a semiautomatic weapon in his apartment complex before setting fire to his own apartment. He was shot and killed by a SWAT team.

June 17, 2015: Charleston, South Carolina; Dylann Roof, 21, walked into a historic black church in Charleston, South Carolina and kills nine people.

Oct. 1, 2015: Roseburg, Oregon; Christopher Harper-Mercer entered Umpqua Community College in southwest Oregon, opened fire, and killed nine, wounding seven others before police shot him to death.

November 27, 2015: Colorado Springs, Colorado: Robert Lewis Dear stormed into a Planned Parenthood health clinic and killed three people and wounded nine.

December 2, 2015: San Bernardino, California; A man and a woman, both armed with assault weapons, walked into a holiday party and killed 14 people and wounded 17 others.

June 12, 2016: Orlando, Florida; Omar Mir Seddique Mateen, 29, killed 49 people and injured 53 at Pulse—a popular gay nightclub. President Barack Obama described the horrific event as an "act of terror and hate."

October 1, 2017: Las Vegas, Nevada; Stephen Paddock, 64, opened fire from the 32nd floor of a Las Vegas hotel during a country music concert located at the Mandalay Bay Resort and Casino, killing more than 50 people and injuring about 200 others.

November 5, 2017: Sutherland Springs, Texas; Devin Patrick Kelley, 26 entered First Baptist Church during service, killing at least 26 people and wounding at least 20.

February 14, 2018: Parkland, Florida; according to federal officials, Nikolas Cruz, a 19-year-old former student at Marjory Stoneman Douglas High School, walked into the school and killed 17 students before taken into police custody.

April 22, 2018: Nashville, Tennessee; Travis Reinking, a 29-year-old man, opened fire at a Waffle House restaurant in Antioch, a Nashville neighborhood, killing four people and wounding two. An AR-15 rifle was found at the scene.

May 18, 2018: Santa Fe, Texas; Dimitrios Pagourtzis, 17, walked into Santa Fe High School and opened fire, killing at least eight people including fellow students. According to Reuters, the male student entered the school around 8 a.m.

June 28, 2018: Annapolis, Maryland; At least five people were killed at *The Capital* newspaper in Annapolis, Maryland. Police and witnesses say the suspected gunman was taken into police custody around 5 p.m. EST.

October 27, 2018: Pittsburgh, Pennsylvania; Robert D. Bowers walked into the Tree of Life Congregation synagogue shouting anti-Semitic slurs, opened fire and killed 11 people using an AR-15-style assault rifle.

November 7, 2018: Thousand Oaks, California; A man dressed in all black and carrying a handgun opened fire inside the Borderline Bar & Grill, a country and western dance hall, killing at least 12 people, including a sheriff's deputy who arrived at the scene to provide assistance.

February 15, 2019: Aurora, Illinois; Gary Martin, a 45-year-old factory worker killed five people at the Henry Pratt Co. manufacturing plant in the suburbs of Chicago with a .40 caliber handgun. He was later killed by police in a shootout.

May 31, 2019: Virginia Beach, Virginia; DeWayne Craddock, a 40-year-old civil engineer working for the Virginia Beach Public Utilities Department, fatally killed 12 people. All but one of the people fatally killed were city workers. Craddock was shot and killed by police.

August 3, 2019: El Paso, Texas; Patrick Crusius of Allen, Texas, killed 20 and injured more than 26 others at a WalMart.

August 31, 2019: Midland and Odessa, Texas; Aaron Ator killed seven people after being fired from his job.

It's obvious from these and the many other violent interactions that no community is immune from acts of violence. Could some of these tragedies been avoided if organizations employed professional security officers as a part of their workplace violence prevention plan?

Summary

Organizations must base their protective force policies on a realistic understanding of interpersonal workplace conflict and violence and the unique challenges that security officers face when preventing and responding to workplace violence and managing and resolving interpersonal workplace violence.

Recommendations

1. Enact a workplace violence prevention plan based on reality, not how it ought to be.
2. Enact situational protective force policies enabled by reliable training and effective supervisory leadership for security officers.
3. Create a security department mission statement that focuses on protective activities and integrates with the organization's global mission.
4. Assess the actual job duties currently being performed by security officers to define and delineate protective duties from non-protective ones.
5. Reassign non-protective duties to other stakeholder groups.
6. Develop an accurate job description based on the newly created security officer job duties.
7. Recruit, interview, hire, and retain security officers based on the newly developed job description.
8. Create incentives to encourage officers who resist the newly defined security officer protective job duties to find other positions within or outside the organization.

Reference

Wilmot, W.W., Hocket, J.L., 2007. Interpersonal Field Conflict (seventh ed.). McGraw-Hill, New York.

Chapter 7

Protective Force and Organization Risk Management (ORM)

Problem

Organizations are unable to formulate effective protective force policies that prioritize the protection of people without creating unreasonable financial, legal, and civil exposure.

Introduction

To manage workplace conflict and resolve violence and protect people, security officers will need to use protective force. Therefore, they will need effective policies to guide their actions when physically interacting with dangerous or violent individuals.

In a private, free marketplace, there's no policy that can mitigate an organization's total liability to zero. Even when an employee acts within policy and the law, the employee and the employer can still be sued civilly. To protect themselves, organizations must enact policies that create the safest workplaces possible while simultaneously protecting against total liabilities, not just civil liabilities, associated with their security officers using force to protect people.

Unfortunately, some organizations make the mistake of focusing exclusively (or obsessively) on policies that attempt to mitigate civil liabilities, associated with certain security officer behaviors, known as risk aversion, but overlook other just as potentially damaging liabilities, such as creating unsafe conditions for security officers, employees, and consumers and protecting their reputation and their ability to compete in their unique market.

Therefore, policies that guide security officers' physical interactions with dangerous or violent individuals, whether they restrain or allow certain behaviors, need to be biased toward actions that protect people. Unlike other behaviors that organizations attempt to influence, conflict resolution activities are some of the most complicated because they involve unpredictable and highly emotional human interactions.

Many organizations prefer their security officers to operate using an observe-and-report safety model, a risk-aversive model, that prohibits or severely restricts security officers from making physical contact, or any contact at all, with dangerous or violent individuals, hoping to avoid liability.

Process

Rarely do organizations, or security directors/managers, clearly define their security officer's protective force boundaries through a written protective force policy defining the circumstance that allows or requires the use of protective tactics and tools. Some senior corporate managers don't think they need to because their use is prohibited, others create narrow limits for their use, while some want it to be vague to allow for any response to either fit or to be prohibited. Or, security officers are authorized to use protective force but only if they can guarantee that no one will be injured or file a complaint, so no one does! Since no policy or procedure, no matter how well written or executed, can stop security officers from intervening under all conditions, prohibiting intervention is unrealistic, impractical, and ineffective. A better approach to risk mitigation is to craft policies that provide reasonable boundaries, encouraging certain behaviors while discouraging other behaviors.

The Role of Policies in Conflict Resolution

Organizational stakeholders often live in a constant state of denial when it comes to workplace violence prevention and the effectiveness of their approved protective force policies. Some senior non-security managers don't understand the *business merits* of allowing (or requiring) their security officers to use protective force to protect people and prevent workplace violence. Perhaps the most obvious reason that organizations enact restrictive protective force policies is that they don't trust their security officers (or their security director/manager) to act responsibly during high-stress, interpersonal conflict.[1] Some fear that if security officers are given too much leeway to act or to use protective tactics or tools, they'll regularly resort to the most extreme physical options, even when dealing with low levels of resistance. Other stakeholders believe that forbidding or severely restricting officers from using physical options to protect themselves or others will keep security officers from using them.

Situational Protective Force Policies and Reframing

Policies guiding security officers' use of protective tactics and tools need to take into consideration the unique set of circumstances that officers may face and allow for a broad range of options for dealing with the various types of workplace conflict. When security officers are faced with dynamic field conflict and use situational protective force policies, they're better able to calculate the level of risk they face and choose the best risk/benefit option that both *serves and protects*. Protective force policies should be framed in the affirmative to account for the totality of risk based on inaction, not the risk associated with action. Too often, policies are written in a form such as "don't do that," or "this is not allowed."

Interestingly, even when protective force is authorized, security officers rarely use it. This infrequency sometimes confuses stakeholders and may make it even more difficult to understand why force is ever necessary. First, since most organizations don't operate in a *war zone* and have the support of their local law enforcement agency, there aren't a great number of aggressive interactions that need to be resolved using force. In fact, even in organizations where there are a high number of conflicted interactions,

---

[1] Another example of the Trust Tautology.

the use of protective force is still a rarity because its use is only authorized under very narrow circumstances. Lastly, even when organizations authorize the use of force to resolve violent workplace interactions, there's still an "atmosphere of fear" associated with using force because too often the protective force policy is inconsistently applied and security officers believe they'll be unfairly disciplined or fired.

In 1989, the U.S. Supreme Court, in *Graham v. Connor,*[2] developed a constitutional standard to evaluate law enforcement (non-deadly) use-of-force challenges and determined that hindsight was an unfair standard for evaluating whether law enforcement officers were justified in using physical force. The current federal legal standard for judging the decision to use force is *objective reasonableness,* based on the totality of circumstances (TOC).[3] Although the objectiveness test specifically applies to government-employed law enforcement officers, we think it's a useful standard for evaluating a security officer's decision to use protective force. The *Graham v. Connor* decision makes it clear that there are unique challenges associated with trying to protect people from violence.[4]

Graham v. Connor: **The Legal Standard**

1. Judged from the perspective of the officer.
2. Examined through the eyes of an officer on the scene at the time force is applied.
3. Based on the facts and circumstances confronting the officer without regard to the officer's underlying intent or motivation.
4. Based on the knowledge that the officer acted properly under the established law at the time.

---

[2] U.S. Supreme Court, *Graham v. Connor,* 490. US 286 (1989), No. 87-6571.

[3] The Fourth Amendment "reasonableness" inquiry is whether the officers' actions are "objectively reasonable" in light of the facts and circumstances confronting them without regard to their underlying intent or motivation. The "reasonableness" of a particular use of force must be judged from the perspective of a reasonable officer on the scene, and its calculus must embody an allowance for the fact that police officers are often forced to make split second decisions about the amount of force necessary in a particular situation.

[4] AB392 became law in California January 1, 2020 modifying the conditions that allow law enforcement officers to use deadly force from *reasonable* to *necessary.* The law was written, in theory, to induce officers to use de-escalation and crisis intervention techniques, if possible, before using deadly force.

Private Security Officers and Objective Reasonableness

How is object reasonableness defined in a private (non-sworn) context?

In short, a reasonable security officer decides to use force based on the objective behaviors of a subject and uses their available tactics and tools based on their training. Merriam-Webster's Dictionary of Law defines a reasonable man (person) as:[5]

> a fictional (hypothetical) person with an ordinary degree of reason, prudence, care, foresight, or intelligence whose conduct, conclusion, or expectation in relation to a particular circumstance or fact is used as an objective standard by which to measure or determine something.

This hypothetical person serves as a comparative standard for determining the rightness of an action or to assign liability.

When applied in a private, free market context, the use of protective force by security officers should be used to protect people (and only under exigent circumstances - property) by reasonable security officers who use objective criteria to assess an individual's behavior and then choose and apply a reasonable solution. The solution needs to account for the TOC known to the security officer at the time the force was used, and its use must be:

1. within policy,
2. proportional to degree of subject resistance,
3. pragmatic,
4. necessary,
5. moral/ethical, and
6. legal.

An ethical and effective protective force policy needs to define objective reasonableness and then train its security officers on how it should influence their decision-making.[6] To help security personnel apply the objective reasonableness standard to a subject's verbal and/or physical resistance, we developed a chart, known as the *Situational Protective Action Risk*

---

[5] https://www.merriam-webster.com/legal.
[6] Training is discussed in Chapter 10.

Continuum chart, or SPARC chart, that helps personnel determine their best available responses to workplace conflict or violence.[7]

Hindsight

The reality is that no employee in any department, including security officers, could ever be required to effect behavior change if their employment status depended solely on meeting a hindsight standard. Using a hindsight standard to evaluate less space a security officer's protective force decision-making processes creates unproductive and hesitant officers. Since people's behavior during interpersonal conflict is highly unpredictable, officers need to be focused on making the safest choice, given the unique circumstances in which they find themselves, not hyper-focused on how their choices may impact their employment. For a good person (and I assume that reflects the character of most security personnel), just knowing that force may be necessary to protect people (the theory) naturally stimulates a low-level cognitive dissonance because protecting someone (including one's self) may require using a protective tactic or tool (the application) that creates enough pain to stop an attacker from continuing to victimize another. The use of hindsight to judge a security officer's decisions often heightens this awareness, increasing cognitive dissonance, and causes a *hesitancy to act*, decreasing officer and organizational safety.

Leaderless

A lack of leadership among senior corporate managers and senior security managers feeds these false protective force assumptions. There are persistent and underlying sociopolitical fears among some senior corporate managers that if they authorize security officers to use protective tactics and tools, they may be forced to defend their actions (not that they always want to!). For some senior security managers, learning that their security officers have been involved in a physical interaction is their worst nightmare! It's not that they're insensitive to people being injured, but an incident may end up jeopardizing their employment because they may have some culpability for

---

[7] We discuss the SPARC chart in greater detail in Chapter 12.

training or supervision. Moreover, they often force security leadership into the uncomfortable position of having to defend their employees' actions to senior stakeholders who are socially or politically situated much higher in the organization.

Unfortunately, these interactions and the corresponding "fault-finding expeditions" often lead to security officers being *thrown under the bus* to satisfy organizational, social, or political agendas. This is especially common when physical force is used to stop a violent aggressor and individuals are injured. Physical injuries resulting from attempts to protect people naturally generate a lot of interest among various senior corporate managers. However, security officers need to be assured, through policy and practical demonstrations of faith, that if they need to use force to protect people and they operate within policy, their organization will stand by them.

In 2011, in what is thought to be a highly unusual organizational response to a critical field incident involving physical injuries, a hospital security officer was forced to kill a subject while attempting to resolve workplace violence, and his organization defended him (Cavatti, 2011). While working as a uniformed security guard at WellStar Cobb Hospital in Austell, Georgia, Jerry Evans got into a physical altercation with a patient, and the patient subsequently died. Evans, the security officer, was subsequently arrested and charged with involuntary manslaughter and reckless conduct. However, after reviewing surveillance video and conducting an internal investigation, the hospital's senior stakeholders determined that Evans wasn't at fault, nor did he violate any organizational policies. The hospital decided to defend Evans and even helped him obtain an attorney. Unlike the circumstances surrounding this incident, senior stakeholders too often apply an unrealistic hindsight analysis to decisions made by security officers, especially when the interaction results in injuries. Although the business community generally doesn't support a hindsight standard, organizations often apply it to employee discipline.

Like many of my readers, I've been to various leadership seminars and read many good leadership books. Unfortunately, when security officers are socially or politically situated at the lowest levels of their organization's sociopolitical power structure, it's challenging to exhibit effective leadership characteristics without paying personal, professional, social, or employment consequences. Although both security and non-security stakeholders are responsible for these leadership failures, senior non-security stakeholders share the *greatest responsibility.*

Bottom-Up Leadership

Unfortunately, these leadership failures are often self-fulfilling prophecies; security managers are afraid to exert leadership, senior non-security stakeholders fail to trust their security manager's leadership abilities, and security managers socially withdraw and become timid and ineffective followers. This leaderless cycle is responsible for neutering many seemingly professional security directors/managers and has subsequently created a stockpile of discarded, but competent, unemployed security professionals. Again, these leadership challenges can be traced back to one of the recurring themes of this book; organizations typically position the security function and its security officers low in the organizational hierarchy making *bottom-up leadership* practically impossible.

In fact, in 2011, Joseph Wambaugh, the famous former LAPD detective and author, wrote an op-ed article for the *Los Angeles Times* in which he commented on the sociopolitical environment at the University of California and the consequences of taking a leadership role. In November 2011, UC Davis police officers pepper-sprayed students who were sitting peacefully on the ground after refusing to move. The publicity surrounding this incident led to the police chief's resignation. Wambaugh wrote, "… instead of doing what most police chiefs routinely do (including Bratton[8]) and issuing a pension-saving CYA statement and throwing her cops under the bus. That loyalty probably cost her [Spicuzza] the chief job" (Wambaugh, 2011). In the end, Annette Spicuzza, the UC Davis police chief, took responsibility for her officer's actions and resigned, and other police officers were subsequently disciplined or fired.[9]

Part of the long-term solution to these leaderless environments is both individual and organizational. Individual security professionals need to find ways to create personal relevance in their organizations,[10] and all senior stakeholders need to encourage (and practice) the sharing of organizational, political, and social power, with their subordinate security department directors and managers.

---

[8] William Bratton was the LAPD Chief at the time of the incident.

[9] In an email to the Sacrament Bee in California, Spicuzza wrote, "As the university does not want this incident to be a defining moment, nor do I wish it to be mine. I believe in order to start the healing process; this chapter of my life must be closed."

[10] We cover the benefits establishing standards in Chapter 9.

Paradoxically, one plausible reason that explains why senior non-security stakeholders are resistant to share organizational power with their own chosen security leaders may be their preference for hiring police-oriented personnel who don't share their business, educational, philosophical, or social background. The truth is these two personality types have very little in common!

Organizational Risk Management (ORM)

The process of developing appropriate protective force policies that determine the acceptable limits for the use of protective tactics and tools involves logical, social, and emotional considerations. Attorneys, human resource managers, risk managers, insurance providers, police managers, business executives, and even the mass media have influence over these policy decisions. Unfortunately, too often senior non-security managers fail to take their senior security directors'/managers' experiences and opinions seriously when developing their organization's protective force or other related security department policies. The undeniable truth is that it's impossible to create effective policies for any department (especially protective force policies) without integrating the thoughts, experiences, and opinions of the end users of a policy. When it comes to developing policies meant to guide an employee's response to violent behaviors and mitigate organizational risk, there's often a big "theory versus application" disconnect; some ideas on paper just don't work.

Unlike other organizational processes, managing passive–aggressive behaviors and trying to keep behaviors from escalating to workplace violence are some of the most complicated *business* activities that organizations need to get right. Therefore, it's imperative that personnel who have actual experience dealing with aggressive and violent individuals in a private, free-market, security context are involved in the process of creating policies that determine their security officers' behavioral boundaries for interacting with resistant individuals. Corporate personnel who have never been personally involved in resolving workplace conflict and violence often make false assumptions about how to best process it. The solutions range from an overreliance on communication to a fear that if force is authorized, it will be regularly used, injuring people and creating unnecessary liability and unwanted attention.

The truth is, even if it were possible, with detailed policies, procedures, and ongoing training and supervision, to guarantee that every security officer would adhere perfectly to a restrictive protective force policy, under all circumstances, no policy can control what dangerous subjects will do!

The Risks and Benefits for Using Protective Force

Human resource managers, risk managers, and attorneys typically have the greatest, or only, influence over what protective tactics and tools are available to security officers and how and when they should be used. Since preventing and responding to workplace violence may require security officers to use force to protect people, organizations need to determine the risk/benefits for its use. Practically, there are only two ways to respond to risk: mitigate it or transfer it. Since organizations can't usually transfer the risk, they have to enact policies that will mitigate it.[11] But how are those protective force policies determined? It's understandable that organizations want to protect themselves, but they must also consider how their policies impact a security officer's ability to protect themselves and others, under highly volatile, violent interactions, not simply based on *difficult* consumer interactions.

Consider what options a security officer might want or need, and how an organization's protective force policies may impact a security officer who's confronted by a violent individual, perhaps under the influence of drugs and alcohol, at 2 o'clock in the morning, who's actively assaulting employees or consumers. If the security officer in this hypothetical scenario were seriously injured or killed trying to subdue this criminal, will the corporate managers who prohibited the security officer from using every available protective tactic or tool to protect their life, lose personal, professional, social status, or their employment for limiting the security officer's options? There are real-life consequences for security personnel when their protective force options are limited.

---

[11] Some organizations believe that by using a contract security vendor they can transfer the liability. It may lessen some liabilities, but not the organization's total liabilities. In tort law the organization with the greatest assets ("deepest pockets") pays the greater costs.

Unfortunately, it's hard not to think that *a lack of trust* is the real, or primary, motivating factor to explain why human resource managers, risk managers, and attorneys overestimate risk associated with their security officers' activities.[12] Since a lack of trust is a factor (or the factor!) in determining risk, then limiting access to certain tactics and tools may seem like a sound way to mitigate it, but it's not. A lack of trust shouldn't be used to determine the appropriate risk/benefit for action/inaction. Rather, human resource managers, risk managers, and attorneys should use *lack of trust* as a motivating factor to advocate for the establishment of security officer competency standards for applicants and employees, which naturally improves reliability and trust.[13] Security officers should be provided every advantage possible for protecting themselves and others.

Shifting Liability

Even under ideal circumstances, the practical impact of instituting overly restrictive protective force policies isn't mitigating actual negligence claims; rather, it shifts the responsibility from individuals to the organization. Even if one were to assume that any action taken by security officers would increase civil liability because of injuries to employees or resistant subjects, it's just as likely that any action taken by security officers would mitigate potential civil liability by stopping or reducing potential injuries. Negligence claims not only create civil liability, they also impact a community's perception of the organization and could damage its reputation. Organizations that turn a blind eye to their organization's safety concerns, such as failing to protect them, damage their reputation, which in turn makes it even more difficult for the organization to compete in their marketplace, thus creating unnecessary financial instability.

When security officers have no *affirmative* requirement to protect employees, consumers, or others, potential civil liability is shifted, transferred, or passed from the employees to the organization. It's hard to hold security personnel accountable for something they're not responsible for.

---

[12] Again, the Trust Tautology.

[13] Paradoxically, they are often the ones that resist the establishment of nonnegotiable security officer standards.

There are both personal and financial costs or *transfer fees* associated with these interpersonal transactions. Although vicarious liability, the responsibility of the superior for the acts of their subordinates, a strict secondary liability, accounts for these failures, when personnel have no obligation to protect others, especially when they *appear* to be able to help, naturally increases an organization's liabilities.

Effective and responsible protective force policies that guide security officers' actions (or inaction) should be based on calculated risk. Calculated risk is a time-constrained decision matrix used by security officers in the field to decide the safest available method(s) for neutralizing a threat to protect people, based on the TOCs and their ability, ethics, expertise, training, law, and policy, as compared to all other known and available choices. Regrettably, protective force policies are often based on risk aversion, a strong disinclination to take risks, and exacerbate unsafe conditions. Protective force policies based on calculated risk create outcomes that have the greatest *total* benefits for security personnel, employees, and consumers, as compared to outcomes based on risk aversion. Since all protective force choices are naturally comparative, policies based on calculated risk allow security officers to choose their best available option to them at the time of the interaction to effectively and safely resolve workplace violence. Unlike risk-aversion policies, calculated risk-based protective force policies create affirmative behaviors that security officers should take, not behaviors they should avoid.

Restricting or prohibiting security officers from making physical contact with individuals may cause more problems than it solves. Protective force policies that forbid security officers from making physical contact delay help from being rendered to potential victims in a timely manner. Waiting to act is only beneficial when workplace conflict doesn't involve the potential for physical injuries.

When employees are restricted from physically interacting with resistant subjects, there are unintended consequences. Since all organizations have a "duty-of-care" responsibility and must maintain safe environments that protect all people who frequent their property, having security officers seemingly available to help but who are actually prohibited from acting may increase the potential of a negligence claim for breach of duty. Restricting security officers from physically interacting with resistant subjects also means that community members must rely on other resources to protect them from aggressive subjects, no matter how long it takes them to arrive. Because workplace conflict comes in varying sizes and degrees of trouble, there will naturally be some low-level interpersonal conflict that security officers could easily resolve by preventing simple interactions from becoming serious ones.

Organizational Malpractice

From the community's perspective (and civil juries too), presenting security officers as *available* but unable or too incompetent to protect them could be interpreted as organizational malpractice. When community members need help and security officers don't respond in the way they expect, regardless of the actual policy, the community may perceive officers as *unwilling* to act to protect them; inaction creates negative public perceptions. Community members will interpret a lack of willingness to help a person in distress as a moral failing. Even in organizations where community members are knowable about their security departments protective force policies (which is rare), no community education program can override a community's tendency to expect *Good Samaritans* to come to their aid when they're being victimized.

Expectations of Service and Workplace Conflict

Expectations play a powerful role in creating interpersonal tension and influence perceptions of service. Communities naturally expect uniformed security officers to perform many organizational safety tasks, including protecting them from being victimized. In fact, when uniformed security officers dress like law enforcement officers, wear law enforcement-type duty gear, and drive law enforcement-type vehicles, it elevates community members' expectations of service. Unlike security officers, law enforcement officers have access to vast resources and training to help support their community's safety needs. Dressing like law enforcement officers creates an expectation that security officers *should* be able to perform many of the same high-level community safety tasks as law enforcement officers, including coming to community members' aid under very complicated and potentially violent circumstances. There's a natural relationship between perceived expectations of service and actual service. From the community member's perspective, not providing the same level of service as law enforcement officers ("especially since you look like a cop...") may be perceived as a cruel joke. Failure to meet the community's expectations, especially when the community feels duped, creates negative community attitudes toward security officers and an organization's safety program. This is especially paradoxical when organizations that enact restrictive protective force policies while employing security officers that dress and look like law enforcement officers!

Although it's difficult to calculate actual loss in revenue based on negative public perceptions of safety, consumers will avoid frequenting a location if they feel unsafe, no matter what product or service is provided there. There are numerous examples where a damaged reputation based on safety concerns was costly to the organization and brand. For example, the LA Dodgers' organization lost millions of dollars in revenue in 2011 because a fan, Brian Stow, was severely beaten, and the assault created public perceptions that the stadium was unsafe. Fans, including Brian Stow and his family, that attended baseball games at Dodger stadium reasonably expected to be protected from violence.[14]

Underground Behaviors

Restrictive protective force policies may lead to *underground* security officer practices; these practices create unintended civil and criminal liability for organizations. When there's strong disagreement with an organizational policy, regardless of the actual written policy, employees will often passively or actively resist them. Resistance to protective force policies is played out in various ways by security officers. Passive-resistant security officers simply become unproductive employees; they avoid any interaction that may involve potential conflict. On the other hand, actively resistant officers may become overly aggressive with subjects, to prove their organization's protective force policies are ineffective. Furthermore, these underground practices create an additional burden for supervisors. Supervisors must keep *policy resisters* from developing cliques that undermine the organization's safety mission and create negative officer morale.

Forbidding security officers from using physical strategies to resolve workplace violence also creates employment uncertainty. Since security officers are constantly processing complicated interpersonal behaviors and

---

[14] Dilbeck (2011).

potentially violent situations, they're continually challenged to make *snap* protective force decisions, sometimes choosing between ethical behaviors (self-protection) and policy compliance. This uncertainty has the potential to decrease security officer safety because their attention is focused on avoiding behavior that could get them fired rather than making the safest decision.

Moreover, restrictive protective force policies cannot protect employees, visitors, or others when they're being actively and savagely assaulted while waiting for the law enforcement to arrive. If an employee or consumer is assaulted while security officers stand by and "do nothing," especially if the interaction is recorded and posted on the various social media outlets, how would it impact an organization's online reputation? Consumers don't react positively when an organization's security officers refuse to help people while they're being victimized.

Summary

Risk managers are (partially) right! Allowing untrained and incompetent security officers the option of using physical force to resolve workplace conflict is a bad decision and may increase various liabilities. However, on balance, it's clear that when trained professional security officers use physical force to protect people and resolve workplace conflict, it creates greater *total benefits* than total risks for people and organizations.

To protect people and successfully resolve workplace conflict, organizations need to create effective policies that guide their security officer's behavior for interacting with dangerous or violent individuals. To minimize financial loss, maximize safety, and mitigate potential liability, organizations enact protective force policies that are thought to mitigate organizational risk.

Recommendations

1. Enact situational protective-force policies based on calculated risk and provide security officers access to a full spectrum of conflict resolution tactics and tools.
2. Involve the security personnel, *end users,* in the process of creating (or rewriting) protective force policies.

3. Support and recognize security officers who use protective force ethically to protect people from harm.
4. Use a calculated risk matrix to develop protective force policies with a bias towards action.

References

Cavatti, R., 2011. Hospital backs guard accused of killing patient. WSBTV, 31 October 2011; Web: <www.wsbtv.com> 03.03.12.

Dilbeck, S., 2011. Attendance at Dodger Stadium continues to plunge. Dodger Now, Los Angeles Times, 13 May 2011; Web: <www.latimesblogs.com> 10.07.12.

Wambaugh, J., 2011. Op-Ed Columnist: Joseph Wambaugh solves the great UC Davis pepper-spraying incident. Los Angeles Times, 27 November 2011; Web: <www.articles.latimes.com>.

Chapter 8

Involving People in the Process

Problem

Organizations continue to recruit, hire, and retain security officers who don't reflect their organizational safety priorities.

Introduction

Today, it is extremely challenging to find *qualified* security officer candidates. When the economy is good and law enforcement departments are hiring, security directors/managers simply cannot find *quality* security officer candidates to hire.[1] It takes unique individuals to successfully process workplace conflict involving dangerous or violent individuals. The success of an organizational safety program depends on employing personnel with the right temperament, morals, and skills to process interpersonal workplace conflict and violence.

Every unique department within an organization has a preferred employee profile based on the assigned duties and certain personal and professional characteristics, which may include aptitude, intelligence, integrity, experience, education, or even availability, to name just a

---

[1] There are two additional associated problems: the organization hasn't defined those characteristics, or they have, and their organization won't let them screen for them.

few items. These desired, preferred, or required characteristics and prior work experience are thought to be necessary for maximizing an employee's productivity in a unique job setting. Most job descriptions contain a reality gap between what the official job description states and the actual duties that employees perform. But the typical security officer job description is often disconnected from the kind of protective activities they're actually assigned. Unfortunately, too often the "other assigned duties" morph into actual duties that security officers regularly perform. When the organization doesn't define the duties accurately, recruiting, hiring, and retaining the ideal security officer becomes impossible.

Processing workplace conflict is often demanding and sometimes dangerous, and organizations need to be assured they're recruiting, hiring, and retaining the right type of individuals who can manage interpersonal conflict and protect employees, consumers, and others from violence.

Process

Based on current hiring trends, most senior security and non-security senior stakeholders, corporate managers, and human resource personnel believe that police-oriented individuals are best equipped to process workplace conflict and violence and meet their organizational needs, at both the line officer and at senior security leadership positions.

But how did these hiring preferences become embedded in organizational culture? What is the ideal security officer profile?

Currently, police-oriented individuals are the most desired security officer applicant types. Some believe police-oriented individuals are an asset because the task of processing workplace conflict requires individuals who are physically and mentally disciplined to deal with the risk associated with interacting dangerous or violent individuals. On the other hand, police-oriented individuals tend to overemphasize physicality as their preferred method for processing conflict, while minimizing collaborative, more customer-focused, interpersonal solutions.

The current assumptions about the ideal security officer candidate are not always based on a rational assessment of a security officer's job duties or mission. In fact, they may be the result of unexamined and perhaps faulty assumptions about the nature of free-market, private organizational safety and organizations not clearly defining their security officer's mission and related tasks.

Nothing in Common

As we've discussed throughout the book, and a recurring theme, stakeholders often *conflate* the *superficial* visual similarities between uniformed public law enforcement and private security officers and *assume* that police-oriented individuals can replicate their public community safety success in their private organizational context. The truth is, other than wearing a similar uniform, working 24/7/365 shifts, and interacting with criminal behavior, there are *no* job task similarities (or, there shouldn't be!). Although it's true that these professions have similar missions, such as protecting people and maintaining safe environments, they accomplish it using different principles and processes, and operate in a very different context. Private security officers use protective activities to accomplish their primary mission, managing face-to-face, employee/consumer disputes and protecting people. Conversely, law enforcement officers achieve their mission primarily by enforcing laws and arresting people. These unique job task differences are nicely summarized in the excellent book *Hospital and Healthcare Security.*

The writers define security officer activities as organizationally defined, privately funded, and profit-driven, and they include the protection of people and property, prevention of incidents, and administrative remedies, whereas law enforcement activities are publicly defined, taxpayer-funded, and results-driven and include the enforcement of laws, apprehension of offenders, protection of society, statutorily defined, and legal remedies. The authors go on to note, "Although some common ground may exist between security and law enforcement, at least 90% of their respective activities are different" (Colling and York, 2010 p. 20).

Role Conflicts: Law Enforcement versus Private Security

There are substantive differences between processing face-to-face employee/consumer disputes that occur within a private organizational setting and processing interpersonal disputes in the public, and in nonorganizational settings (e.g., when the conflict is expressed in a workplace). The primary reason that private organizations employ security officers is to influence people's behavior and protect employees as a component of their overall workplace violence prevention plan. When disputes arise in face-to-face commerce, there's at least one employee and one nonemployee consumer involved, each bound by laws, rules, and expectations of socially acceptable behavior. There's a much narrower range of acceptable behaviors for employees than for consumers. In a dispute with a consumer, an employee's behavior is *strictly* guided by organizational policies, and possibly regulatory ones, while consumers have few constraints. Their behavior is *loosely* guided and determined by societal norms and personal preferences for communicating their dissatisfaction with employees. A dissatisfied consumer who verbally or physically threatens an employee may still maintain their *customer status*.[2] Conversely, if an employee behaved in the same manner toward the consumer, they'd lose their *employee status*; two different interpersonal standards regulate these interactions.

Unlike conflict that occurs in a private workplace setting, public interpersonal disputes are typically between two or more people who have deep emotional, psychological, romantic, and familial connections, who may also be under the influence of drugs and alcohol. The parties themselves, and the communities they socialize in, may even accept verbal or physical abuse as a socially acceptable way to resolve their disputes.[3] When law enforcement officers are called to these *domestic* disputes, the combination of deep emotional connections between the aggrieved parties and the intoxicating effects of drugs and alcohol make them the most dangerous types of human interactions that law enforcement officers face.

Unlike private security officers, law enforcement officers rely on statutory authority, scope of employment immunity, extensive officer training, and access to various law enforcement resources to suppress crime, arrest law breakers, process public disputes, and maintain safe communities. In fact, ask any former law enforcement officers currently working in a private security role and they'll provide firsthand accounts of

---

[2] In fact under some circumstances, even an individual who is not a consumer creates additional expenses for the organization and has no legitimate reason for being on an organization's property can demand, and be awarded *customer status*, and is then expected to be treated like one.

[3] As an example, physically assaulting a person as *payback* for abusing one's romantic partner.

how difficult it is to maintain high levels of personal and organizational safety *without* these statutory attributes and resources. When law enforcement officers leave the law enforcement vocation, their authority stays behind. Even though law enforcement officers have extensive training in dealing with difficult and dangerous individuals, their law enforcement training has much less value in a private setting without its enabling statutory authority and scope of employment immunity. It doesn't take long for former law enforcement officers to get their first introduction to the perceived insignificance of their perceived authority, when called upon to process a workplace dispute. Without statutory authority and scope of employment immunity, it would be impossible for law enforcement officers to create safe public communities. Since private security officers don't possess these enabling attributes, attempts to enforce laws, policies, or rules often exacerbate interpersonal tension. This is one of the many reasons why it's counterproductive to train private security officers using law enforcement-based standards.

Many senior corporate managers don't understand these distinctions and assume that a law enforcement officer's conflict resolution expertise will simply transfer into a private workplace setting. In some instances, this confusion may lead to a flawed hiring paradigm where police-oriented individuals are prioritized over security candidates with no prior law enforcement experience.

Unlike private organizations, public communities generally give law enforcement officers wide latitude in the methods and tactics they use to create safe and secure communities. In fact, it's not unusual for an organization's approved methods and tactics for processing workplace conflict resolution to have very little impact on preventing workplace violence; they just happen to be the only ones acceptable to the influential organizational stakeholders. For instance, in a private security setting, even the perception of being "too aggressive" with potential conflict makers may lead to negative public perceptions, community dissatisfaction, and a loss in market share. Conversely, if law enforcement officers are perceived as "too soft" on criminal behavior, it may lead to increases in criminal activity, decreases in community satisfaction, and negative public perceptions.

Additionally, police-oriented personnel don't typically possess the type of private, free-market customer service skills or personality traits that are generally required to process the ambiguity and the unique challenges associated with managing interpersonal workplace conflict in a competitive market, such as preferring communication over more physical solutions.[4] In fact, this conclusion is supported by a recent University of California report.

In response to an allegation of excessive force in 2012 by police officers from the University of California Davis campus, Mark G. Yudof, the University of California president, ordered a fact-finding review of the incident. One of the tentative findings reported in the "Response to Protests on UC Campuses, draft for public comment," written by University of California Dean Christopher F. Edley, Jr. and University of California General Counsel Charles F. Robinson, concluded that the UC system should hire police officers with the "right temperament" to deal with the unique challenges of managing conflict on a college campus. The authors wrote, "No matter how robust our policies are, we cannot avoid breakdowns in the police response to protests and civil disobedience if individual officers on the ground do not have the appropriate outlook and temperament" (Edley and Robinson, 2012 p. 46). In other words, even effective policies (and supervisory controls) can't make up for failures to hire the right personality type.

As a vocational group, law enforcement officers have been extremely effective at convincing senior corporate managers that their actual (or perceived) law enforcement expertise provides an added benefit for private organizations. However, there's nothing inherent about law enforcement work that *naturally* prepares individuals for the unique challenges of free-market, private security employment.

Paradigm Shift: From Law Enforcement Officers to Business Professionals

In some cases, law enforcement experience may be an impediment to success in a private, free-market organizational safety setting. Since many organizations don't want their security officers to physically interact with resistant subjects or they place extreme limitations on their interactions, it's unrealistic to require (and expect) police-oriented individuals to refrain from *acting like* law enforcement officers when confronted with potential criminal behavior.

---

[4] Both law enforcement officers and private security officers receive communication training, but they use communication much differently based on their unique contexts. See Chapter 11 for more detail on the use of communication.

There are many talented former law enforcement officers who have made a successful transition to private, free-market security officer roles. However, others have struggled making this transition from an environment where they had authority, power, prestige, and social influence, to an environment without those positive attributes. This is especially true for those former law enforcement officers or managers who become security directors/managers without prior private, free-market security employment, and/or have never been employed in the market they're now employed in. They quickly find out that the dynamics of leading non-sworn, private security officers, especially with no experience in that field, is much more challenging than leading sworn law enforcement officers, in their profession.

In sum, it takes a unique personality type to successfully process interpersonal workplace conflict and violence; a police-orientation does not necessarily qualify an applicant. Again, this is not a critique of an individual's character; rather it's an incompatible feature of the setting where one applies their experience. The truth is, an honest assessment of these biases benefits security officers who want to become law enforcement officers, former law enforcement officers transitioning out of law enforcement and into the private security market, and the public and private organizations they represent. There are plenty of opportunities for police-oriented individuals to gain a better understanding of the challenges that private (non-sworn) security officers face in the private, free-market security field *prior* to leaving a law enforcement career.

The Business-Minded Security Officer

To improve customer service and organizational safety, and mitigate the effects of workplace violence, organizations need to recruit, hire, and retain security officers who are more like business stakeholders and less like law enforcement officers; this refocus will be a challenge. To be clear, we are not proposing that police-oriented individuals (or former military personnel) be dissuaded from private security employment. The truth is these individuals embody many of the required personality and character traits necessary for success in the private security market. However, placing police-oriented individuals in noncontact, observe-and-report settings, where physicality is discouraged, naturally creates unreasonably high levels of cognitive dissonance for individuals that often manifests itself in inappropriate behaviors.

Police Academy Graduates

Police academy graduates make up a high percentage of the line personnel in the security industry. Academy graduates are generally young men and women who don't yet have actual law enforcement experience but are police trained. Security directors/managers desire this employee profile type because police academy graduates are typically physically fit, have personal discipline, and are trained to process dangerous behaviors. Academy graduates choose private security employment because it's often viewed as a stepping stone to becoming a law enforcement officer. From the academy graduate's perspective (and the hiring agency's perspective), working in the private security sector provides an excellent opportunity to develop necessary communication and conflict resolution skills. This relationship benefits the academy graduate/employee and the hiring law enforcement agencies, but it doesn't always benefit the private organizations that employ them, primarily because academy graduates have a high turnover rate when they move on to become law enforcement officers.

Former Police Officers

Former police officers make up another significant percentage of private security employment, especially at the senior security management level. Former police officers are typically older males who have actual law enforcement experience and become employed in the security industry as a second career. These individuals are looking for supplemental income or potential second careers until they retire (again). These relationships benefit the former police officers/employee, but they don't always benefit the private organizations that employ them. The two primary challenges for former law enforcement officers transitioning into the private sector are the significant learning curve, and for those who have a solid pension, a lack of financial motivation. These challenges are especially true for former law enforcement officers who are hired to lead security departments who have never performed the job duties of the personnel they're hired to lead. Paradoxically, organizations that prefer to hire former police managers as their security director/manager, with no security experience and no experience in a particular sector (e.g., education, healthcare, or retail), don't typically fill other senior corporate positions with individuals who have no prior experience in that job category! Again, this is not a criticism of the honorable men and women who have had success in law enforcement; rather it's a failure of organizations to truly understand the differences between these two distinct professions. Providing protective services for a private organization has little in common with providing law enforcement services to the public.[5]

Both police-oriented employee types use the security industry as a placeholder. For police academy graduates, it's a stepping stone; for former police officers, it's a second career.

The high numbers of police-oriented individuals employed in the private security industry may be responsible for exacerbating three longstanding security industry myths:

1. There are no other necessary prerequisites or requirements for security employment other than prior law enforcement training or experience.
2. Law enforcement training or experience naturally prepares individuals for private security employment.
3. Security employment is much easier than police work.

It could be argued that providing security services in a private free market is more challenging than police work because success is primarily the result of cultivating, developing, maintaining, and influencing free-will relationships without using of coercion. (Unlike security officers, when law enforcement officers can't get people to *act right*, they can always use force or an arrest.[6]) Moreover, it also requires security personnel to occasionally use force to protect people, but its use can't interfere with an organization's ability to remain financially viable! Additionally, the infrequency of processing violent behaviors creates other challenges resulting from complacency. The personality traits required for these tasks are much different than those needed for success in a law enforcement context.[7]

---

[5] A better method for orienting former law enforcement personnel to private sector security work is to place them in a subordinate position to an experienced security professional.

[6] Whether they use reasonable or probable cause, or other less ethical means to influence behavior.

[7] The good news is that law enforcement applicants who have success in a private, free-market security settings are much better prepared for the challenges of law enforcement because they've learned how to use communication to influence difficult people without needing to use force.

Vocational Relevance

These myths, and other unexamined assumptions about the security industry, are partially responsible for the high levels of vocational irrelevance for today's security officers. It's unfortunate, but security work is primarily thought of as a job and not a vocation. For many, the vocation was, or will be, a law enforcement career. These ideas are reinforced by the numerous police-oriented individuals who enter the private security industry and consider it a *step down*. One representative example of this belief occurred when a security officer applicant for my contract security company, who was a former law enforcement officer, threated to sue me because he failed to meet our health, wellness, and fitness standard and therefore wasn't offered employment.[8] In short, he thought that since he was qualified to be a law enforcement officer in his current health and wellness condition that he was qualified to be a "security guard." Like many others, he had low expectations about the qualifications necessary for success in the private security industry, but my clients don't! These industry myths and false assumptions interfere with the professionalization process and make it much more difficult for security officers to create vocational relevance.

No industry can maintain a high degree of professionalization or vocational relevance when a large percentage of its personnel (in this case, security officers) continually cross back and forth between other industries. The security industry cannot create vocational relevance if they continue to rely on law enforcement departments for their talent; however, the inverse relationship does!

One of the primary challenges of hiring individuals who are in *career holding patterns* is that their employment status tends to turn over at a high rate. Academy graduates eventually end up getting hired by law enforcement agencies, and former law enforcement officers often become disenchanted by the constraints of the private security market and quit. Constant employment turnover is a deficit in any field and makes it impossible for organizations to maintain continuity and highly productive workforces. The task of maintaining violence-free organizations requires a cohesive, experienced, productive team of unified personnel who are highly

---

[8] As the owner/operator and leader of our organization, I typically perform our health, wellness, and fitness assessments alongside of our job applicants. As of this writing, I'm 59 years old and can still run a 10 K under 60 minutes.

committed to the goals and objectives of their organization and the security departments that employ them. The need to constantly recruit, hire, and train new security officers creates serious financial and productivity costs for organizations. When individual employees are more focused on their personal circumstances than on the organization's needs, it negatively affects employee productivity and organizational safety.

Hiring the Right Security Officer

Although there is no perfect matrix for hiring the ideal security officer, following is one reliable path to success:

1. Create a distinct security officer mission statement that supports and integrates with the organization's global corporate mission.
2. Determine the specific job duties required to meet the corporate and departmental missions.
3. Identify those duties that require a significant level of health and wellness to safely perform.
4. Determine the ideal employee profile and required competencies that are necessary to successfully perform the job duties.
5. Create a job description based on the mission-focused duties and employee profile.
6. Write policies and enact processes that enable security officers to perform those duties.
7. Create a job flyer that accurately lists the required duties for recruiting applicants.
8. Require applicants to perform as many of the required competencies as possible to become employed.

Unfortunately, since security directors/managers are often prohibited from screening for the required competencies, they have no choice but to ask the applicant if they can meet them.[9] Moreover, organizations often hire (and retain) the wrong security officer applicant type because they haven't determined the required competencies or the *ideal* employee profile required to successfully perform the job; they just need to hire *someone*.

---

[9] We call this process "qualified by personal affirmation" or QPA.

Provided below is a representative example of a Southern California healthcare organization's job flyer, posted to Indeed.com, on April 8, 2020, seeking to hire a security officer (or guard).[10] The listed job description focuses on the protection of the hospital's physical assets and *not* on the people. The type of person that applies for this job will reflect the advertised employee profile which *clearly* doesn't demonstrate the importance of protecting its employees and consumers.[11]

> Job Summary: Performs under the supervision of Security Supervisor, Performs a variety of duties related to the security of the hospital building and rounds to prevent fire, theft, vandalism, illegal entry and to assure the personal safety of employees, patients and visitors.
> Essential Job Duties:
>
> ◼ To perform Building and ground patrols to assure the safety of the hospital.
> ◼ To investigate any thefts, disturbance, suspicious activity.
> ◼ To assist staff with patient restrains and intervention of disruptions by patients, visitors or staff.
>
> Facility access Control. Including the identification of individuals entering the facilities, controlling access to and from sensitive areas, locking, unlocking and restricting traffic at various times. To activate and deactivate anti-theft alarm system. To report crime and have open communication with local law enforcement.
>
> ◼ To observe and report activities on daily activity report, question any unauthorized individuals and escort them out as need it.
> ◼ To provide timely response to reports of violent activity or request for the assistance in the restraining violent and aggressive patients of visitors.
>
> Based on this job flyer, it's obvious that this organization is operating on a 20th century *security* mindset and has failed to upgrade its security posture to focus on the protection of people.

---

[10] The flyer is copied as it was published. We didn't correct syntax or grammar deficiencies.
[11] This job flyer looks like one that may have been used 10 years ago!

Impediments to Hiring

In most organizations, the hiring process is a collaboration between each unique organizational department and the human resources department. Often, these processes apply to all organizational candidates and allow for no variances to address the unique role of hiring security officers. Under most circumstances, the senior security director/manager is subject to the processes that the human resources department has established and approved for interviewing and screening potential security officer candidates. It's true these employee screening challenges are not unique to security departments and occur to some degree in every organizational department. Since there's only one employee category, security officer, whose job responsibilities include protecting people from harm, confronting violent behaviors, and carrying protective weapons, there needs to be additional screening processes to identify the emotional and physical qualities necessary for interacting with these types of harmful behaviors. The standard screening processes that are used to qualify non-security applicants cannot accomplish this goal.

To qualify security officer candidates, the human resources department needs to rely on input from the senior security department director/manager to create additional, legal, processes to properly screen and qualify applicants. Unfortunately, since the senior security department director/manager is typically located low in the organization's sociopolitical organizational hierarchy and the human resources department processes are thought to be nonnegotiable, challenging the hiring policies is discouraged and often comes at a high personal cost.

Qualifying Security Officers: Risks/Rewards

Security officer candidates *should be* required to demonstrate the verbal and/or physical attributes that are needed to successfully perform the required job duties *prior* to being hired. Unfortunately, this rarely occurs, which results in hiring security officers who are incapable of performing the most important organizational tasks: managing and resolving interpersonal conflict and protecting people. Instead of requiring applicants to demonstrate these necessary attributes, the typical hiring process instead requires applicants to "qualify themselves by personal affirmation," or QPA. Phrases like "must be able to demonstrate" or "must possess the ability to" (and similar ones) are found in most security officer job flyers. But how can QPA qualify a security officer candidate? Every applicant will answer these or similar questions in the affirmative for obvious reasons; there's no risk to *not* affirming them since they probably won't be required to demonstrate them prior to being hired and there's no organizational risk for asking these questions. Paradoxically, most organizations don't take an applicant's word when it comes to criminal background checks, vehicle driving records, former employment, to name just a few areas. It's true there are potential organizational risks and additional effort involved in requiring applicants to orally and physically demonstrate the required job skills during the screening process; but there is a huge upside to it.[12] The greatest organizational risk is not from security officer applicants who are denied employment based upon an allegation of unlawful or discriminatory hiring processes but results from an employee acting inappropriately or failing to act when interacting with a combative person and being sued for negligence.

The most practical ways to improve the probability of hiring the right type of security officer is to require applicants to complete a series of active roleplay scenarios where their decision-making, verbal, tactical, and physical skills can be *practically* evaluated. Unlike written roleplay scenarios where an applicant is asked to verbally respond to a theoretical scenario while seated in a low-stress environment, active scenario roleplay requires applicants to solve problems in an environment that recreates the emotional, social, and cultural dynamics of real-live workplace conflict. Active scenario roleplay assessments can be facilitated using live actors or computer simulation.[13]

A Diverse Workforce

An added benefit of deprioritizing police-oriented applicants and law enforcement philosophies, and seeking business-minded security officers is attracting a more diverse workforce. This refocus will naturally create more racial, ethnic, and gender diversity. Diversity has many benefits, and it's generally thought to be a positive attribute of successful organizations

---

[12] Another downside I've been told is a reduction in the qualified applicant pool. But employers who are desperate to fill open positions often hire desperate people.

[13] See Chapter 10 for a greater exposition on advantages of scenario roleplay.

(Forbes Insights, 2012). Diversity has the potential to improve problem solving by involving a multitude of perspectives.

Unfortunately, the failure to deemphasize physicality as the primary method for processing workplace conflict keeps the private security industry from becoming more gender and culturally diverse. Deemphasizing physicality and law enforcement training or experience as a prerequisite for employment will also provide more opportunities for women. Women naturally have a difficult time breaking into traditionally male-dominated industries (Kwok, 2010). Since the typical security job description is geared toward male-dominated personality traits, it may inadvertently discourage women from considering a career in the private security industry. The infusion of more women into the security industry will have a positive effect on conflict management since women typically rely on more collaboration methods, such as compromise, accommodation, and negotiation, for solving interpersonal disputes. One of the reasons some organizations struggle to effectively process workplace conflict is an overreliance on aggressiveness and physicality, in lieu of less intrusive means. However, since physical conflict resolution methods may be needed, prospective security officers, whether male or female, need to be comfortable using physical methods to process violent behaviors.

Athletes: An Untapped Resource

I'm often asked where to find the best security officer applicants. One area that I think is overlooked are sports and athletic teams. Athletes have a lot in common with police academy graduates, such as a high degree of self-discipline, being physically fit, and the experience of working in teams. However, unlike police academy graduates, athletes may also provide organizations the added benefit of lower turnover rates because athletes may be more apt to seek a *career* in the security industry, versus looking for a (temporary) job. Athletes are one employee profile type often overlooked by organizations that should be considered when recruiting for security officers.

Mentoring

Organizations often create unnecessary hiring impediments and additional costs when trying to fill their vacant security positions because they haven't mentored personnel or developed their own "farm team." Organizations should cultivate current personnel and create a robust internal promotional system to prepare for growth and attrition within their own security departments. Every security director/manager should be mentoring select individuals on their staff to be their eventual replacement. By creating an internal promotional system for current employees, security departments can develop internal candidates and alleviate the need to constantly recruit personnel from outside their organizations. Additionally, security officer candidates can be recruited from other internal non-security stakeholder groups. Hiring from within affords several benefits: internal applicants understand the social and political nuisances of the organization, there's a much shorter orientation phase, and there is a greater allegiance to the organization's values.

Summary

Managing and resolving workplace conflict and violence and protecting people in a private setting takes a unique personality type. The differences in processing interpersonal conflict in private versus public settings need to be incorporated into the preferred security officer employee profile and determine the types of security officers that organizations recruit, hire, and retain.

Recommendations

1. De-emphasis law enforcement and military experience as a prerequisite for employment.
2. Develop an in-house farm team and recruit security candidates from internal stakeholders.
3. Don't hire an individual to lead a security department with no experience leading private non-sworn security officers in a free-market organizational safety context, and/or has no employment experience in the particular market (e.g., retail, education, or healthcare).
4. Mentor security personnel and prepare them for upward mobility.
5. Only hire security officers who are excellent communicators and have the personality and temperament to process interpersonal conflict in a free-market setting.
6. Recruit athletes to the security vocation.

7. Recruit, hire, and retain business-minded security officers.
8. Regularly assess currently hired security officers to assure they remain competent.
9. Screen/assess all applicants to determine if they can meet the required competencies.

References

Colling, R.L., York, T.W., 2010. Hospital and Healthcare Security (fifth ed.), Butterworth-Heinemann, Boston, MA.

Edley, C.F., Robinson, C.F., 2012. Response to Protests on UC Campuses. Report draft for public comment, 4 May 2012; Web: <http://campusprotestreport.universityofcalifornia.edu> 05.05.12.

Forbes Insights, 2012. Diversity & Inclusion: Unlocking Global Potential Global Diversity Ranking by Country, Sector, and Occupation, n.d.; Web: <www.forbes.com/forbesinsights> 05.07.12.

Kwok, L., 2010. Female entrepreneurs venture into male-dominated industries and thrive. [New Jersey] Star-Ledger, 11 April 2010; Web: <http://blog.nj.com/business> 10.05.12.

Chapter 9

The Role of Standards

Problem

Organizations recruit, hire, and employ security officers that don't meet reliable core competency standards necessary for preventing workplace violence.

Introduction

To prepare security officers for the role of managing and resolving workplace conflict and violence, and protecting people, organizations must establish a core set of security officer competencies to be screened for during the preemployment processes and that currently employed security officers must maintain.

However, for some stakeholders, the fear of establishing nonnegotiable security officer competency standards may trump the fear that employees could be left unprotected. There may be no other way to explain the status quo and the overwhelming stakeholder resistance to establishing competency standards. Establishing standards means that not everyone will qualify, meaning less time, energy, and resources spent on individuals who either can't or won't be able to perform the necessary job duties and more time devoted to those who can.

Process

There are a multitude of benefits for establishing nonnegotiable competency standards and some perceived downsides. Standards assure that the people hired can perform their most important job duties, especially the ability to protect people from violence. Additionally, requiring applicants, and currently employed personnel, to meet competency standards means less time and energy invested in trying to make the *wrong* hire right and more time and energy investing in developing and maintaining the *right* hire. Moreover, standards may significantly reduce the pool of available applicants; standards will discourage some applicants (those you don't want) while encouraging others to apply (the ones you do want). In a competitive free market, organizations will always look to reduce and control costs and expenses. And one of the main reasons that standards are often resisted is because they will initially increase the cost of doing business. However, the return on investment will far outweigh the costs in establishing standards. The truth is, there are certain competencies required to successfully perform the job even if the employer doesn't test for them.

SOS: Responding to Standards

Security personnel will react in various ways to an organization's decision to enact competency standards; some will appreciate them while others may react negatively out of fear. These reactions are especially noticeable if organizations decide to enact a health and wellness competency standard. However, nonsecurity, line employees, who are *in the trenches*, love them! The bottom line is that every organization consciously maintains employees who have survived for years without having to meet minimum competency or performance standards; the fear of losing one's job is a real concern. Likewise, employees who know that they can't physically perform their jobs are not going to walk into their boss's office and resign. The truth is that the job of protecting people and preventing workplace violence is not for everyone. It requires certain unique attributes and a minimum level of health and wellness that not every applicant or employed security officer possesses. Under some circumstances, security personnel may have initially been able to meet the minimum competencies, but over time their health and wellness or other abilities may have deteriorated, and they've become incapable of safely performing their job. This is one of the many weaknesses of hiring personnel who meet the minimum competencies without requiring that they maintain them to remain employed. It's not unusual for people's motivations to change over time, and unless the organization provides extrinsic motivation (policies and incentives) for maintaining the required minimum competencies, over time some personnel will naturally become unwell, unhealthy, and/or inept.

Even though it may involve a certain amount of organizational risk, incompetent security officers should not be put in a position to be a danger to themselves or others just to avoid the unpleasant organizational challenges and legal consequences of rehabilitating or removing them from duty. The reality is that some security officers already know that they can't perform their jobs but are afraid of acknowledging it because it will impact their employment. Human resource personnel know that within their respective organizations there are certain job duties that require a minimum level of physicality to perform and that eventually some long-term employees in good standing will become unable to perform them. For employees who *can't* meet a newly enacted or currently enforced standard and want to stay with the organization, they should be given ethical options for transferring into other jobs within the organization or for leaving the organization. However, for personnel who *won't* meet the standard because they refuse to cooperate in the organization's rehabilitation program, they should be discharged from the organization. Since most organizations don't have many personnel who fall into these circumstances, they often have little experience processing these circumstances. Human resources personnel know that this is perhaps the greatest organizational challenge to plan for when considering whether to establish and enforce competency standards. This is one of the many reasons they often balk at the idea of requiring current employees to meet a new standard.

Protecting People and Required Competencies

The job of protecting people requires security personnel to be healthy, well, and fit, and meet certain verbal and physical competencies. Prior to being hired, security officer applicants need to *prove* that they can meet them and currently hired personnel need to prove they can *maintain* them. There are various methods used to screen applicants against required competencies, but unfortunately most organizations use the *qualified by personal affirmation* or QPA approach in lieu of actual verbal or physical assessments. A key is to develop competency assessments that reflect the standards that are legal, fair, and accurately measure the required competencies.[1]

Verbal Competencies

Communication is perhaps the most important and most often used skill needed to effectively manage and deescalate passive–aggressive behaviors and keep emotional instability from escalating to violence. Therefore, security officer applicants and currently employed security personnel should have to meet and maintain a verbal communication competency standard.

Physical Competencies

Physical competencies, both the application of *protective tactics*, such as control and restraint techniques and weaponless protective measures, and the use of *protective tools*, such as OC/pepper spray, defensive baton, Taser and firearms, and a minimum level of health and wellness standard, are the most important skills and abilities needed to effectively neutralize danger and protect people. Therefore, security officer applicants and currently hired personnel should have to meet and maintain protective tactics and tools competency, including a minimum level of health and wellness, and regularly demonstrate their proficiencies. Tactical and physical competencies naturally degrade over time and continually need to be practiced to maintain proficiencies. Moreover, to safely operate and maintain control of protective tools, security officers must maintain a minimum level of health and wellness. Likewise, it's impossible to safely conduct training when security officers are unhealthy, unwell, and unfit.[2] Security officers who are unhealthy, unwell, and unfit and who use protective tactics or tools when interacting with combative subjects may elevate harm to themselves or others and create civil liabilities and possible criminal liabilities.

---

[1] PSOST.org has some excellent examples of verbal and physical competencies.
[2] See Chapter 10 for a greater exposition on training and health and wellness.

Fit for Duty: Health, Wellness, and Fitness Standards

It may well be that the primary reason that security officers have historically struggled to achieve high levels of organizational and vocational relevance and performance is based *solely* on their generalized lack of health, wellness, and physical fitness. Although these truths are self-evident and have been widely known for many years, there's a high degree of denial in organizations that employ security officers and in the security industry writ large and denying this reality has created many organizational dilemmas.

1. Organization can't establish reliable competency standards that rely on health, wellness, or physical fitness.
2. Unhealthy, unwell, and unfit officers cannot provide high levels of physical protection for employees and others.
3. Organizations can't establish reliable training programs that rely on health, wellness, and physical fitness.[3]
4. Unhealthy, unwell, and unfit officers cannot establish necessary social control (authority) for influencing behavior or protecting people.
5. Unhealthy, unwell, and unfit officers are more easily injured on the job, take more time to recover from an injury, file a greater number of workers comp claims, call in sick more often, require more work accommodations and create morale issues.

The Elephant in the Room

How does being unhealthy, unwell, or physically unfit *improve* the efficiency or effectiveness of any regularly performed job duty? On its face, this may seem like a foolish question to pose. But the answer is both obvious and instructive for this discussion on security officer health, wellness, and physical fitness. Obviously, health, wellness, and physical fitness play an important role in the performance of any job duty. However, it may have little discernable effect on many of the job duties that organizations regularly perform. For instance, there are many sedentary job assignments

---

[3] Physically unfit or obese officers are much more likely to be injured during attempts to control resistant suspects than physically fit officers. See a study by Dr. Alexander Eastman on police officer injuries, reported in the Force Science Institute #207; www.forcescience.org.

that officers perform, where being overweight, obese, injured (temporary or permanent), or ill would have very little impact on an employee's ability to competently perform. Protecting employees from potential workplace violence is not one of them! Unhealthy, unwell, and physically unfit security officers cannot protect employees (or themselves) from dangerous and violent individuals.

It's plainly obvious to everyone that security officers are historically some of the most unfit individuals in the workforce. A CDC (Centers for Disease Control and Prevention) study determined that protective services workers, which includes security personal and law enforcement officers, have the second highest percentages of obesity rates of all occupations measured, ranging from 32% to 50%! (Interestingly, the employment category with the highest rate for obesity is transportation personnel.)[4] The prevalence of obesity when categorized by age reveals an additional organizational challenge: 35.7% among young adults aged 20–39 years, 42.8% among middle-aged adults aged 40–59 years, and 41.0% among older adults aged 60 and older (CDC, 2020).[5] For security departments that employ a high number of long-term older employees, health, wellness, and fitness are even greater organizational challenges.

For some reason, organizations, and to a lesser degree, the security officers themselves, have decided that health, wellness, and physical fitness are *not* required to successfully perform the job of a "professional security officer." This is partially the result of organizations in the 1980s deciding to start their own in-house security departments and move away from using contract security officers. When organizations began this transition, they absorbed and recruited unfit security officers from the contract security industry. There have been some improvements since then, which are primarily the result of private organizations hiring police academy graduates, who are generally younger, healthier, and more physically fit than non-police-oriented applicants. However, the contract security industry still employs the greatest number of obese and morbidly obese security officers.

---

[4] I'm writing this during the COVID-19 pandemic and isolation and medical professionals are now arguing that obesity is an underlying factor for acquiring the disease and fighting it.

[5] https://www.cdc.gov/obesity/data/adult.html.

Mission-Driven Health and Wellness

Below is an example of a healthcare provider's corporate mission statement that we used earlier in our text. Here we use it to illustrate the importance of security officer health and wellness:

> Our mission is to help people keep well in body, mind, and spirit by providing quality healthcare services in a compassionate environment.

When organizations create mission statements like this, their target audience are consumers who will seek out their services or products. But shouldn't the organizational values embedded in a corporate mission statement also apply to applicants and employees? If so, shouldn't job applicants be screened to assure that organizations aren't hiring people who may not be "well in body, mind, and spirit"? Additionally, shouldn't organizations be concerned about employees who are not "well in body, mind, or spirit"? How should organizations practically demonstrate these mission-driven values toward employees? One practical way to assure security officer applicants and employees are "well in body" is to institute a minimum health and wellness standard.

Lifeguards versus Security Guards

As a thought experiment, and to really drive home the point that the failure to require security officers to be physically fit to perform their job duties competently and protect people, consider the similarities and differences between a lifeguard and a security guard. Believe it or not, these two jobs have some commonalities. Both lifeguards and security guards spend most of their workday sedentary; lifeguards sit in elevated towers while security guards sit at stationary locations, sit while riding in vehicles, or stand posts, both scanning their respective environments looking for potential dangers. Then when they observe danger, or they're alerted to danger, they must quickly respond from their low-stress sedentary activities to high-stress life-saving ones; this process is physically, mentally, and emotionally stressful on the human body. Being healthy, well, and physically fit is a key to performing well under these conditions. In fact, unfit officers who try to perform life-saving or protective duties not only place others in danger, but they also create a situation where they may need to be rescued!

Moreover, consider which of these two jobs has genuine vocational relevance, a better public image, more prestige, better pay and benefits, better working conditions, serious pre- and postemployment hiring and training standards and requirements, perform their jobs with greater efficiency, are more trustworthy, and have greater levels of observed health, wellness, and physical fitness? I realize that this comparison is rhetorical and not real, but it should help reinforce this point: Not requiring professional security officers to meet a minimum health, wellness, and physical fitness standard is another example of the "no-standard standard" that's unfortunately become *the standard* for many organizations that employ security officers. In fact, when public entities recruit for lifeguards, 100% of the applicants show up to interview and test for the job, meeting all the rigid physical job requirements. Likewise, when public beaches have lifeguard openings, it's not unusual for hundreds of lifeguard applicants to apply for very limited open positions. In contrast, when organizations have open security officer positions, many of the applicants who apply are often overweight and physically unfit. The reason that unfit lifeguards don't show up for a job interview is twofold; it's well known that employers have high standards and the person knows they're not qualified. Moreover, even when an applicant is obviously qualified, they still have to pass a grueling preemployment assessment, such as running in the sand, swimming against an active sea current, rescuing an unconscious person from the water, and bringing them safely back to shore.

Let's try another thought experiment. Think of a lifeguard and then try to conjure up a mental picture of an obese person wearing a swimsuit. You can't do it! Next, think of a security guard and then try to conjure up a mental picture of an obese person wearing a security uniform. Easy to do! This thought experiment gets right to the heart of the culture change that needs to take place in organizations and the security industry. It takes healthy, well, and physically fit security officers to protect employees, consumers, visitors, and others from violence.

Next, let's consider how obesity impacts law enforcement officers. Security officers, like law enforcement officers, have high obesity rates (both are considered within the protective services category) associated with the number of hours they spend in sedentary behaviors, like patrolling in their police vehicles. Unlike most security officers, law enforcement officers begin their career physically fit because a high degree of physicality and fitness are required to successfully complete a police academy. However, within just a few years after completing a physically demanding police academy, a great number of these law enforcement officers become overweight, obese, and sadly, some are morbidly obese (Otu, 2015).[6] But unlike obese security officers who *can't* safely perform their protective duties, law enforcement associations, law enforcement unions, and a large percentage of law enforcement officers believe they *can* adequately perform their jobs since they are universally against requirements for officers to maintain a minimum physical fitness level as a condition of employment.

In fact, even when the State of Texas tried to adopt a fitness standard for its public safety officers that required their law enforcement officers to keep their waist size under 40 inches for men and under 35 inches for women, its public safety officers union sued the State. Richard Janovsky the union's president commented, "Not only is this policy demeaning, it is damaging to our troopers and to our citizens … Not all physically fit troopers are of the same body type, the same height or the same genetic makeup (Barragan, 2019)."[7]

Technology, Safety, and Fitness

Law enforcement officers have advantages that offset or minimize the impact of obesity on job performance and safety, which security personnel don't have.[8] For instance, if an individual law enforcement officer can't bring a resistant suspect under control by themselves because of injury, poor health, or fitness, they can call for additional resources, such as backup police personnel, not only from their own law enforcement agency but also from other adjacent agencies or use advanced tactics and tools, such as Tasers, including K9 officers, special operations teams, and if needed, helicopters. These technological advances are partially responsible for significant increases in officer safety, but paradoxically, they may also contribute to increased obesity rates. Resources such as digital portal radios, cell phones, in-car computer systems, and GPS provide access to resources that weren't readily available to law enforcement officers before 1985. Before that, law enforcement officers had to rely much more, or exclusively, on their own

---

[6] This portion of the study is listed under the heading, "Process of Growing from Healthy Weight to Obese Police Officers," in the Journal of Social Sciences Research. V6. No. 3.

[7] James Barragan. The Dallas Morning News. 10.3.19. "Texas troopers sue over new fitness standards that require waistlines to be measured."

[8] Unlike, law enforcement departments, many fire departments have strict requirements for their personnel to remain fit. (See CPAT as an example fitness testing for fire firefighters.)

physical abilities to control resistant suspects, and not being physically fit created a much greater risk for law enforcement officers than it does today. Oddly, these advancements in officer safety may also create disincentives for officers to maintain a healthy lifestyle.

Today law enforcement officers working a *slow shift* may spend up to six hours or more patrolling in their vehicle get their food through a fast food drive-through, eat in their patrol vehicle, communicate with their dispatcher through their in-car computer, and never exert more energy than walking to it after briefing and from it at the end of shift. Unlike law enforcement officers, security personnel typically have very limited resources and training, work alone, and even if they had a portable radio, no one else may be working, or if another security officer were available, that officer may be less competent than the one calling for help! The bottom line is that security officers *must* rely on their personal abilities to keep themselves safe and perform their protective duties. For a security officer, being unhealthy, unwell, or unfit creates serious impediments for personal and corporate safety and job performance. Additionally, unlike police officers, security officers rely almost exclusively on *public perceptions of effectiveness*, based primarily on how they look and their ability to project confidence, more than *actual* effectiveness.

Let's be honest; obese security personnel may be able to safely perform some *limited* job duties such as walking around and sitting to observe and report various behaviors, typical untrained, unsupervised, and inexperienced security guard duties. But professional security officers cannot safely perform the kind of duties necessary for preventing and responding to workplace violence and protecting people if they're unhealthy, unwell, or physically unfit. Organizations, professional security associations, and the individuals employed as security officers need to accept that meeting a minimum level of health, wellness, and physical fitness is *required* to be considered a security professional, even when organizations don't require it![9]

Risks, Rewards, and Costs

So why do organizations continue to recruit and employ unhealthy, unwell, and physically unfit security officers and assign them protective duties?

---

[9] According to the CDC, physical activity is one of the best things people can do to improve their health because it's vital for healthy aging and can reduce the burden of chronic diseases and prevent early death.

There are several reasons that explain an organization's resistance to requiring security officer applicants and employees meet a minimum level of health, wellness, and physical fitness; some are pragmatic, others are social, and some are thought to be legal. From the security director/manager's perspective, it limits the pool of available candidates, to others it may seem unfair to force a person to do something they can't control, while risk managers argue it increases liability. Paradoxically, many of the same organizations that argue enacting standards increase risk succeed in their respective markets because they take (or took) unreasonable risks to sell or provide their services or products to their consumers.

In truth, every organization that employs security personnel will be sued by an aggrieved individual and their attorney for either taking an action or for failing to act. And every organization that begins the process of requiring security officer applicants and employees to meet a minimum health and wellness standard will open themselves to legal, social, and ethical challenges. Likewise, organizations that continue to allow their unwell, unhealthy, unfit security officers (whether they're fully aware of their particular conditions or operating under plausible deniability) to interact with potentially violent individuals will eventually be sued by an injured security officer, employee, consumer, or visitor for failing to train or for failure to meet a due care standard but are guilty of a greater sin: fearing potential liabilities over the actual human costs of protecting victims from workplace violence.

The reality is that every action or nonaction involving an employee creates potential risks and rewards; there are no risk-free or reward-free behaviors. Employing security officers who are unhealthy, unwell, or unfit is a greater risk than the risk associated with requiring them to meet a minimum health, wellness, and fitness standard. Organizations have many financial, social, legal, and ethical responsibilities. But protecting their employees, consumers, visitors, and others from violence is one of their primary responsibilities.

Moving beyond QPA

To determine that security officers can protect employees, consumers, visitors, and themselves, security officer candidates must be required to *demonstrate* that they can meet the established set of core competencies by successfully performing them *prior* to being offered a job. Too many organizations allow applicants and employees to qualify themselves by personal affirmation or QPA, instead of being required to demonstrate they're competent. An organization's initial goal should be to keep *unqualified* individuals from becoming employed. Likewise, once hired, and as a condition of continued employment, security officers must be required to *maintain* a set of core competencies by participating in the department's ongoing and continuous training programs. Security officers who fail to meet/maintain the required core competency standards should be subject to remediation, and if necessary, corrective action and discipline. Corrective action should include a process for identifying potentially deficient security officer competencies that need rehabilitating. However, security officers who are unable to be rehabilitated need to be retired, transferred to other departments, or if they refuse to participate in the rehabilitation process, they should be discharged from employment.

Fit for Duty

The most basic qualification of a security officer is to be healthy, well, and fit. Employers can teach an employee who is healthy, well, and fit, and has a positive attitude and good moral character how to use the tactics or tools necessary for protection. But it's virtually impossible to inculcate a healthy lifestyle or fitness mentality to individuals who don't possess it when they apply for the job. In fact, if an unhealthy, unwell, and unfit individual applies for an open security officer position, they've communicated a message and mindset to the employer that *being fit is not a requirement to do the job.*[10] However, I have personally seen unhealthy, unwell, and unfit security officers make dramatic changes in their lifestyle, health, wellness, and fitness when their organizations decided these were not just *ideals* but were important organizational values.[11]

---

[10] Although it's difficult to know the extent of an applicant's (or an employee's) overall health and wellness without testing them, it's easy to determine if they're overweight, obese, or morbidly obese by observing them. However, nonobservable (hidden) illnesses, and injuries may be of greater concern to individuals and organizations.

[11] If an organization values its employee's health and wellness but doesn't support methods to encourage and require them to be well, it's easy to assume that other organizational concerns are a greater priority than their health and wellness.

Actual versus Theoretical Employment Discrimination

Unfortunately, when discussing requiring security officers to meet a minimum health, wellness, and fitness standard, too many stakeholders, both nonsecurity and, sadly, even security stakeholders, continue to focus exclusively on the potential of employment discrimination over their ethical and legal obligations to be honest with their employees about their health, wellness, and fitness and how it impacts their ability to prevent workplace violence. This is true even for organizations that require, either directly or indirectly, that their security officers intervene to protect employees from dangerous people. A risk aversive focus communicates a lack of ethical (and legal) concern for their employees' health and increases the potential that low-level interpersonal conflict will escalate to workplace violence. It's true that it would be irresponsible not to consider the total liabilities and the administrative costs of requiring security officers to be healthy, well, and fit, but the *greater* concern should be providing the safest possible workplace for employees, consumers, and visitors and assuring that an organization's security officers remain healthy and well.

Truthfully, requiring security officers to meet a minimum health and wellness standard creates much less (if any) liability than the current methods used by many security directors/managers to screen applicants. Departmental managers in all organizational departments, not just security directors/managers, have become experts at *getting around* official HR policies that impact recruiting, hiring, and leading security personnel. These workarounds create much greater liability than using an objective standard to screen individuals.

The various methods used by security directors/managers to screen out overweight security officer applicants are often *de facto* discrimination. The most common method is to simply disqualify overweight applicants after observing their physicality. Another typical method is to prefer or require applicants to be recent police academy graduates because they're usually young and physically fit. One of the more creative methods of screening out overweight or obese applicants I've heard of was from a security manager who would call an applicant on the phone and ask them what size shirt or pants they wore. If the applicant responded with a shirt size larger than XL, or a pants waist size greater than 40 inches, the manager simply moved on to other applicants. Of course, the real reason that these applicant types are disqualified is never admitted to (plausible deniability). But security directors/managers know what is obvious to most honest stakeholders: unwell, unhealthy, and unfit security officers cannot provide the kind of protection that is necessary to prevent workplace violence and protect employees, consumers, visitors, and others. And if human resources and risk managers are not going to allow security applicants to be screened for required competencies, including screening for health and wellness, then security directors/managers will continue to use creative, and possible discriminatory, screening processes to hire more qualified applicants, with or without the tacit approval of other stakeholders.

Organizational Risk Management and Health and Wellness

Of all the organization safety issues I discuss with my clients (and potential clients) requiring a health and wellness standard is the one that creates the most controversy. Logically, every decision and nondecision an organization makes involves potential risk. And which expert the organization relies on to determine the level of acceptable risk will determine if a policy will or won't be enacted. Rarely, when I discuss the benefits of establishing a security officer's health and wellness standard do nonsecurity stakeholders enthusiastically engage me in a conversation. They typically respond with the boiler-plate risk aversion statement, "we'll be sued," even though they're currently operating with legal exposure due to employing unwell, unhealthy, and unfit security officers. Likewise, initiating a security officer's health and wellness standard will create other liabilities. However, once a security officer's health and wellness standard become embedded in organizational culture, these liabilities will be mitigated to virtually undetectable risks. The truth is that every day that passes without adopting a security officer's health and wellness standard, the organization's current liabilities remain, and a resultant lawsuit may create the inability to remain financially viable.

The truth is, an organization can be sued civilly for its hiring practices or wrongful separation. The cost of potential liabilities for requiring security officer candidates to meet job-related competencies prior to being hired is much less (if any) as compared to the actual costs of hiring incompetent candidates, including the time, resources, energy, and potential liability associated with negligent hiring. The real employment liabilities, both pre- and postemployment, are not based on requiring an applicant or employee to meet a standard that's a normal business practice in most employment contexts; it's based upon discriminatory employment practices. A key to avoid claims of discriminatory employment practices, the standard must:

1. Be consistent with business necessity.
2. Bear a manifest relationship to the employment in question.
3. Measure a minimally necessary skill to perform the job.

Professionalized Vocations

Professionalized vocations such as attorneys, doctors, nurses, and teachers are characterized by their individual and collective influence, high degrees of relevance, productivity, effectiveness, and trust are highly compensated (pay, fringe benefits, and retirement) and upwardly mobile. In those industries, the establishment of high competency standards played an important role in the professionalism process and *turning jobs into vocations*. Similarly, the successes noted in the law enforcement community are partially based on having serious physical fitness (at least initially) and high training standards.

Employing physically fit security officers improves personal and organizational safety. Physically fit security officers are less likely to have their authority questioned and less likely to be physically challenged. In fact, positive public perceptions of a security officer's physical fitness reduce the number of uncooperative interactions and officer assaults. On the other hand, when security officers need to exert themselves, like having to run a distance, run up a flight of stairs, or physically defend themselves or others against a violent subject, physically fit security officers are able to maintain an adequate level of physical stamina necessary to overcome an attacker, survive the encounter, and gain control over the subject. Conversely, unfit security officers are often a danger to themselves and others and become a liability when they need to physically defend themselves. Additionally, when physically fit security officers are involved in physical interactions, they're less likely to be injured, reducing potential workers' compensation claims, payouts, and increase workers' compensation insurance premiums.

Tiered Classifications

Change is always hard. But trying to convince senior corporate managers and security officers on the value of a health, wellness, and physical fitness program is a challenge—especially when most of an organization's security personnel are unhealthy and couldn't meet the new standard. Some organizations are willing to *encourage* health and wellness, but few are willing to make it a nonnegotiable standard. Enacting a tiered security officer program may be an effective way to improve the health, wellness, and physical fitness of security officers and avoid claims of employment discrimination. To initiate a tiered program, all currently employed security personnel would automatically qualify for tier one (or status quo) and nothing about their job requirements would change. But to qualify for the *tier two* security officer classification, currently employed personnel would have to meet additional required competencies, along with a health and wellness standard to apply for the new position, which may be accompanied by a higher hourly pay rate. This may be a good option for establishing many of the necessary (and required) competencies without violating human resources policies or creating perceptions of bias. Moreover, creating the two tiers of security officer classifications may create healthy competition and incentivize all officers to voluntarily *upgrade* their competencies. If a security department has significant vacancies, they need to fill, this may be a great option.

Summary

The role of managing workplace conflict, resolving violence, and protecting people requires security officers to be proficient and competent. All professionalized industries have high regard for standards and ongoing and continuous training to assure their respective industries that their personnel are certified and qualified. Unfortunately, the failure of organizations to establish minimum security officer competency standards has created a *no-standard standard* that no one is disqualified from. Absent reliable competency standards, organizations can't recruit, hire, and retain highly efficient and effective security officers who can prevent and respond to workplace violence and protect people.

Recommendations

1. Create a list of required verbal and physical core security officer competency standards.
2. Create tiered security officer classifications with additional benefits.

3. Develop legal and practical ways to assess applicants and employees from the list of required competencies.
4. Ensure that human resources creates a fair and legal process for adjudicating personnel who can't or won't meet the required competencies.
5. Institute a reliable health and wellness standard for applicants and currently hired security officers.
6. Require applicants to go beyond QPA to determine if they can meet the required competencies.
7. Require human resources personnel and risk and legal stakeholders to voluntarily share sociopolitical organizational power with security directors/managers to develop and maintain a core set of security officer competency standards and legal methods for screening for them.
8. Require security officer applicants and currently hired security officers to meet the required competencies.

References

Barragan, James, 2019. Texas troopers sue over new fitness standards that require waistlines to be measured. The Dallas Morning News, 10 March 2019.

Centers for Disease Control and Prevention (CDC), 2020. <https://www.cdc.gov/obesity/>

Otu, Noel, 2015. Obesity warning for police officers. J. Soc. Sci. Res. 6. 1073–1082.

Chapter 10

The Role of Training

Problem

Organizations employ security officers who aren't adequately trained to manage or resolve workplace conflict or violence and protect people.

Introduction

Security officer training plays an important role in an officer's ability to successfully manage workplace conflict and resolve violence, protect people, and fulfill their duties. Organizations need to establish a set of core security officer competencies that must be taught, accurately assessed, and monitored. Once core competencies are established, officers must be regularly assessed to assure that they are maintained. Moreover, processes must be instituted for rehabilitating, disciplining, or discharging personnel who can't or won't meet them.

Process

Successful organizations rely on highly trained and proficient employees who sell or deliver their services and products. Interestingly, many of these same organizations don't require the same level of professionalism from their security personnel. The process for improving security officer performance and accountability is challenging and requires adequate funding.

Successful organizations need to establish a set of core security officer competencies that are required to perform their job duties. These core competency standards are then incorporated into the security officer's job description and form the basis for recruiting and hiring. Applicants, and current hires, will have to meet these requirements to become employed or to remain employed by the organization. Additionally, the organization needs to educate employees on the importance of enacting security officer competency standards and the necessity of the culture change. The organization must:

1. Establish a reasonable timetable for enacting the changes.
2. Explain how a security officer's employment status will be affected if they can't or won't meet the standard.
3. Enact legal and ethical employment processes to rehabilitate, reassign, or discipline personnel who don't meet the new standard.
4. Develop a requisite training curriculum to support the competencies.
5. Deliver training using a qualified instructor, using appropriate training and learning methodologies, that allow for practice and measures and tests for competency in order to provide assurances that classroom training competency translates into field competency.
6. Establish a significant training budget to support the training program.
7. Require security officers to receive ongoing and continuous training to maintain the required competencies.
8. Properly supervise security officers to identify and correct deficiencies and to issue disciplinary action or to prepare documentation for personnel who refuse to participate in the program.
9. Create processes to deal with program resistors who create negative employee morale. Organizational change is never easily accepted, and some personnel may become outwardly hostile and resist it.

Charles P. Nemeth, a recognized security expert, suggests that the security industry will be held to its own professional (or nonprofessional) standards. Nemeth writes, "What is certain is that the security industry will be held to its own standard of professional conduct and that injuries that result will be scrutinized in accordance with our expectations of performance and due care owed" (Nemeth, 2005 p. 136). In other words, liability resulting from attempts to process workplace conflict will be evaluated based on the standards an organization creates or fails to create. This admonishment is a reminder that failure to create reliable security officer training standards is an organizational disaster in waiting.

Training Approaches: Law Enforcement versus Private Sector

Although there is a substantive difference between the private security industry and the law enforcement industry, the law enforcement community should be emulated for its success in establishing and maintaining competencies and for developing universally accepted training standards. Standards are responsible for the high levels of professionalism noted among law enforcement officers and for overcoming the *Barney Fife* law enforcement caricature on *The Andy Griffith Show* in the 1960s to today's highly respected and admired police vocation.[1] The private security industry and organizations that employ security personnel, unlike the law enforcement community, have failed to create reliable competency and training standards. This failure is one of the primary reasons for the nearly universal negative public impressions of "security" and a lack of vocational and organizational relevance.

Although it's obvious that law enforcement officers have a dangerous job, it's surprising to many that private security employment is similarly dangerous. The Bureau of Labor Statistics (BLS) estimates that there are over 800,000 municipal law enforcement officers and over 1 million security officers employed throughout the United States. Law enforcement training standards are so effective at creating high levels of officer safety that in spite of being involved in billions of potentially dangerous encounters (PDEs) every year, law enforcement officers on the whole are relatively safe.[2] (We define potentially dangerous encounters or PDEs, as an interaction between an officer and physically resistant individuals when an officer needs to intervene to control or to deescalate harmful behaviors.) We estimate that law enforcement officers are involved in approximately 4 billion PDEs

---

[1] A similar example that could be used for the security industry is the "Paul Bart, Mall Cop" security guard caricature.

[2] Police officer PDEs are calculated based on an average of 10 PDEs per week, per officer. These statistics were calculated based on interviews with local law enforcement officers and are estimates. Although anecdotal, they provide a realistic view of the dangers that officers face.

per year, while private security officers are involved in approximately 52 million PDEs per year.[3]

According to the 2017 BLS "Fatal Occupational Injuries by Occupations" report, 44 law enforcement officers were killed in 2017 during "assault and violent acts" (down from the previous year of 66 fatalities), whereas 74 security officers were killed in the same category.[4] We estimate that on average, 1 police officer is killed for every 74 million PDEs, whereas on average 1 security officer is killed for every 1.5 million PDEs. However, for both vocations the number of nonfatal injuries, both temporary and permanent, requiring time off work, is significant. However, security officers are much more likely to be injured when interacting with violent subjects than law enforcement officers due to being unhealthy, ill-trained, and not having access to protective tools or to additional *backup* officers.[5]

Based on the quantity and quality of police interactions with resistant individuals, it's easy to draw two obvious conclusions from this data: First, training makes a substantial contribution to officer safety, and second, security officers are more vulnerable to harm than law enforcement officers.

Over the years the national law enforcement community has developed a consistent and unified standard for the use of force (or protective action). This professionalized standard is so refined that a police officer can transfer employment from a law enforcement agency in one part of the country to one in another part of the country with only minor use-of-force policy differences. Unlike the law enforcement industry, the private security industry's protective force *guidelines* often differ from organization to organization—and sometimes from moment to moment! As an example, in response to the UC Davis pepper-spray incident in 2011, one of my clients suggested removing pepper spray from their security officer's duty gear because they were concerned that the public outcry resulting from the UC Davis police officer's alleged use of pepper spray on innocent victims could negatively impact their organization. The client who was not in proximity to this campus justified leaving their security officers "defenseless" based on possible negative public perceptions associated with *their officers* carrying

---

[3] Security officer PDEs are calculated based on 1 PDEs per week, per officer. These statistics were calculated based on personal experience, officer interviews, and opinion surveys conducted with local security officers. Again, although anecdotal, they are useful for discussing the differences between private security and law enforcement officers.

[4] North American Industry Classification System or NAICS Codes: 5616, 56161, 561612, and 561613.

[5] Later in the chapter we discuss health, wellness, and fitness.

pepper spray. They made a conscious choice that protecting their reputation had a greater value than the protection that pepper spray offered their security officers or its consumers.[6]

Every organization that takes workplace violence prevention seriously and employs security officers as part of their workplace violence prevention plan approaches organization safety through an enforcement and/or a protective philosophical lens; there are advantages and disadvantages to both perspectives. Security officer training should be geared toward improving an officer's ability to communicate with difficult people and critical field decision-making, not on forced compliance (enforcement). Protection-based training supports an SAP deployment model and doesn't interfere with an organization's ability to meet its consumer's needs, while easily integrating into an organization's basic business operating structure. Unlike protective-based training, enforcement-based philosophies work best when used by law enforcement officers in a public law enforcement context which relies on statutory authority and scope of employment liability protections.

Historically, the private security industry has relied on law enforcement (or law enforcement-like) training in lieu of creating unique private security best practices or standards. Unfortunately, the failure to create one has created confusion in the security industry and within organizations that employ private security personnel. Too often law enforcement training is a requirement, or it's highly preferred, just to apply for a security officer position.[7] Unfortunately, it exacerbates the current state of confusion due to security officers having to reconcile these two distinctive philosophies and processes. Moreover, the use of POST law enforcement training amplifies the (negative) effects of "Security Attire Identify Dissonance" (S.A.I.D.).

Liabilities: Failure to Train

Organizations that do not adequately train security officers open themselves up to various civil and criminal liabilities. Negligent training lawsuits are one of the most difficult and costly for organizations to defend. Community members, including legal and civil institutions, *expect* adequately trained

---

[6] After further consideration they decided against it.

[7] In California, many organizations *require* PC 832 law enforcement training for private, non-sworn security officer employment.

officers in all job categories. However, because security officers perform a specialized role, which includes interacting with dangerous individuals, protecting employees and consumers, and sometimes carry protective tools, including tools that can seriously injure and kill others, institutions should *require* their security officers to be held to high training and behavioral standards. Failing to require adequate training will become a serious liability when the organization is sued!

As an example, in the U.S Supreme Court case, *The City of Canton, Ohio v. Harris* (1989), the city was sued for allegedly not properly training their law enforcement officers (although this decision relates to law enforcement, the underlying legal concept is well established in tort law and could easily be applied to private entities and security officers). In April 1978, Canton police arrested Geraldine Harris. At the police station, Harris slumped to the floor on two occasions and was eventually left there to prevent her from falling again. When asked if she needed medical attention, she responded with an incoherent remark. No officer summoned medical assistance for her. After her release about an hour later, Harris went to the hospital by an ambulance provided by her family and was diagnosed as "suffering from emotional ailments." She remained in the hospital for a week and then required outpatient treatment for a year after. Years later, Harris brought claims of negligence against the Canton Police Department. She argued that her Fourth Amendment right to due process was violated when the police failed to provide her medical attention while in custody. The case went to the U.S. Supreme Court in November 1988. In February 1989 the Supreme Court ruled that local governments can be liable for monetary damages when deliberate indifference to the need for training and failure to train officers result in constitutional violations.[8]

The two basic vulnerabilities for organizations are:

1. A lack of training in an area where there's a patently obvious need for training.
2. An established pattern of conduct by officers that would put the final policymaker on notice and the policymaker failed to respond to it with adequate training and policies.

---

[8] https://www.acluohio.org/archives/cases/city-of-canton-ohio-v-harris.

In another example, in the case of *Weaver v. Event Staffing et al.,* claimant Daniel Weaver sued Event Staffing, a security company, and its security officer, alleging they were responsible for Weaver's physical injuries that left him a quadriplegic. The lawsuit claims that Event Staffing "failed to properly train" its employees, which led to Weaver's injuries (Associated Press, 2012, "Man Sues over Paralyzing Injury at West VA Event"). This is only one of the thousands of claims made each year against security officers who aren't adequately trained by their organizations for the realities of processing workplace conflict and violence.

Professionalized Industries

In most professionalized industries there are stringent personnel training requirements and standards that need to be met to be certified or to maintain certifications, but not for the security industry or its security officers. Unfortunately, this has created an industry characterized by a "no-standard standard." Most states that license security personnel require a minimal level of training, often eight hours or less, to become a licensed contract security guard, and rarely is there any significant training requirement to maintain licensure or an enforcement mechanism to assure compliance. In many instances these certifications only apply to officers who are contracted by private security firms to work at various organizations and don't apply to professional security officers who work directly for an organization. Although many private organizations require their proprietary security officers to have these contract security certifications when they're hired, they are not always required.

The lack of universally accepted professional security officer standards has led to a smorgasbord of approaches, or best practices, usually created by each organization and heavily influenced by nonsecurity organizational stakeholders. Worst yet, in the absence of *standards* many organizations have opted to train security officers in the only thing they're familiar with— POST law enforcement practices. But when dealing with difficult people, the use of POST training may increase the likelihood that private security officers will use physical measures over more collaborative approaches, which in the end increases other liabilities.

A risk and vulnerability assessment should be performed to determine the specific core security officer competencies required to protect people and prevent workplace violence. Additionally, they provide the basis for determining the appropriate training needs and the selection of duty gear required for each unique organizational context. Finally, security officers should receive training in the business basics and the protective arts.

The Business Basics

Regardless of the environment where a product or service is sold or provided, such as education, healthcare, and retail communities, *every* security officer should receive training in:

1. Business-focused principles such as supply and demand, profit and loss, and customer service.[9]
2. The processes involved in selling or providing an organization's specific products or services to their unique market.
3. Risk management and business law.[10]

Prior to engaging disruptive behaviors, professional security officers need to be trained on how an organization's unique product or service is sold or provided to its market and how their specific activities impact their organization's ability to deliver it and remain financially viable, as well as provided a clear understanding of how their activities support the organization's overall mission. Likewise, to function as a business stakeholder also means understanding how risk is determined, how it's applied to various policies, and what laws govern the organization's activities.[11]

Unfortunately, some stakeholders falsely believe that since safety is a security problem and not a business problem, security officers don't need to know anything about their business. The truth is, it's a business problem that's often solved by professional security personnel using principles of protection. Unfortunately, most security officers don't have a clue about

---

[9] Security officers need to know who the revenue generators are that fund the security department and security officer's payroll (expense).

[10] Since the use of protective organizational safety strategies doesn't require extensive knowledge of criminal law, with the few exceptions of understanding the elements of assaults, batteries, or trespassing, I've excluded criminal law for the basic requirements.

[11] It may be useful for new security officer trainees to work in the sales or customer service departments to gain a practical understanding of these business concepts.

the basics of business and how their activities create relevance for their organizations. This is especially true when security officers focus on forced compliance (enforcement) and not protective activities. Ignorance is partially due to a lack of integration and coordination between security departments and other organizational departments. To make training useful, it must be clear on how it benefits the organization and its security officers must prioritize the organization's needs over their own; this is true of all employee training, not just security training. Too often the individual officers' idea of organizational relevance is far removed from the organization's expectation and it impedes productivity.

The Protective Arts

To improve the potential of successfully managing workplace conflict, resolving violence and protecting people, security officers need to be trained in a core set of protective tactics and tools. Since communication is the most often used tactic for processing workplace conflict, security officers need to regularly train on how to deescalate interpersonal tension using communication.[12] This is especially true since many private security officers don't carry any protective tools. In some instances, effective communication may be the only way for security officers to protect themselves or others from harmful behavior. Regardless of the environment, anytime uniformed security officers are deployed to create a visual deterrent and discourage inappropriate behavior, there's always a possibility that they will be confronted by dangerous subjects, and they need reliable and ethical ways to protect themselves and others.

The minimum training requirement for security officers, regardless of the level of environmental risk should include:[13]

1. Basic personal protective measures,[14]
2. Behavior analysis and SPARC Matrix,
3. Protective-force theory, and
4. Basic de-escalation communication techniques.

---

[12] Communication is discussed in greater detail in Chapter 11.
[13] Additional training may include medical support, first aid and AED, to be included in the basic training.
[14] Also known as *weaponless self-defense*.

Additionally, *professional* security officers should be authorized and trained to use additional protective tactics and various tools such as:

1. Advanced personal protective measures,
2. Health, Wellness and Fitness
3. Control and restraint techniques,
4. Defensive baton,
5. Firearms,
6. Handcuffs,
7. OC/pepper spray, and
8. Taser.

It's irresponsible for any organization or security director/manager to assign security officers to field duties without first providing the above-listed *minimum* training, and in higher risk environments, they must allow personnel to carry and use protective tools. Depending on the complexities of the unique employment environment, security officers may require additional training in other protective tactics and tools. However, since a firearm is also capable of harming innocent victims, security officers who carry a firearm must meet a reliable health and wellness standard to be assured they can maintain control of it if a dangerous individual attempts to disarm them. Unfortunately, organizations continue to employ armed private security officers who are unhealthy, unwell, or unfit and are a personal and organizational liability. To be clear, I am an advocate for employing armed private security officers under three minimum conditions: when there is a significant potential for armed violence, when there is no way to limit access to the property to screen people entering it, and when the officers must meet nonnegotiable health, wellness, and fitness standard. Additionally, every security officer should be trained to use and carry a Taser. It is the safest, most effective, and the simplest, nonlethal personal protective tool to use for private security officers.[15] Training also needs to include the opportunity for security officers to practice using the requisite tactics and tools and testing for competency.

---

[15] We discuss the use of a Taser in more detail in Chapter 12.

Coached Practice: Applying Theory in Context

Effective training must include significant time for *coached practice*. Whether training involves newly acquired or already acquired competencies, coached practice is necessary for learning new skills or for maintaining them. The adage *practice makes perfect* is an important and underused training axiom. Practice provides a safe environment for security officers to personally test out various verbal and physical tactics, or how to apply a tool. Practice provides a safe opportunity to try, fail, recover, and refine skills, and develop confidence while receiving vital feedback and correction from a qualified instructor. Ideally, the practice and testing environment should recreate the realities of the true field conditions security officers will face. Since processing live workplace conflict involves interacting with emotionally unstable people, the training environment must replicate the emotional tone of real human interactions. Training in a sterile environment doesn't help security officers learn how to make critical decisions while processing strong emotions. Unfortunately, most security training environments are emotionally void.

Emotionally Rich Training Environments

To prepare security officers to deal with the realities of workplace conflict and keep simple interpersonal conflict from escalating, officers need to understand how failed expectations or unmet needs create emotional instability that can trigger unsafe behaviors that have the potential to cause harm. Emotional instability can impact employees and consumers equally. Ideally, training should help inoculate officers against the physiological and cognitive effects (generally called stress) that naturally occur when emotions become unstable, especially when interacting with verbally and physically resistant individuals. Unfortunately, when a security officer's emotions become unstable, it becomes a reciprocal and self-reinforcing process; the more emotionally unstable they become, the greater the likelihood the other party will become emotionally unstable. During stressful encounters security officers often experience cognitive disruptions in their mental processing, and they respond in ways that exacerbate and/or enable more aggressive tendencies. Emotionally rich training environments help inoculate security officers against the effects of stress and condition them to respond with defense resistant triggering strategies to offset their effects.[16]

Scenario Roleplay: Creating Emotionally Rich Training Environments

A key to preparing security officers for the realities of workplace conflict is injecting the emotional complexities of live, human interactions into the learning environment. The most effective way is to use scenario roleplay (SRP). A key to effective SRP learning is progressively interjecting increasing levels of interpersonal resistance into the learning environment, without exceeding a student's emotional capacity, to allow the student to safely experience how stress impacts critical thinking. The main reason that low-stress, peer-to-peer roleplay is rarely effective is that it's difficult to interject interpersonal resistance into the learning environment without inadvertently triggering a student's strong emotions and creating an uncomfortable or hostile work environment. Unfortunately, to avoid these potential liabilities, most training environments remain emotionally sterile, and uncharacteristically safe, unlike the security officer's real work environment.

There are two types of SRP: Interactive Simulated Video (ISV) and Live Actor. Both types of SRP are extremely effective for teaching security officers on how to effectively manage the physiological and cognitive changes that occur when processing interpersonal workplace tensions.

Interactive Simulated Video SRP

ISV SRP learning provides a productive and safe platform for officers to practice what they've learned using highly contextual conflict scenarios. During ISV sessions a videoed image is projected onto a video screen allowing the security officers to interact with prerecorded actor scenarios. The video screen acts as an "emotional wall of protection," allowing the security officer to safely interact with realistic consumer behaviors while learning to stay within their emotional limits. Unlike face-to-face,

---

[16] We discuss inoculation in greater detail in Chapter 11.

peer-to-peer scenario roleplay that limits the use of intense and realistic language and behavior, which are naturally present in real-life human interactions, ISV SRP learning uses gender, racial, ethnic, cultural representations, and realistic language (e.g., vulgarity and slang) and allows the teacher/trainer to introduce the appropriate levels of emotional intensity into the learning environment without it inhibiting learning or creating unnecessary liabilities. ISV SRP learning creates the kind of physiological and cognitive responses necessary for practicing and learning how to influence behavior during intense employee/consumer interactions.[17]

Live-Actor SRP

A more effective learning methodology that incorporates many of the advantages of Simulated Interactive Video learning is the use of live actors to roleplay conflicted scenarios. Unlike ISV learning which uses prerecorded video snippets, live-actor SRP provides real-time, continuous, and highly dynamic and interactive sessions that allow employees to interact face-to-face with actors. First, the actor's responses are instant and natural, and can quickly adjust to the changing relational dynamics between the security officer and the actor/roleplayer. Next, since the officer and actor have no relational connection, their interaction is more natural. The downside to using live actors is the cost, including training actors to understand the client's unique context and limits.

Improving Access: Mediated Live Scenario Roleplay

Although live actor SRP is a good option, mediated live SRP, a cloud-based option that allows security officers to remotely interact with live actors in highly contextual roleplay scenarios may be better. Mediated live SRP uses a proprietary internet connection (like Zoom) that allows security officers/trainees to remotely access live actors using a desktop, laptop, or tablet. The device used to access the program creates a degree of emotional protection for the student/trainee (like the way a video screen functions

---

[17] We use and recommend TI Training software and applications based in Denver, CO. (titraining.com).

when using ISV SRP). The remote live actors can present realistic cultural representations, and use representative language, without creating an unsafe environment for the officer/student.

Assuring Training Outcomes

Employees, consumers, and other organizational stakeholders (and the security officers themselves) need to be assured that training translates into field competency. Competency testing must include:

1. Written tests,
2. Hands-on proficiency testing, and
3. Realistic SRP.

One of the greatest impediments to organizational success, vocational relevance, and security officer effectiveness is a failure to require security officers to be tested against reliable competency standards prior to being *certified* to perform their duties. Unbelievably, most security training is delivered with no way to fail! The practical result is that no one can be disciplined, disqualified, fired, or reassigned for not maintaining competencies. (I am often surprised when I ask other trainers how they deal with personnel who fail their courses. I'm told that no one fails!)

Computer-Based Instruction: Delivering Information Remotely

To complicate matters, many organizations rely *exclusively* on computer-based instruction, or CBI, that can't test for tactical proficiencies. Although CBI is *not* training, it's a cost-effective method for *delivering information* and is useful for developing the theories that underlie the use of protective tactics and tools. However, to establish and maintain these physical competencies, *training* must take place in-person, be hands-on, be instructor lead and involve opportunities for students/officers to practice, and then be tested for competency. The use of CBI is extremely effective when used in a hybrid teaching format; it benefits the students/officers, instructors, and organizations. Students can learn the underlying theories at their own pace and complete the written intellectual testing prior to attending the training. Instructors benefit by maximizing the limited time they're given with students/officers and can focus on practice and competency testing. Organizations benefit because students/officers complete training at a faster pace and spend less time away from their regularly assigned duties.

Distinctions: Instruction versus Training

The distinction between instruction and training needs to be made clear. KIP, or *knowledge is power*, is an often-heard maxim in the education community. In some contexts, theoretical knowledge alone may be empowering, especially when philosophizing. However, the *power* required to effectively manage workplace conflict, resolve violence, and protect people requires security officers to contextually *apply* their knowledge. The application of knowledge is difficult to learn if training doesn't take place in person.[18] Too often the measure of *highly trained* security personnel is based on the number of *training hours* security officers have acquired through CBI. CBI can supplement learning and be effectively used in a hybrid training environment, but it's *not* a reliable substitute for *training*. It's possible to learn *theories* of protection using CBI, but it can't prepare officers to provide *actual* protection. CBI is useful for establishing and testing for theoretical competence but not for teaching applications. Employees, and all organizations stakeholders, need to know their security officers are competent in the application of protective measures, not just *theoretically* competent.

Validating Proficiency

To validate proficiency, officers must satisfactorily demonstrate how to properly use the protective tactics and tools their organizations require to successfully perform their job duties. Ultimately, the ability to translate *theory to practice* is key to becoming proficient in the use of the various protective

---

[18] The good news is that virtual learning and new and emerging remote technologies have provided access to information for more people.

tactics and tools. Additionally, there need to be processes in place for identifying and removing officers from service who can't/won't demonstrate the required competencies during training sessions and for determining if individual officers should be rehabilitated, retrained, and returned to service or their employment severed. This is one of the primary reasons that many organizations are reluctant to require that students/officers demonstrate proficiency during training. The truth is that most organizations don't know what to do with security officers who can't/won't meet standards. Additionally, many organizations don't have adequate staffing to replace sidelined officers and they're unprepared to deal with the sociopolitical issues that arise when security officers fail to meet certain standards and are determined to be *unfit* to remain on active duty.

Security Officer Training and Fitness

Truthfully, it's impossible to create reliable training standards that support competencies that involve various levels of physical exertion when a large percentage of an organization's security officers are unhealthy, unwell, or unfit.[19] Preventing and responding to workplace violence involves interacting physically with combative subjects; therefore the training environment must also require a high degree of physical exertion to create and maintain core security officer competencies and test proficiency. Unfortunately, if security officers are unable to practice and test their physical competencies in a safe and controlled environment, the only other environment left to *test* it in is an actual work environment! The *inability* to practice using the various tactics and tools and to test for competency in a realistic training environment increases risk and leads to a greater number of field injuries, work time lost, and increased workers' compensation claims.

As a trainer there have been numerous occasions when I was contracted to train an organization's security officers in various protective tactics and tools, and prior to the start of the training session, a significant percentage of their personnel informed me that they couldn't participate or they were limited in their participation because of an injury (or being unfit), while others simply went through the motions of training but were obviously "taking it easy" because of illness, injury, or being unfit. Paradoxically, many of these same security officers were still assigned to their regular duties and

---

[19] We cover physical fitness in greater detail in Chapter 9.

often returned to work after the training session! These officers were not healthy, well, or fit enough to train (or they just wouldn't train), but they still thought (and so did their employer!) they were competent to perform their respective job responsibilities. In some instances, their employers didn't know their security officers had physical limitations, while others knew but since they were so short staffed, they looked the other way. If an employee is unable (can't) or refuses to train (won't) and is still considered fit for their regular assigned duties, their job description needs to be rewritten or the officer needs to be removed from service to avoid creating unnecessary liability.[20]

Over the years I've continually surveyed my senior security manager/director clients to gauge their interest in implementing a security officer health and wellness program. The vast majority said that they'd like to implement one, but only a few of my clients have. My informal surveys revealed two basic reasons that account for a failure to implement health and wellness programs: resistance from their human resources department over potential civil liability and the fact that most of their current security officers couldn't meet the standard! Based on working with several of my clients who have successfully implemented a health and wellness program, there are several sociopolitical, legal, and pragmatic considerations that have been challenging.[21] Paradoxically, most organizations that authorize their security officers to carry and use protective tools don't require their officers to meet health, wellness, and fitness requirement and are *walking liabilities*.[22]

Law Enforcement Influence on Private Security Training

What makes a person qualified to train security officers? Historically, the assumption has always been that current or former law enforcement officers are subject matter experts and *de facto* qualified trainers. But are law enforcement officers the best choice for training private security officers? Trainer qualifications are rarely discussed in the private security industry. Using LE trainers may be another unexamined security industry assumption that

---

[20] Some officers can be rehabilitated and returned to active duty, while other can't be and need to be removed.

[21] We have a great turnkey program for helping organizations implement a security officer health and wellness program.

[22] Personnel who are unwell, unhealthy, and unfit are vulnerable to having their protective tools taken from them by combative subjects.

has become naturalized over the years. Ideally, to meet their organization's protective mission, security officers need to be trained using private free-market, protective principles and taught by instructors that not only understand the unique challenges of providing security services in a free-market context but have actually been employed in it. The substantive differences between the law enforcement and private security industries make it untenable to create one training standard that meets the needs of both industries.

In fact, attempts to create a single standard have created a confused private security training standard that has resulted in decreases in organizational safety and increased potential civil and criminal liabilities because private security officers often try to emulate law enforcement officers' behaviors. Since a great number of senior security directors/ managers are former law enforcement officers, and even if when not, they still tend to have a natural affinity for law enforcement personnel and philosophies, and typically choose law enforcement officers to train their personnel. In the end, these training preferences may create unintended consequences for private security officers and their organizations.

Law Enforcement Trainers

Although many law enforcement trainers are experts in the use of certain defensive tools (e.g., firearms, baton, OC/pepper spray, or Taser) and tactics (such as weaponless self-defense) and are skilled instructors, they rarely have experience using them in a non-sworn, private free-market security context. A lack of actual experience using the tactics or tools in the context they are meant for could become a liability. Not understanding the legal, ethical, or social considerations for physically interacting with resistant subjects exposes private organizations to unnecessary liabilities. In fact, law enforcement trainers who train private security officers may create additional areas of vulnerability for private organizations, such as being drawn into a training lawsuit involving private security officers they've trained.

Trainer Qualifications

How would a law enforcement officer testify to their own experiences using the tactics or tools they teach when they've never actually applied them while employed as a private security officer? This question is not new to law enforcement trainers or to law enforcement training. It's the same concern that helped develop the rationale law enforcement officers use for prohibiting civilian (non-police) security trainers from training law enforcement officers. In the law enforcement industry, private (non-sworn) trainers are rarely accepted as qualified to instruct law enforcement personnel.[23] In fact, the POST training standards are so strict they typically prohibit former or retired law enforcement officers from instructing active-duty law enforcement officers. To become a POST-approved instructor, the instructor must be an active-duty law enforcement officer, and the curriculum and the facility must be POST-approved. The law enforcement community has very high standards for both the individuals they accept as qualified to teach and for the training curriculums used. These rigid POST-training standards are partially responsible for the relatively high degree of peace officer safety. Paradoxically, the law enforcement trainers I've talked with don't think POST's methodology and reasoning for qualifying law enforcement trainers should be used as a model by private organizations to qualify private security trainers. The overwhelming majority of law enforcement officers, security managers, and senior stakeholders assume that active, former, or retired law enforcement officers make the best security trainers. In short, law enforcement trainers believe that law enforcement experience is necessary for training law enforcement officers, but actual private free-market security experience is not necessary for training security officers. These unexamined training assumptions are inaccurate and are an impediment to the creation of unique, private security industry training standards.

Law Enforcement Training Challenges

The concern with teaching private security officers, law enforcement theories, and tactics is that it creates confusion and cognitive dissonance, leading to the false belief that once security officers receive the training, they also acquire the effectuating power of statutory authority and scope of employment immunity that law enforcement officers enjoy. On its face this may seem ludicrous, but there are security officers who can't become law enforcement officers who still fantasize about becoming one, and law

---

[23] There are rare exceptions for certain subject matter experts.

enforcement training creates both an excitement and a level of confusion and dissonance. This dissonance causes some security officers to emulate the types of behaviors that law enforcement officers engage in when interacting with resistant individuals. However, when private security officers interact with consumers like law enforcement officers often do, it has the potential to increase interpersonal tensions, decrease personal safety, and create other liabilities.

Most private organizations, especially organizations that employ their own proprietary (in-house) security officers, hire police-oriented personnel (academy graduates and former or retired law enforcement officers). In fact, many of these older police-oriented individuals have extensive law enforcement experience and POST training. However, once these former law enforcement officers "suit up" in a non-sworn, private free-market security setting, they lose a great deal of influence over uncooperative behaviors because they can no longer rely on statutory authority or scope of employment immunity to influence behavior.[24]

Law enforcement training also confuses private security officers by minimizing and conflating (directly or indirectly) the substantive principal differences between these two industries. This confusion is further exacerbated, since many security officers are former law enforcement officers, which make them more susceptible to social-psychological law enforcement influences, such as mimicking law enforcement behavior or preferring law enforcement conflict resolution tactics over uniquely collaborative, private free-market methods for process workplace conflict.

It's been well established that the effectiveness of law enforcement training is primarily the result of statutory authority and scope of employment immunity, not on the specific individual's character, training, pay, or the tools they carry. A rookie police officer has the same statutory authority and scope of employment immunity protections that a seasoned police veteran has. Likewise, a former veteran police officer who becomes employed in the private market has the same authority as any private security officer with no law enforcement experience.

Training private security officers in law enforcement, tactics, or protective tools has the potential to increase potential civil and criminal liability.

---

[24] While some have also lost the physical advantages they had over suspects when they were younger and physically fit.

Private security officers operate as agents of the owners of the property to which they're assigned. Unlike law enforcement officers, private security officers typically have narrow physical interaction limits for resolving workplace conflict. Under most circumstances, organizations don't want their security officers to use hands-on force when processing workplace conflict. (In extreme cases, security officers are prohibited from using force, even when it may help protect their own lives.) Unlike security training, law enforcement training emphasizes the use of force to influence behavior and suppress crime.

Context, Training, and Trainers

Although the law enforcement and private security industry operate under very different legal, philosophical, and cultural principles, many decision-makers, both security and nonsecurity stakeholders, continue to conflate these two industries based on their superficial similarities (e.g., wearing similar-looking uniforms, carrying law enforcement equipment, or interacting with criminal behavior). Law enforcement tactics and defensive tools are applied in a unique public context where law enforcement officers have statutory authority, the scope of employment immunity, extensive training (up to 1,000 hours prior to working in the field, supervised field training, and ongoing and continuous post-employment training), and high levels of community support. Unlike law enforcement officers, security officers employed by private organizations have none of these advantages. In fact, in the private sector, if a private security officer takes the initiative and intervenes (or if he or she decides not to act), the security officer and the employer could be sued, even if the security officer's actions were both legal and ethical.

Even though it may seem counterintuitive, relying on law enforcement officers to set the training standard impedes the security industry's professionalization process. Although we don't recommend using POST training, we do recommend that the private security industry and trainers adopt training principles similar to POST, such as requiring actual private security work experience, the use of certified training courses, and mastery of free-market business principles, intellectual vitality, and dedication to the security vocation.

Funding and Budgets

Establishing a responsible training budget and funding for security training is and will remain the biggest challenge for every organization that employs security personnel. Security officer labor and payroll is another related funding and budget concern. A question that's often posed is how many security officers we should employ. As a general observation, most organizations should employ more security personnel, and if they're professionally trained, they're probably underpaid (and underappreciated).[25] Some security officers who are initially hired have an impressive training résumé but over time since the employer isn't scheduling or paying for training, they never maintain or upgrade their protective competencies, and since tactical skills are perishable, they naturally degrade over time.[26] Although training is not really an option for responsible organizations, adequately budgeting and funding the training program often is! Every organization needs to prioritize spending but often the needs of the security department and its personnel are low on the list and are often the first places to cut during lean times. From a business perspective, it's challenging to justify spending money on any support, nonrevenue-generating department that creates ongoing and regular expenses; that's true of all support departments, not just security. However, allocating funds to support security personnel and organizational safety is both an expense and a *saving*.

Return on Investment

The most obvious way that trained and highly competent (professional) security personnel protect its employees from harm (physically and emotionally) is providing them a safe place to be productive serving its consumers. Employees have options. In a competitive, private, free-market setting, good employees are hard to find and keep. Workplace safety impacts where and when people work, how committed they are to their employer, and if they will seek to work elsewhere when they feel

---

[25] We've decided not to take a position on the best methods for determining the *correct* number of security officers that organizations should employ or their pay and benefits.

[26] This also communicates to security personnel that training is not an important organizational value. It's easy for personnel to conclude that if it's not important to them, then why should it be important enough to me to spend my own money and time to train?

unsafe at work, increasing turnover.[27] How much money is *saved* when employees feel safe at work?

Consumers have options, too. Trained security personnel protect consumers from harm (physically and emotionally) by providing them a safe place to visit and purchase products and services without worrying. In a competitive business context, a consumer will *not* spend their hard-earned money or time where they feel unsafe, even if it means traveling to a more distant location to consume similar products or services. If a consumer is seriously injured or killed at *your* location, how would sales, revenue, and profit be impacted when consumers feel it's unsafe to frequent it?

Criminals have options as well! They can victimize *your* organization and people or try elsewhere. People who may have a propensity to act out during times of crisis can recognize an *easy mark* and need to be disincentivized from acting in an unsafe manner and know they'll be dealt with swiftly if they do. Trained, professional security officers discourage bad actors and help the *good people* feel secure knowing that someone is available to help them. There are tangible savings for discouraging violent incidents from happening.

Conversely, when security personnel are *not* competency trained, and people are harmed, there are legal, civil, and public liabilities and *actual* costs. Even when an organization is sufficiently insured against various liabilities, they may still be responsible for costs that exceed their coverage, and general liability insurance premiums and workers' compensation *costs* soar. But maybe the greatest cost is how the public responds! Consider the example of the LA Dodgers. It's estimated that the total *costs* for a fan, Bryan Stow, being severely injured in 2011, was over 100 million dollars to the organization and the owner Frank McCourt, including a loss in revenue and financial liabilities for alleged "cutbacks in security and antiquated facilities including light fixtures dating from 1962 contributed to the brutal attack." (Kim, 2011, Victoria. LA Times. 5/24/11. "Byran Stow's Family Sues the Dodgers"). Stow's family sued the LA Dodgers for:

1. Negligence,
2. Premise liability,
3. Negligent hiring, retention, and supervision,
4. Negligent infliction of emotional distress,
5. Assault, battery, and false imprisonment, and
6. Intentional infliction of emotional distress.

---

[27] As an example, I once quit a good job because my car kept getting broken into in my employer's parking lot, even though my workspace was safe.

Moreover, after Stow was injured, the LA Dodgers spent a significant amount of money to upgrade their security personnel and facilities. It took several years for the LA Dodgers to regain the public's trust, rebuild their brand, and become financially viable (again).

Besides the human factors related to organizational safety, there are other reasons for employing professionally trained security officers. Organizations are *required* through OSHA regulations to have a plan to prevent and respond to workplace violence, and in some industries, there are regulatory and accreditation requirements which professional security officers help maintain.

The *total costs* of mitigating all organizational liabilities, using both proactive and reactive organizational safety strategies involving the deployment of professionally trained security personnel, are far less than the costs for failing to do all things possible.

According to OSHA, in their pamphlet on *Training Requirements in OSHA Standards*, "Training in the safe way for workers to do their jobs well is an investment that will pay back over and over again in fewer injuries and illnesses, better morale, lower insurance premiums and more" (Occupational Safety and Health Administration [OSHA], United States Department of Labor, 2020).[28]

Part of the solution to this training dilemma is for senior security managers to become experts at quantifying the benefits and liabilities associated with training security officers, educating their senior stakeholders on the importance and value of training, and being honest about the consequences for failing to train. The bottom line is that spending on security officer training is an excellent investment and has quantifiable practical, financial, and ethical organizational benefits.

Impediments

Perhaps the greatest impediment to communicating these training imperatives to senior stakeholders is structural; most organizations situate their security function and their senior security director/manager low in the corporate hierarchy. Rarely is the senior security director/manager afforded an opportunity to defend their training principles directly to the

---

[28] The Guide to Training Requirements in OSHA Standards. https://www.osha.gov/Publications/osha2254.pdf.

senior stakeholders who make the budgetary decisions; it's often filtered up through the chain. In some instances, they must rely on their immediate, nonsecurity, direct report to make the case. These individuals may have little to no practical security experience or have competency in social, personal, and corporate agendas. A lack of relevant security experience may create an ignorance about what should be required, the person responsible may not be motivated to learn what's needed, or they simply don't have the time to spend with the senior security director/manager to become educated. Finally, when there are competing agendas, direct reports may make spending decisions based on personal circumstances rather than the security department's training needs.

Summary

To prevent and respond to workplace conflict and violence, and protect people, organizations need to employ professional security officers who are trained to reliable competency standards. Security officers should be trained by qualified trainers who understand the unique challenges of providing security services to the free market. Training should be ongoing and continuous, and officers should be supervised to identify and correct training deficiencies, and for transferring officers who can't meet standards or to discipline or discharge officers who won't meet competency standards. Finally, the organization needs to financially support security officer training with a fair training budget.

Recommendations

1. Allocate the appropriate funds necessary to support a reliable training program.
2. Create a system to rehabilitate personnel who are unable to maintain the required competencies.
3. Develop a list of required competencies that must be maintained to successfully perform the job.
4. Discharge personnel who refuse to participate in training or rehabilitation programs.
5. Implement an ongoing and continuous training program to maintain the required competencies and to identify personnel who may be deficient.

6. Implement preemployment screening processes to assure that only qualified applicants are hired.
7. Require all employees to meet a reliable health and wellness standard.
8. Train personnel using free-market–based protective tactics and tools.
9. Use trainers that have actual private free-market–uniformed security officer experience.

References

Associated Press, 2012. NY man sues over paralyzing injury at W. VA. event. Wall Street Journal, 17 May 2012; Web: <http://online.wsj.com/article/APb83daae0af2c4a96a52b2800dbcdd888> 07.06.12.

Kim, Victoria, 2011. Byran Stow's family sues the Dodgers. LA Times, 24 May 2011.

Nemeth, C.P., 2005. Private Security and The Law (third ed.), Elsevier. Boston, MA.

Occupational Safety and Health Administration, United States Department of Labor, 2020. The Guide to Training Requirements in OSHA Standards. <https://www.osha.gov/Publications/osha2254.pdf>

Chapter 11

Communication: A Key Tool for Processing Workplace Conflict

Problem

Security officers aren't adequately trained to use of communication to process workplace conflict and keep unsafe behaviors from escalating.

Introduction

A key to preventing workplace violence is keeping minor interpersonal workplace conflict from escalating. Security officers are often the first ones called to assist customer service personnel when conflict arises. However, to determine the potential effectiveness of communication, security officers need to conduct a behavior analysis to determine a consumer's initial level of cooperation/resistance and emotional stability.[1] To assure safe employee/consumer interactions, there needs to be a clear understanding of the different interpersonal processes involved in managing workplace conflict and resolving violence and the various communicative strategies and their limits. Moreover, when conflict is

---

[1] We discuss behavior analysis in greater detail in Chapter 12.

effectively managed it also reduces the need for security personnel to use force to protect employees and consumers.

The methods used for keeping passive–aggressive behaviors from escalating to workplace conflict are different from those used to keep directly aggressive behavior from escalating to violence. As an individual's behavior escalates to direct aggression or violence, it's virtually impossible to *manage* behaviors. Proactive collaborative communication strategies, such as active listening, dialoguing, responding, accommodating, compromising, and negotiating, become less effective, or completely ineffective, as unstable emotions and behavior escalate. Conversely, attempts to resolve conflict require reactive communication strategies, such as direct and forceful communication, but may also require the use of physical force.

Moreover, the misapplication of reactive communication strategies to passive–aggressive consumer behavior often exacerbates the conflict and increases emotional instability, which may lead to unnecessary customer service complaints. However, the greater risk is created when employees misapply proactive communication strategies to directly aggressive consumer behaviors, which may enable or activate a consumer's more violent tendencies, leading to employee or consumer injuries. Once a consumer's behavior escalates to violence, communication ceases to be effective at reestablishing emotional stability and deescalating unsafe behavior, and physical strategies may be necessary to protect people or to gain control of the individual.

All employees who interact face-to-face with consumers should be trained to manage passive–aggressive behaviors. But only a select group of specially trained personnel, and all security officers, should be required to intervene to keep unsafe behaviors from escalating it to violence. Once an individual's behavior escalates beyond passive aggressiveness, the risk to employees and consumers is too great for line personnel without specialty training to be involved. In short, assaultive behaviors cannot be managed and not all crises can be solved nonviolently.

Process

A key to managing passive–aggressive behaviors is the effective use of collaborative communication strategies, such as active listening, dialoguing, responding, accommodating, compromising, and negotiating. The University of California (UC) report supports the contention that communication training is imperative for officers who regularly interact with uncooperative individuals. Although the report focuses on law enforcement officers and their interaction with college students (their consumers), the report highlights a lack of verbal skills training by their police officers as a contributing factor for a campus protest turning violent.[2]

In a report written by UC Dean Christopher F. Edley, Jr., and UC General Counsel Charles F. Robinson in response to an allegation of excessive force on the part of UC Davis police officers, the writers concluded that UC police officers lacked training in verbal de-escalation and made a recommendation that the UC system should only hire police officers who have the right temperament to deal with "taunting and other disrespectful behavior … without resorting to physical force" (Edley and Robinson, 2012).

Perspectives on Communication

Keeping interpersonal conflicts from morphing into passive–aggressive behaviors and then escalating to workplace violence are keys to workplace violence prevention. This is accomplished through the effective use of communication especially when a consumer's emotions begin to become unstable. Although communication is a key, it can be used instrumentally or relationally, to influence behavior. When communication is used *instrumentally* the goal is to achieve the desired end state, when using *relationally* its goal is to create, develop, or maintain an interpersonal connection. A key to managing interpersonal workplace conflict is knowing how and when to use communication to influence escalating behaviors. As an example, consider a typical drive-through restaurant interaction. You drive up to the speaker box and use *instrumental* communication to order your food, "I'll take a hamburger." You drive up to the window and pay but before you drive away, you look in the bag and find a chicken sandwich. You then reengage the employee and use *relational* communication. "Excuse me I hate to bother you, but I think you may have given me the wrong order, I ordered a hamburger and instead got a chicken sandwich."

---

[2] The report also notes the importance of possessing the *right temperament* to deal with verbal abuse.

The employee apologizes, gives you a hamburger, and you drive off.[3] When ordering you're not concerned (or much less so) about how a lack of interpersonal connection with the employee will affect your interaction. But when attempting to solve the problem and avoid creating defensiveness (and making sure the employee doesn't add anything *extra* to the sandwich) you attempt to ingratiate yourself, creating a *mini interpersonal connection* that helps both parties achieve their behavioral goals. When interacting with passive–aggressive behaviors, security officers need to know how to use communication to keep behaviors from escalating and if it does, find effective ways to de-escalate it.

Personnel whose job requires them to regularly interact with difficult people often have a different perspective on the role and effectiveness of communication than those who don't. Unfortunately, both security officers and nonsecurity employees often make critical communication assumptions about the role of communication in managing conflict. Over time, and through the continued exposure to difficult consumers and *resisters*, customer service personnel, and security officers, often try to use communicative short cuts to create influence. However, this approach tends to exacerbate interpersonal tension and escalates dysfunctional behaviors. When customer service personnel take short cuts, they often end up calling security to *bail them out*, whereas when security officers take communicative short cuts, they end up needing to use more physical solutions to de-escalate conflicts. However, security officers, customer service personnel, and senior corporate managers all agree that most interpersonal workplace conflict can be managed, and some lower levels of escalating tensions, mitigated, with the proper use of communication. But security officers are still more skeptical than nonsecurity personnel that communicative solutions will generally lead to peaceful resolutions.

A key to successfully de-escalating workplace conflict is gaining the involved individual's cooperation early in the conflicted interaction before emotions become unstable. Ideally, the organization should create an environment that makes it difficult for consumers *not* to cooperate with its employees and employees should become relational communication experts at influencing behavior to increase the possibility that initially uncooperative individuals will cooperate. The reality of workplace conflict is that not all attempts to keep interpersonal conflict from escalating will be successful. This is especially true when individuals are in a heightened

---

[3] Moreover, you'll probably use affirming nonverbal communication to show empathy.

emotional state, under the influence of drugs and/or alcohol, or in mental or emotional distress, this can be an extremely complicated task. Resistant individuals are not easily convinced of what's in their best interests during times of crisis.

The Ability to Influence

In a private, free-market environment, social power helps create noncoercive influence that's necessary for processing interpersonal workplace conflict and keeping passive–aggressive behaviors from escalating to violence. Since private security officers don't enjoy statutory authority and most organizations limit their influence through policies, they need to create influence through effective communication and social power.

Kathy Henning (2012) identifies five social power types that influence conflict:

1. Coercive power is the ability to punish.
2. Expert power is a possession of special knowledge or experience.
3. Legitimate power is being hired, elected, or appointed to a position of power.
4. Referent power is created from positive interpersonal attributes (being liked).
5. Reward power is having the ability to reward.

According to Henning, one of the keys to managing conflict, or if subsequently needing to resolve it, is determining which party has the greater power level and then creating solutions based on those power imbalances.[4] Although Henning lists five social *power types*, we've expanded the power list to seven by rounding out the list with two additional power types:

6. Ethical/moral power is the embedded universal values that most community members share with the organization's security officers.
7. Physical power is the visually obvious physical advantage a person has over their adversaries, such as height, weight, muscular build, speed, or fitness.

---

[4] Hence the sayings, "Evening the score," "Having the upper hand," or Getting even."

Individuals involved in processing interpersonal conflict may embody and demonstrate power, deliberately withhold power, or exercise more than one of these power types simultaneously when attempting to de-escalate interpersonal tension and process conflict.

For instance, a parent may be able to physically discipline (punish) a child or reward the child with ice cream—two power types to overcome the child's resistance to cleaning their room. However, unlike the frustrations associated with trying to get a child to clean their room, frustrations associated with workplace conflict, without understanding the role that social power plays may create power imbalances that lead to unsafe, violent, or even deadly consequences for employees, consumers, and security officers. Since most private security officers are not typically afforded high levels of legitimate power by their organizations, they need to develop and rely on expert, physical, and/or ethical/moral power to influence unsafe behaviors and protect people.

Check Yourself before You Wreck Yourself

Security officers, including those who have received extensive communication training, often communicate in ways that end up exacerbating interpersonal tension when interacting with difficult people. There are thousands of examples of these interactions captured on police body cameras and bystander videos posted online.[5] There is an obvious disconnect between the communications training an employee receives and the employee's ability to effectively use communication to process workplace conflict. There are two possible reasons for this disconnect. Some employees are just conflict averse and don't like being engaged with others when interpersonal tension arises. The other is the result of failed learning methodologies. When employees process face-to-face, employee/consumer workplace conflict, certain cognitive, physiological, and emotional processes are naturally activated. Typically, when employees are learning how to process workplace conflict, the training takes place in an *emotionally void* training environment. Many of the most popular conflict training programs utilize CBI, PowerPoint, video presentations, or similar

---

[5] Since most security officers don't use body-worn video devices, most examples of officers either appropriately or inappropriately using communication to manage interpersonal conflict are police officers.

learning methodologies, as their primary, if not the only, methodologies used to prepare employees/students to process workplace conflict. These approaches often fail because the training environment doesn't replicate (or even try to) the emotional tone of real interpersonal conflict and students have limited opportunities to practice.[6] Unfortunately, when employees/students experience emotional instability during live, field, workplace conflict, and not in a safe training environment, they're more apt to react inappropriately.

Resistance, Vulnerability, Defensiveness, Emotional Instability, Stress, and Decision-Making

Understanding the cognitive, emotional, physiological, and psychological processes that are activated when employees are confronted by resistant consumer behaviors is important for refining the learning methodologies needed to improve the training environment, training outcomes, and real-world success. During a live employee/consumer interaction if an employee's initial verbal and nonverbal responses fail to control or stabilize the conflicted interaction, employees often begin to feel emotionally and/or physically vulnerable which activates verbal, nonverbal and/or physical defensive responses that are attempts to reduce feelings of physical and emotional vulnerabilities (fear). Initially, these cognitive and physiological changes (called arousal) prepare our bodies by sharpening our senses to potential dangers. However, when initial defensive responses fail to reduce feelings of vulnerability (e.g., they don't work), physiological changes spike, commonly known as stress arousal. As stress increases, employees may experience cognitive deficits such as narrowing of attention, loss of memory, or deficits in performance or emotions (such as frustration, annoyance, withdrawal, or aggression) from becoming *overly aroused*, which often creates a fight, flight, or freeze response.

On the low end of stress arousal, and within controllable limits, physiological and cognitive processes sharpen mental focus and prepare the body for battle. However, if stress exceeds controllable limits, and arousal increases to acute levels (e.g., acute stress), cognitive and physiological

---

[6] See Chapter 10 for more detail on inoculation training.

changes interfere with mental processing, making it difficult to recall training and it severely impacts decision-making. As stress levels rise, an individual's mental processes (schemas) shift from controlled to automatic; under acute stress employees end up *reacting* to an event, rather than *acting*. Under acute stress security officers often respond as though they've never been trained!

These emotional, psychological, and cognitive processes explain why even trained officers often say and do things during attempts to process workplace conflict that seem outrageous and counterproductive. To effectively offset the effects of stress arousal caused by nonphysical (or verbal) defensiveness,[7] personnel need to develop defense-resistant triggering strategies.

One useful defense-resistant triggering strategy is to depersonalize the interaction by separating the *problem from the person*, and not interpreting the attack *personally*. An offending consumer often attacks an employee, not as a person, but as the *business's* representative, who they interpret as *the one* responsible for keeping them from satisfying a need or want or meeting their expectations.

Sarcasm, for instance, a typical verbal defensive response (and one overused by public safety officers), is only useful for reducing emotional vulnerabilities when used with people we've previously developed a relationship with or who appreciate it. When sarcasm is used with people we know, it's usually interpreted as humor and doesn't negatively impact the relationship. But when used in a workplace setting, especially during interpersonal conflict, sarcasm is usually interpreted as passive aggressiveness and considered an inappropriate form of communication, increasing interpersonal tension. Similarly, consider another often used, nonverbal defensive response, *the eye roll*, and how it would be interpreted when used in a workplace setting versus among friends. Unfortunately, under some conditions these types of verbal defense responses may activate or enable the worst possible instincts in a consumer and lead to violent behaviors.

Similarly, a typical defensive response to feeling physically vulnerable (to an attack) is to move away from danger and change one's body positioning, and if available, access a protective tool. This *physical*

---

[7] Most defensiveness is created by verbal infractions, not physical attacks. We use the generic term *attack* since even words can *feel like*, and be responded to, like a physical attack.

defensive response is very effective at reducing vulnerabilities, stabilizing emotions, and keeping physiology and cognition from creating impediments to decision-making.

Attack, Fear, Defend, Attack (AFDA) Response Pattern

Below we've mapped out a typical workplace employee/consumer interaction pattern that results from a dispute over needs, wants, and expectations. To be clear, the offending or offended party can be the employee or the consumer and what both parties say or do during the interaction has the potential to improve or escalate it. However, since the employee represents the organization and has an affirmative responsibility (and training) to process and overcome verbal resistance, we describe these processes from the employee's perspective. Moreover, these patterns and these processes occur during both verbal and physical attacks. Although most employee/consumer disputes involve passive–aggressive (nonviolent) behaviors, some can escalate and become physical. We call these responses, the "attack, fear, defend, attack" (AFDA) pattern:[8]

- An employee and the consumer become involved in a dispute over needs, wants, or expectations.
- The consumer says or does something that the employee interprets as a personal and/or physical attack, feels vulnerable, and then responds defensively.
- The employee says or does something to reduce feelings of vulnerability. The consumer responds in a positive way and the interaction remains productive and safe.
- Or, the employee's attempt to reduce feelings of vulnerability doesn't work.
- This failure creates low-level cognitive and physiological changes, within manageable ranges, such as increases in adrenaline and heartbeat, and changes to blood pressure, which activate mental processes. These processes initially sharpen senses, and training schemas are retrieved from memory. As a result, the employee applies the proper conflict

---

[8] These processes are similar to conflict that occurs outside of a workplace and between intimates, but employee/consumer disputes have some unique qualities.

management strategy, the consumer's behavior de-escalates, and the employee's vulnerabilities reduce and remain productive and safe.

■ Or, the employee's attempt to reduce feelings of vulnerability doesn't work.

■ This time, the failure creates higher levels of cognitive and physiological changes that are less/not manageable, resulting in greater increases in adrenaline, heartbeat, and blood pressure. As a result, mental processes now degrade and attempts to retrieve training schemas from memory fail. The employee then says and does things outside of training and policy, the consumer's behavior escalates, the employee's vulnerabilities spike, and the interaction becomes risky.

■ As each successive attempt to reduce vulnerabilities fails, the greater the physiological and cognition changes, elevating stress to *acute* levels which interferes with critical decision-making. This most critical junction in a conflicted employee/consumer interaction can lead to an escalation in behavior some will interpret as justification to resort to violence.

The Battle Lines Are Drawn

When employees become overwhelmed (battle weary) by their inability to bring the interaction under control and feel like they've *lost the battle*, a fight, flight, or freeze response is often activated. A *fight* response could be employees yelling profanities or physically assaulting consumers, a *flight* response could be an employee simply walking away from the consumer and disengaging, while being silent or not being able to physically move could be a *freeze* response. Unfortunately, these responses can lead to customer service complaints or employee and consumer injuries and could seriously impact an organization's reputation and financial viability.

A key to keeping interpersonal employee/consumer workplace conflict from escalating to violence is twofold. One, employees should be trained to process passive–aggressive consumer behaviors, including how to process their own emotional triggers. Two, when customer service personnel reach their cognitive, communicative, emotional, or psychological limits, they need to safely transfer the responsibility for interacting with the consumer to other expert stakeholders who have greater capacities and abilities to process escalating behaviors. Security personnel should be involved if the conflict continues to escalate and the consumer's behavior has the potential to cause harm.

Shoot–Don't Shoot

So, how do we prepare employees and security officers to keep these internal processes from impacting their ability to effectively and safely process workplace conflict? It's much easier to teach an employee/student the limited set of physical defensive responses to feelings of *physical* vulnerabilities than it is to teach them the appropriate set of *unlimited* verbal responses to emotional/psychological vulnerabilities. The simplest response to feeling *physically* vulnerable is to create as much physical distance from the threat as quickly as possible. In public safety parlance we call this "tactical retreat." If carrying protective tools, an appropriate response to feeling physically vulnerable may be to draw a baton, pepper spray, Taser®, or firearm and direct it at the threat. Physical threats are more obvious and easily quantifiable, and the set of appropriate defensive responses is narrow. For instance, if an individual pulls a knife and threatens an armed officer, the officer pulls out a gun. The knife creates extreme feelings of vulnerability; drawing and pointing a firearm at the person holding the knife reduces feelings of vulnerabilities. This is one reason that typical "shoot–don't shoot" scenario roleplay training for armed officers is somewhat effective for testing physical threat detection and decision-making.

However, on the other hand, teaching employees/students *what to say* in response to feeling emotionally vulnerable is extremely complicated. The same words, used in the same context, may be interpreted several ways by many different people. Meaning is determined by the person decoding the message; it's not transmitted through the words. When *trained* employees are confronted by verbally abusive and/or physically assaultive consumers, during attempts to process workplace conflict, employees who haven't experienced the physiological or cognitive effects of stress in a controlled training environment, and learned how to effectively process them, typically resort to their naturalized, untrained, interpersonal defensive habits that have "worked" for them over their lifetime. Employees need to develop appropriate and ethical defense-resistant triggering strategies to keep their cognitive, emotional, and psychological changes at manageable levels and avoid exacerbating interpersonal conflict.

Overcoming Poor Habits

Changing the way adults communicate is a difficult task. By the time humans arrive at adulthood they've spent over 100,000 hours *perfecting* the best way for them to communicate in various situations. In a sense, all their communication practice has turned them into experts! Over time, these functional and dysfunctional communication habits become naturalized (hardwired) and stored in a person's subconscious. All of us have developed certain communicative and behavioral scripts that we automatically draw on when we interact in unique settings. Some scripts help create more intimate relationships, while others result in greater emotional and physical distance. As we age, from infant to adolescent to adulthood, every human goes through this trial and error process of figuring out the best way to communicate with particular people, in specific settings. Some people become attuned to their dysfunctional communication habits and are intrinsically motivated to improve them. Others, however, are forced into the process of change because they have difficulties maintaining personal or professional relationships, or because their livelihood depends on it.

Often, communication trainers fail to address these basic communication axioms and integrate them into their conflict management training programs. One flaw is they fail to acknowledge the simple truth that humans begin their communication training (or programming) at birth, not when they're hired and assigned to a conflict management class! Moreover, a few hours of CBI will rarely change how an employee interacts with difficult consumers. However, it may change how a student/employee *feels* about their ability to process conflict after participating in the instruction. When employees are surveyed after taking conflict management training, employees will often self-report that they "feel more confident" about their ability to process workplace conflict. Unfortunately, when conflict management training is facilitated using CBI, or when it takes place in sterile learning environments, rarely is there quantifiable evidence of long-term behavior modification. There is a disconnect between how students *feel* after training versus how they *perform* using CBI.

By the time employees are confronted with difficult customer service behaviors, they've already established, over the many years of practice (trial and error), "what works and what doesn't work" for them in various contexts. If responding to someone they disagree with by saying, "F-off" works for them—then it's useful and they may repeat its use again until they determine it has lost its usefulness.[9] Successful linguistic training involves reprogramming verbal behavior; inoculation is a key. Unless employees are inoculated against the effects of acute stress, during attempts to manage or resolve intense interpersonal conflict they're more likely to resort back to pretraining behavioral schemas, or naturalized behaviors, and say and do things that are contrary to trained behaviors.

When faced with interpersonal conflict, employees conduct behavior analysis to determine the individual's emotional state, their stated and unstated unmet needs, motivations, and expectations, to forecast the individual's behavior and determine the optimum path to de-escalation and recovery.

The Role of Expectations on Workplace Conflict: Better/ Worse Than Expected

Expectations play a powerful role in the creation of interpersonal tension and with attempts to de-escalate it. Before a conversation even begins, communicators, both employees and consumers, enter the interaction with certain expectations and needs. The scaled and relative difference between the communicator's pre-contact expectations and their point of contact experience influences their emotional stability and their post-contact experience (e.g., their corresponding behaviors such as being cooperative, passive-aggressive, directly aggressive, or violent). Although these relative emotional and behavioral factors are difficult to measure precisely, the below matrix is useful for gaining a better understanding of the root causes of interpersonal tension, workplace conflict, and violence and how best to process it.

Emotional Intensity: How Much Worse Than Expected?

Although failing to meet expectations increases emotional instability, failed expectations that are internally cataloged as "much worse than expected" or "worse than expected" are correlated with directly aggressive and violent behavior. Very few consumers who are/become emotionally unstable when

---

[9] This may occur after they get fired from a job or when someone punches them in the nose!

interacting with employees will ever become disruptive or violent, but there is a significant number who will. Gaining a better understanding of the role that failed expectations play in workplace conflict will help employees formulate effective responses.

Expectations, Emotional Stability, and Behavior

Initial: Pre-Contact

Prior to making face-to-face contact (Pre-C), all involved parties (the consumer and/or their affiliates and employees), begin the interaction with a range of expectations about how the interaction should proceed, and respond with varying initial levels of emotional stability. These expectations are formed by both rational and irrational means. For instance, a consumer may have talked with a friend who said they had an awful customer service experience at a particular organization, or they read an unfavorable experience on Yelp about the organization. So, when the consumer begins to interact with the organization's employee, they have an expectation of being treated poorly and have their defensive responses prepared and ready to launch.

Process: Point of Contact

At the point of face-to-face contact (POC), all involved parties make tentative and evolving evaluations about the likelihood that their Pre-C expectations and their overall level of satisfaction will be realized. These process evaluations influence emotional stability and corresponding behaviors. Using the above example, an employee may or may not be able to respond to the consumer's expectation in a way that keeps interpersonal tension from rising. This is especially problematic if the employee has an expectation that the consumer will not launch a defensive attack.

Terminal: Post-Contact

After making contact (Post-C), all involved parties make final (terminal) determinations about the totality of their actual experience (expectations and satisfaction) and say or do things consistent with their terminal experience. Responses to these terminal assessments may be instant or noticed within seconds of Post-C. The involved parties compare their Pre-C expectation with their Post-C experience to determine their overall level of satisfaction (the satisfied/dissatisfied quotient). The scaled difference between their Pre-C expectation and the POC experience determines their Post-C satisfaction/dissatisfaction level and correspondent behaviors.

The POC experience affects employees and consumers alike. Sometimes when an employee's expectations go unmet, they respond by saying and doing things they weren't trained for, which exacerbates the interaction. However, unlike an employee, if a consumer's expectations go unmet, they may become emotionally unstable and become violent.

Satisfaction and Expectation Gaps

The greater the terminal Post-C expectation gap (EG) and the greater dissatisfaction, the greater the likelihood that emotional instability will increase, and the consumer's behavior will become dysfunctional.

Terminal expectation gap is the scaled numerical difference between Pre-C and POC expectation levels. This is calculated by using a seven-point satisfied/unsatisfied Likert scale to measure satisfaction levels ranging from highly unsatisfied (−3), unsatisfied (−2), somewhat unsatisfied (−1), neutral (0), somewhat satisfied (+1), satisfied (+2), to highly satisfied (+3).

Below is a chart that is helpful for plotting a consumer's range of failed or realized expectations and is an effective visual aid for gaining a better understanding of how failed expectations and expectation intensity influence workplace conflict.

	Highly Dissatisfied	Dissatisfied	Somewhat Dissatisfied	Neutral	Somewhat Satisfied	Satisfied	Highly Satisfied
	−3	−2	−1	0	1	2	3
Expectation							
Actual							
Difference							

To better understand these relationships, consider how a consumer's prediction that their experience interacting with an organization's personnel will be highly satisfying (+3) and their actual POC experience is interpreted/evaluated as somewhat dissatisfying (−1), resulting in a terminal EG of 2, will impact their emotional stability and corresponding behavior. Terminal EG ratings range from zero, meaning that expectations were perfectly met, to 6, indicating the greatest relative distance from an expectation. The greater the terminal expectation gap, the more likely that emotional instability will increase, and behaviors will become dysfunctional.

Expectation Valence (EV)

In addition to the expectation gap, expectation valence (EV) is another important expectation measurement. Expectation valence (EV) is the value (positive/negative) associated with the expectation gap. Negative expectation valences (NEV) are directly correlated to increased emotional instability and lead to poor consumer service outcomes and/or verbal and physical abuse. Negative expectation valences increase the potential for simple interpersonal conflict to escalate into workplace conflict or violence.

Expectation Valence Examples

To understand the relationship between expectations, expectation gap, expectation valence, emotional stability, and exhibited behaviors, consider the following three examples dealing with the relative wait time to receive service (or simply—"wait time"):

1. You decide to go to the U.S. Post Office at lunchtime (noon). Prior to leaving for the Post Office, you expect that there will be a longer than average (relative) wait time. You show up at the Post Office and encounter a long line, your EG is zero or 1, your EV is positive, your emotions are stable, and your behavior remains functional. In this scenario, experiencing a long line at the Post Office didn't create interpersonal tension or dysfunctional behaviors.
2. You decide to head to the Post Office at 2:00 p.m., expecting shorter lines and arriving to discover long lines after entering the building. Your EG is 3 or 4, your EV is negative, and your emotions become unstable and your behavior becomes dysfunctional. In this case, being confronted with a long line at the Post Office negatively impacted your behavior; however, if the line to get into the building wrapped

all around the outside of the building, your EG may be 5 or 6, creating extremely unstable emotions and possible disruptive behaviors.[10]

3. You decide to go to the U.S. Post Office at lunchtime (noon). Prior to leaving for the Post Office, you expect that there will be a longer than average (relative) wait time. However, when you show up at the Post Office, there are no lines (no waiting); your EG is 5 or 6, as in the second example. But in this scenario, even though you experience a large expectation gap, your expectation valence is positive, and your emotional levels remain stable (or euphoric!) and your behavior is rational and functional.

Negative Expectation Valance: The Gateway to Workplace Violence

Unlike the above benign customer service examples, consider how individuals would respond differently to these failed expectations if they were experiencing a personal crisis such as being physically ill and needing to go to a hospital. Failure to meet expectations is the primary driver of verbal interpersonal workplace conflict which can be managed effectively using communication strategies. However, negative expectation valence leads to decreases in emotional stability and unpredictable or dysfunctional behaviors that increase the potential for workplace conflict to escalate to violence.

Why some highly emotionally unstable individuals resort to violence is still unclear and the reasons are vigorously debated. One practical explanation posits that consumers who constructively process difficult emotions typically take responsibility for the way they feel and blame themselves for choices they've made that lead to emotional instability. ("It's my fault.") While irrational and/or violent individuals who destructively process difficult emotions often blame other people's choices for their feelings. ("It's their fault.") Decreases in emotional stability are then perceived as an injustice that needs to be "righted." In some instances, these perceived injustices are *righted* with verbal abuse and violence. Unfortunately, consumer service employees bear the brunt of this misplaced blame, anger, and dysfunctional behavior.

---

[10] These responses may involve verbal outbursts of frustration or low-level nonpersonally directed destruction such as punching the car's steering wheel.

Obviously, even highly emotionally unstable consumers will rarely act out; but difficult emotions that seem to result from unmet consumer service expectations are contributing factors for negative consumer service interactions, including poor consumer service and potential workplace conflict. Although the relationship between a consumer's expectation of service, emotional instability, and inappropriate behavior are imprecise, they are important concepts for gaining a better understanding of workplace conflict and violence and for developing the best solutions.

BEN: Boundaries, Expectations, and Needs

To successfully process workplace conflict, employees need to know their personal limits, the limits of their organizational authority, and their full range of available solutions. For instance, unless a patient's illness or injury is determined to be immediate or life-threatening (as compared to all other patients), no matter how forcefully the patient demands to be seen by a doctor, the patient must wait to be treated or they must seek care elsewhere. Accordingly, an employee who is dealing with an emotionally unstable patient who demands to be seen may only have one available option: tell them to wait their turn. Under some conditions, a patient may demand that an employee expand their options to include moving them up in the waiting queue to be treated right away. Under some conditions, limiting the number of available options may inadvertently increase emotional stability. Every organization that sells/provides a product or service has its own unique set of customer service complaints that will need solving. For instance, in a patient care setting, the number one recurring complaint (or failure to meet expectations) is "long wait times."

Processing Passive–Aggressive Behaviors

Effective communication is necessary for processing interpersonal tension and keeping emotions from escalating, or for de-escalating unstable emotions associated with passive–aggressive consumer behaviors which consist of:

1. Authoritative presence,
2. Listening/dialoguing/responding, and
3. Verbal assertiveness.

Authoritative presence is the social-psychological influence that's created through verbal and nonverbal communication, tone of voice, body language, and physical appearance, which influences some people, under certain conditions, and at certain times. It's a nonlinguistic (or the nonspoken) process that helps reinforce a message through body language. Authoritative presence is created through the synthesis of body language, physical appearance, tone of voice, and demeanor. The emotional content of a message is communicated primary nonverbally. It's often argued that more is communicated through body language than through the spoken word. To be effective, security officers need to be aware that their body language and their physical appearance "communicate without words," and often occurs unconsciously.

Authoritative presence plays an important role in gaining an individual's cooperation; however, it is temporary, fleeting, and ultimately unsustainable over time. Under some circumstances, authoritative presence quickly dissipates once an individual determines that security officers have little or no real authority or power, creating a power struggle between security officers and resistant individuals, whereas under other conditions initially resistant individuals will fully submit to the security officer's verbal instruction based on their authoritative presence. Power struggles often lead to entrenched physical behaviors and have the potential to quickly escalate to violence. Security officers need to be cautious in attempting to assert themselves into highly emotional circumstances because power struggles can quickly escalate into violent interactions. Once power shifts from security officers to uncooperative individuals, they have a limited time frame in which to apply a verbal strategy before their influence wanes and physical force become necessary. If an uncooperative individual becomes entrenched in their refusal to cooperate with security officers, the interaction may need to be reassigned to another responsible internal or external expert stakeholder for resolution.

The *power of presence* is created through a combination of the security officer's verbal and physical attributes and a community's socialized response for interacting with perceived authority figures in each context. Initially when officers exert authoritative presence, interpersonal conflict may temporarily escalate until social power is balanced. However, once security officers establish an effective authoritative presence, there's a greater likelihood that their influence will affect behavior.

A security officer's appearance plays an important role in creating an authoritative presence and processing interpersonal tension because *perceptions of effectiveness* play an important role in establishing credibility. Although a security officer's *look* or how they are perceived is not verbal communication, it does play an important role in how verbal communication is interpreted. Being perceived as *professional* could be a deterrent to some uncooperative or potentially assaultive individuals. Potentially uncooperative individuals will often "size up" or test a security officer's ability to professionally perform based solely on how they're perceived. Hardened criminals may decide in a matter of seconds whether they perceive security officers to be worthy adversaries. Therefore, even the perception that a security officer is in charge during attempts to process workplace violence plays a role in deterring a potential physical assault.

A security officer's tone of voice can communicate control or weakness during attempts to resolve conflict. It's important for security officers to maintain emotional control of their tone of voice, especially under stressful circumstances. Most content listeners hear is communicated through the way the message is delivered.

The verbal characteristics of tone of voice are:

1. Pace   The speed at which one speaks.

2. Modulation   The rhythm of one's spoken word.

3. Pitch   How high or low one's voice sounds.

4. Volume   How soft or loud one speaks.

Verbal Assertiveness

The challenge for security officers when processing a conflicted interaction is needing to balance being perceived as in control without being punitive. Verbal assertiveness is useful for achieving this goal. It's defined as a formal and authoritative-sounding form of instrumental communication that's used with a serious tone and an increase in volume and intensity and applied with the goal of convincing individuals to immediately stop or start some preferred behavior.

If the pace of conflict allows for it and if it's appropriate, security officers should give strong verbal warnings to an uncooperative individual prior to the application of protective, tactics, or tools, and/or during their application. Verbal assertiveness and authoritative presence should be used simultaneously and in concert with the application of protective tactics.

Since most people are passionate about their rights and the freedom to express themselves, they naturally don't like being told what to do by authority figures, so security officers need to be prepared for verbal and possible physical resistance. These interactions are further complicated when the authority figure is perceived as having little or no authority, which is true for most private security officers. To optimize their success when confronting individuals about their behavior, officers need to be aware of the current social sensitivities. For some, being told their behavior is unacceptable by a "security guard" may be the lowest form of social insult. Security officers need to take these social realities and public perceptions seriously and integrate them into their conflict resolution strategies.

The effective use of communication to de-escalate unsafe behaviors and to negotiate safe outcomes to interpersonal workplace conflict requires a comprehensive understanding of an organization's mission, patience, self-discipline, and self-control. This is especially true when security officers are being verbally *attacked* while trying to process complicated and constantly evolving circumstances. Generally, security officers cannot use protective force against a verbally abusive individual. To justify the application of protective action, an individual must be an immediate or active physical threat, or physically resistant when security officers lawfully attempt to control or restrain them. To effectively manage verbal abuse, security officers must depersonalize the individual's verbal assaults. If security officers fail to depersonalize verbal abuse, it may create emotions that lead to a loss of self-control and the application of inappropriate or unlawful protective action.

Communication Strategies: Separating the Problem from the People

A key to processing verbal resistance is understanding that an individual's verbal abuse is separating the problem from the person, and not personalizing the interaction. An individual's verbal resistance is generally not directed at the security officer but rather at their perceived authority or influence. When interacting with verbally resistant individuals, security officers have several options

1. Deflect it,
2. Acknowledge hearing it,
3. Redirect it, and
4. Ignore it.

When security officers are faced with verbally resistant individuals, their goal should be negotiating an ethical settlement, not enforcing laws, policies, or rules.

LEARNS De-escalation System

Although there are numerous communication/conflict management systems on the market, we've developed a conflict de-escalation management system, LEARNS, that's easy to learn and is useful for managing passive–aggressive behaviors. LEARNS provide communicators (security officers) with a framework for using collaborative communication strategies involving accommodation, compromise, and negotiating, which increases the likelihood that passive–aggressive individuals will cooperate with security personnel. When attempting to manage workplace conflict involving uncooperative individuals, security officers should appeal to an individual's ethical, moral, or pragmatic motivations.

Timing also plays an important role in the successful application of conflict management strategies. To influence behaviors, officers need to move efficiently through the steps to avoid being snared in power struggles with uncooperative individuals. If the process moves too slowly or if the interaction begins at a heightened emotional state, a power struggle may ensue and may create a need to intervene to protect people.

We use the acronym LEARNS to help personnel remember the six-step process of overcoming passive aggressiveness, de-escalating behaviors, and negotiating ethical solutions:

1. Listen,
2. Explain,
3. Ask,
4. Respond,
5. Negotiate, and
6. Settle.

Ideally, security officers should complete the first two steps of the LEARNS process before asking for a change in behavior when the individual's behavior doesn't represent an immediate or active threat.

Step One: Listen

When security officers interact with individuals who are, or appear to be, in violation of an organization's code of conduct or the law, that involves potentially harmful behavior, they should try to keep passive–aggressive behaviors from escalating. To begin the process, we highlight the importance of *listening* in the de-escalation process. Truthfully, most people, including security officers, are not the best listeners. Too often, when faced with passive aggressiveness, security officers have a predetermined response and skip ahead in the conflict management process to the *ask stage*, skipping two important processes. A key to creating a temporary relational base needed to influence behavior is using active listening, dialoguing, productive responses, accommodation, compromise, and negotiating.[11] When individuals *feel heard* they are much more likely to respond positively and cooperate. Security officers must be able to initiate conversations with consumers to create a *positive startup* and develop rapport to maintain productive conversations.[12]

An effective process for developing rapport is for security officers to introduce themselves, by name and job responsibility, and then use a customer service-oriented icebreaker to initiate a productive interaction. Customer service statements that take responsibility for inadequate service or a poorly performing product or apologizing for an employee's behavior, coupled with ego-boosting comments, may help establish goodwill with individuals.

When processing workplace conflict, security officers often say and do things that are counterproductive, interfere with their interpersonal goals, exacerbate interpersonal tensions, and escalate unsafe behaviors, creating a negative startup (Gottman, 2020).[13] Security officers should avoid unproductive comments such as the use of sarcasm or defensive arousing responses to an inappropriate customer comment. Responses, such as telling an individual to calm down or relax, often create the opposite effect and should be avoided. Instead, it's better to respond by saying, "How can I help?"

---

[11] The old adage "We're born with two ears and one mouth for a reason" comes to mind.

[12] A positive startup involves the use of affirming verbal and nonverbal communication, at the initial stages of an interaction.

[13] The effects of positive/negative startups and how they influence conflict are concepts developed by John Gottman (2020), and the Gottman Institute. https://www.gottman.com/blog/softening-startup/

"Let's talk," or "Can we work together?" to de-escalate interpersonal tension. When dealing with difficult customers, it's natural for various unhelpful thoughts to run through one's mind. If spoken aloud, however, they would be counterproductive and increase interpersonal tension.

Being a good listener also involves dialoguing with people. Dialogue is the casual or informal (but professional) banter that's developed between security officers and individuals to discuss ways to solve a problem. Effective dialogue requires active listening and productive responses. Security officers who can quickly develop credibility and trust with resistant individuals are more likely to reduce interpersonal tension and keep conflict from escalating, reducing the need to use physical force.

Step Two: Explain

The second step involves explaining to the individual how their behavior violates the organization's code of conduct or law. If security officers are successful at creating an effective relational base, and the individual is predisposed to cooperation, a verbally resistant individual will usually respond positively after the nature of the conflict is explained and they'll adjust their behavior to conform with the law or the code of conduct.

Security officers should provide a reason for contacting an individual and explain and describe, in as great a detail as possible, how their behavior conflicts with the organization's policies, guidelines, or the law, and why they need to correct it. It may be useful to appeal to authorities, use personal appeals, or refer to an organization's mission statement, posted signs, or specific laws to motivate the resistant individual to adjust their behavior.

Step Three: Ask

Step three is the first opportunity in the LEARNS process for security officers to ask an individual to adjust their behavior to meet the organization's code of conduct or the law. Ideally, security officers shouldn't ask an individual to change their behavior until they've first developed some level of trust with them and explained how their behavior violates the code of conduct or the law. If the individual continues to refuse to cooperate after being asked to adjust their behavior, security officers should ask the individual why they're refusing to cooperate. Sometimes the answer to the question leads to a quick resolution. For instance, if an individual were asked to move their car that was parked illegally, the fact that they don't have the keys would help explain why they can't move it versus why they won't move it.

Step Four: Respond

When responding and trying to overcome a resistant individual's behavior, security officers need to demonstrate empathy and understanding, and create goodwill to respond and overcome an individual's objections to cooperate. Unfortunately, security officers often respond to objections using sarcasm which exacerbates interpersonal conflict. Security officers should identify the policy, procedure, rule, or law that applies to the specific individual interaction. Even typically uncooperative individuals will often cooperate after security officers explain in detail how their behavior contradicts a policy, procedure, rule, law, or other specific conditions.

If individuals still refuse to change their behavior, security officers should next explain the possible options they may employ and the corresponding outcomes for failing to correct their behavior. When explaining and describing the available options and potential outcomes, security officers should present both positive and negative outcomes of each available option. Security personnel should always start by presenting the positive outcomes for cooperating before moving on to the negative consequences. Prior to presenting the potential negative outcomes for being uncooperative, security officers should carefully consider the limits of their influence. Security officers should always look to be as creative as possible when trying to convince resistors to cooperate.

Request Framing: Options/Outcomes

When discussing possible outcomes for failing to cooperate, security officers should always be framed in the affirmative. As an example: "If you do X (good behavior), then something Y (good outcome) will happen." Framing statements in the affirmative improves the likelihood of convincing initially uncooperative individuals to change their behavior to meet the organization's community safety standard. Unfortunately, most requests for behavior change are still framed in the negative. Too often a request for behavior change is framed in the negative, which makes it much easier to resist than positively framed request.

Below are some examples of affirmative and negative request framing:

- Affirmative: If you take your medicine (good behavior), you may avoid needing surgery (good outcome).
- Negative: If you don't take your medicine (bad behavior), you may need surgery (bad outcome).
- Affirmative: If you leave the campus now (good behavior), you'll avoid having to deal with the police (good outcome).
- Negative: If you don't leave the campus now (bad behavior), the police will be called and you may be arrested (bad outcome).
- Affirmative: If you move your car now (good behavior), you'll avoid being ticketed (good outcome).
- Negative: If you don't move your car (bad behavior), it may be ticketed, and it will cost $30 (bad outcome).
- Affirmative: If you move your car now (good behavior), you'll avoid it being towed (good outcome) and save $300.
- Negative: If you don't move your car (bad behavior), it may be towed, and it will cost $300 (bad outcome) to get it out of the tow yard.
- Affirmative: If you lower the volume of your voice (good behavior), we can have a conversation and I may be able to help you (good outcome).
- Negative: If you keep raising your voice (bad behavior), we can't have a conversation and I won't be able to help you (bad outcome).

Step Five: Negotiate

The ability to negotiate with uncooperative individuals may be a security officer's most important personal attribute. Negotiation allows an uncooperative individual to feel like they have some degree of power and influence over their behavior and the outcome which reduces the possibly that the individual will escalate their behavior to get their way. Negotiation involves accommodating and compromising with passive–aggressive individuals to find beneficial solutions to workplace conflict. Negotiation is the give-and-take process that takes place between two or more parties, each with their own aims, needs, and viewpoints, seeking to discover common ground and reach an agreement to settle a matter of mutual concern or a conflict. Negotiating could be as simple as telling a driver their vehicle is parked in an unauthorized location but you'll allow it to remain there for an additional five minutes before taking action, or it could be as unsophisticated as deflecting their verbal abuse by simply leaving the immediate area. However, negotiated agreements shouldn't create unsafe conditions for the uncooperative individuals, employees, consumers, or security officers.

Using Authoritative Presence and Verbal Assertiveness during Negotiations

A key to processing verbally resistant passive–aggressive behaviors is separating the problem from the person. Typically, an individual's verbal resistance is generally not directed at the security officer but rather at their perceived authority or interference. Too often when dealing with verbally aggressive individuals, security officers get drawn into verbal battles, become defensive and inadvertently escalate the interaction. To de-escalate behaviors and achieve safe resolutions, security officers will need to depersonalize the interaction and rely on authoritative presence and verbal assertiveness.

We define authoritative presence is the social-psychological influence that's created verbally and non-verbally using body language, physical appearance, tone of voice, and demeanor, which influences some people, under certain conditions, and at certain times. It's a nonlinguistic (or the non-spoken) process that helps reinforce a message. Since the emotional content of a message is communicated primary, nonverbally, it's often argued that more is communicated through body language than through the spoken word. To be effective, security officers need to be aware that their body language and their physical appearance "communicate without words," and often occurs unconsciously.

Authoritative presence plays an important role in gaining an individual's cooperation; however, it is temporary, fleeting, and ultimately unsustainable over time. Under some circumstances, authoritative presence quickly dissipates once an individual determines that security officers have little or no real authority or power, creating a power struggle between security officers and resistant individuals. Whereas under other conditions initially resistant individuals will fully submit to the security officer's verbal instruction based on their authoritative presence. Power struggles often lead to entrenched physical behaviors and have the potential to quickly escalate to violence. Security officers need to be cautious when inserting themselves into highly emotional circumstances because power struggles can quickly escalate into violent interactions. Once power shifts from security officers to uncooperative individuals, they have a limited timeframe in which to apply a verbal strategy before their influence wanes and physical force becomes necessary. If an uncooperative individual becomes entrenched in their refusal to cooperate with security officers, the interaction may need to be reassigned to another responsible internal or external expert stakeholder to resolve.

The power of presence is created through a combination of the security officer's verbal and physical attributes and a community's socialized response for interacting with perceived authority figures in each context. Initially when officers exert authoritative presence, interpersonal conflict may temporarily escalate until social power is balanced. However, once security officers establish effective authoritative presence, there's a greater likelihood that their influence will affect behavior.

The Look

A security officer's appearance plays an important role in creating authoritative presence and influence for processing interpersonal tension because perceptions of effectiveness play an important role in establishing credibility and trust. Although a security officer's look, or how they are perceived, is obviously not verbal communication, it does play an important role in how verbal communication is interpreted. Being perceived as professional could be a deterrent to some uncooperative or potentially assaultive individuals. Potentially uncooperative individuals will often "size up" or test a security officer's ability to professionally perform based solely on how they're perceived. Hardened criminals may decide in a matter of seconds whether they perceive security officers to be worthy adversaries. Therefore, even the perception that a security officer is in charge during attempts to process workplace violence plays a role in deterring a potential physical assault.

Moreover, when negotiating, a security officer's tone of voice can communicate control or weakness. It's important for security officers to maintain emotional control of the tone of their voice, especially as an individual's behavior starts to escalate. The verbal characteristics of a message, or the tone of voice, play an important role in what the listeners hear, how it's understood and how they respond to it. The verbal characteristics of tone of voice are:

1. Pace   The speed at which one speaks.
2. Modulation   The rhythm of one's spoken word.
3. Pitch   How high or low one's voice sounds.
4. Volume   How soft or loud one speaks.

Verbal Assertiveness

When processing conflict security officers need to be perceived as in control without being punitive. As an individual's behavior begins to escalate personnel will have to become more verbally assertive to de-escalate the interaction. We define verbal assertiveness as a formal and authoritative-sounding form of instrumental communication that's used with a serious tone and an increase in volume and intensity and applied with the goal of convincing individuals to immediately stop or start some preferred behavior. If the pace of conflict allows for it, and if it's appropriate, security officers should give strong verbally assertive warnings to an uncooperative individual prior to using protective tactics, or tools, or during the application of protective force.

Step Six: Settle

Negotiated settlements help keep behaviors from escalating to direct aggressiveness and help resistant individuals *save face*, reducing the need to involve other stakeholders. After negotiating with a resistant individual, security officers need to finalize a course of action. Settlements may or may not include the other party's agreement. A settlement may even mean that security officers submit to the will of the uncooperative individual, as long as it doesn't increase harm, or if behaviors escalate, it may mean require that security officers assert their limited influence and take decisive protective action without consulting the individual. Security officers should try to verbally confirm the individual's choices, repeat the corresponding outcomes, and give the individual plenty of opportunities to cooperate if a reasonable settlement can't be agreed to before security officers physically intervene.

While attempting to manage passive–aggressive behaviors and de-escalate an interaction, security officers should never get into a "push-and-pull" debate with uncooperative individuals. Power struggles can create unsafe conditions for security officers and others in proximity to the conflict. Additionally, security officers should never communicate ultimatums ("or else" statements) to individuals they're not able to legally, ethically, or practically follow through on.

Prior to intervening, security officers need to be sure they're acting within their departmental policy, have requisite legal authority, and have the physical ability to force uncooperative individuals to change their behavior.

Perception Management

The effective use of communication also involves managing the public's perceptions. There's truth in the adage "Perception is reality." Security officers should always strive to act in an ethical manner, and they need to consider how their specific actions may be perceived by organizational members or the community. Sometimes it's best not to take any action, even if an action is ethical. When security officers use communication to influence behavior, they need to be perceived as serious but as flexible as possible when communicating their conflict resolution goals. When interacting with difficult people, the public expects security officers to display a much higher level of patience, self-control, and understanding than they do with the general public.

Summary

Security personnel need to become expert communicators. Communication skills are the most important protective tactics extensively used by security officers to manage workplace conflict and violence. Since most workplace conflicts can be managed verbally, without the need to use physical force, effective communication reduces the need to use protective action to resolve interpersonal conflict. Security officers need ongoing and continuous communications training and practice to inoculate them against the effects of acute stress.

Recommendations

1. Use inoculation and realistic scenario roleplay (SRP) to teach security officers how to process the emotional dynamics of interpersonal tension.
2. Provide generous opportunities for security officers to practice using their communication skills during training.
3. Add communications training to the perishable skills list of security officer training that needs to be refreshed regularly.
4. Train security officers on how to determine when communication is either ineffective or inappropriate to use during a conflicted interaction.
5. Use the LEARNS de-escalation system to process passive–aggressive consumer behaviors.

References

Edley, C.F., Robinson, C.F., 2012. Response to protests on UC campuses. Report draft for public comment, 4 May 2012; Web: <http://campusprotestreport. universityofcalifornia.edu> 05.05.12.

Gottman, John. (2020). The Gottman Institute; Web: <https://www.gottman.com/ blog/softening-startup/>.

Henning, Kathy, 2012. Assessing levels of power. Wisconsin Technical College System, 8 May 2012; Web: <www.wisc-online.com>, 08.05.11.

Chapter 12

Using Protective Tactics and Tools to Protect People

Problem

Security officers aren't adequately trained to use protective tactics and tools to resolve workplace conflict.

Introduction

To prevent and respond to workplace violence and protect people, security officers need access to protective tactics and tools. Although most workplace conflict can be managed through effective verbal communication, there are circumstances when it's necessary for security personnel to use protective force to resolve conflict and violence.

Process

To effectively resolve workplace conflict, security officers need to be trained to assess behavioral risk and have access to a full spectrum of protective actions (PAs). Unlike verbal strategies, the use of physical strategies used to resolve conflict or violence may lead to injuries; this reality concerns risk managers, attorneys, and senior corporate managers. However, it's impossible to create violence-free workplaces without occasionally using protective tactics or tools to protect people.

Authority, Jurisdiction, and Limitations

To safely and legally utilize protective tactics or tools to resolve conflict, security officers need to understand the limits of their legal authority and influence. In a private, free market, an organization's jurisdiction or area of responsibility is limited to the property it owns or controls. Private security officers function as agents of the owner; therefore, they have the same behavioral limits as the owner or the party responsible for the property where officers are assigned. In short, if it's legal for the owner to act, it's legal for security officers to act.[1] The owner's range of protective activities that can be assigned to security officers is limited by the laws that govern the owner's specific jurisdiction. When an individual's mere presence or their unsafe behavior interferes with the organization's ability to serve its consumers, they can be asked to adjust/stop it and/or leave the owner's property. If they don't, and if it's safe to do, security personnel can use protective force to control and/or constraint them, and call the police to process the individual, to assure no disruptions in an organizations' operations.

An organization's policies and procedures guide the security officer's influence, power, and permission to act (or a prohibition from acting) to respond and prevent workplace violence and protect people. Since criminal statutes provide a limited framework for guiding private (non-sworn) security officer behaviors, organizations typically create their own behavioral limits thought to mitigate liabilities. These limitations may or may not actually mitigate claims of negligence because claims are the result of both action and inaction. Forbidding action only mitigates potential liability resulting from unreasonable actions. However, they do nothing to mitigate negligence claims created from falling to act. Although "private person" authority is addressed in various legal codes and social compacts and through situational ethics, the bottom line is that it's up to the employing organization to determine the appropriate behavioral

---

[1] One exception may be that licensed security personnel can legally carry protective tools that property owners can't.

boundaries for their security officers and when they'll utilize their local law enforcement agency's resources.[2]

Law Enforcement Authority versus Private Security Officer Influence

Since private security officers are not government actors, much of the typical use-of-force literature that's often applied to a private-market context will be omitted. However, gaining a basic understanding of the distinctions between law enforcement use of force and free-market use of protective force used to influence behavior is important. Since security officers are not government employees, they cannot ordinarily violate an individual's civil or constitutional rights. However, this doesn't mean that certain behavior, in extreme cases, couldn't violate a law or cause a civil action to be initiated against a security officer or vicariously to the organization.

Behavior Analysis

Once security officers become engaged in a conflicted workplace interaction, they need to determine the level of risk an individual's behavior poses and if they're the *right expert* to process it, by conducting an analysis of the subject's behavior. Behavior analysis (BA) is the initial, tentative, fact-based assessment of an individual's verbal and nonverbal behaviors, including an assessment of their emotional state that helps security officers forecast their near-term behavior. The individual's behavior is then assigned to one of four relative and dynamic behavioral phases (BPs). The totality of behavioral cues is then used to align, or to realign when behavior escalates/ deescalates, and select the most appropriate strategy for managing or resolving the behaviors.

The initial BA may be completed by the employee processing the interaction, or it could be completed by others and communicated to security officers (e.g., a phone call describing the individual's actions or a request for support personnel to assist with an interaction that escalated). However, if someone other than the security officer conducts

---

[2] Just because an individual has acted in a criminal manner doesn't mean it's in the organization's best interest to involve law enforcement officers.

the BA, the responding security officers need to quickly reassess the individual's behavior once they arrive (as behavior often escalates/deescalates rather quickly during the conflict) before deciding the most appropriate response.

Can't/Won't Respond

Under some circumstances an individual may exhibit verbally or physically resistant behaviors due to being under the influence of drugs or alcohol or may result from a mental illness or an emotional disorder. Initially, security officers may conduct a BA and interpret the behavior as an immediate physical threat, when in fact the individual's altered state of mind, physical, or medical condition make it impossible for them to respond to a security officer's commands. It's often difficult to determine, especially under stressful conditions, if verbally or physically resistant individuals *can't or won't* respond to security officer's demands to change their behavior to comply with the organization's code of conduct or the law. All security officers should receive specialized training on how to identify these conditions and how to respond appropriately to these types of behaviors.[3] However, once a subject's behavior turns violent, the reason the individual can't/won't respond to the officer's commands to cease their violent behavior becomes secondary to stopping it. When interacting with unsafe behaviors influenced by mental illness or emotional disorders, it's natural to want to demonstrate sympathy and empathy toward an individual's condition. However, displays of concern should be demonstrated *prior* to an individual acting in a violent manner, if possible, or if they're actively engaged in violence, *after* the individual's potential to harm others is neutralized, not *during* an assault.[4] As an example, an individual who attacks a nurse armed with a scalpel, who is under the influence of drugs or alcohol, or suffers from a mental illness or an emotional disorder can kill that employee just as effectively as an individual who doesn't have those maladies. The officer's response

---

[3] See psost.org for training on how to process conflict with the mental ill, emotional disturbed, or those in crisis.

[4] Specialized training may help officers to keep an individual's behavior from escalating to violence. Although these interactions are challenging, if a security officer chooses to use protective tactics based on the individual's medical or emotional conditions and not on the type of threat their behavior poses, it will create diminution in safety for everyone involved.

to violent behaviors needs to be based on the threat they pose, not on whether an individual can rationally understand and respond to the officer. If an officer has reliable information about an uncooperative individual's mental or emotional status *prior* to engaging them and has the time to involve other protective experts, they should adjust their response to accommodate the circumstances. Unfortunately, some organizations restrict security personnel from using certain protective tactics or tools, regardless of the threat an individual poses, if they are known to have a mental illness or an emotional disorder. Or, worse, they use hindsight to argue that the officer *should have known* that the individual's behavior indicated these illnesses. The safety of the officer, the employees, and consumers must take priority over a violent person's motivations in order to create a safe workplace for everyone.[5]

Emotional Stability

Maintaining, acquiring, or reacquiring emotional stability plays an important role in keeping workplace conflict from escalating to violence. Although an individual's behavior is the primary focus, employees who are involved in processing workplace conflict should try to understand how their communication, and emotional and psychological responses, biases, tendencies, boundaries, expectations, and needs also influence workplace conflict. In truth, some employees are better than others at dealing with high levels of emotional instability, and the accompanying verbal and physical abuse. Maintaining emotional stability is imperative for employees processing workplace conflict.

Behavior Analysis: Determining Intentionality

To create and maintain safe workplaces, prevent and respond to workplace violence, and protect people, security officers need to effectively manage workplace conflict and efficiently resolve workplace violence. Behavioral analysis is the key in understanding an individual's behavioral intentions that are found in the totality of their verbal and non-verbal behaviors within

---

[5] This is sometimes described as a battle of rights: the rights of an individual and the rights of the security officer.

a specific context. Behavior analysis is the initial, tentative, fact-based assessment of an individual's verbal and nonverbal behaviors, including an assessment of their emotional state that helps security officers forecast an individual's near-term behavior. The individual's behavior is then assigned to one of four relative and dynamic BPs. The totality of behavioral cues is then used to align or to realign when behavior escalates/deescalates and select the most appropriate strategy for managing or resolving the behaviors. To assist security officers, we've developed the Situational Protective Action Risk Continuum matrix or SPARC chart, a graphic visual representation of the PA decision-making matrix.

There are four steps to safely processing workplace conflict and violence:

1. Analyze behavior
2. Assign behavior
3. Align behavior
4. Act

Step one, conduct behavior analysis (BA) by assessing a subject's

1. Appearance: Physical appearance
2. Behavior: Actions/lack of action
3. Communication: The words spoken/not spoken and the
                     accompanied body language (nonverbal)

And assess the individual's emotional state as:

1. Escalating
2. Stable
3. Deescalating

Step two, assign the behavior to one of four relative and dynamic BP of cooperation/resistance based on the totality of the individual's behavioral cues:

1. Cooperative   (nonresistant)   customer service
2. Passive aggressive   (verbal resistance) conflict management
3. Direct aggression   (active resistance) conflict resolution
4. Violent   (armed or unarmed)   compliance gaining

Step three, align the individual's level of cooperation/resistance with the corresponding protective response zone (RZ):

1. Customer service
2. Conflict management
3. Conflict resolution
4. Compliance gaining

Step four, choose the most appropriate communicative and/or protective tactics or tools, or PA, based on the totality of the circumstances, the officer's tactical knowledge, the departmental policy, and/or the protective tool array that a security officer carries.

During interpersonal conflict, a resistant individual's behavior may escalate or deescalate, so security officers need to continually evaluate (and reevaluate) an individual's behavior to properly align (and realign) it with the most appropriate and available conflict management/conflict solution. As the individual's cooperation/resistance increases or decreases, the security officer's range of options may change, and they may need to adjust their responses to maintain proper alignment until unsafe behaviors become safe or cease.

Subject Cooperative/Resistance Levels

Typically, emotionally stable people don't suddenly become emotionally unstable without some gradually expressive signs of interpersonal frustration and emotional or behavioral escalation. Under some circumstances, security officers may trigger the escalation of emotional instability by saying or doing something that is interpreted as a *personal attack* (known as 'defense arousal'). An individual's level of perceived cooperation/resistance helps determine the security officers' best strategies for solving the conflicted interaction.

Cooperative

Although initially cooperative individuals usually don't create interpersonal conflict, employees need to be careful not to arouse defensiveness, which creates emotional instability and escalates behavior. The conflict management goal for every employee/consumer interaction is helping individuals to stay at or return to a cooperative level.

Passive Aggressive

Passive aggressiveness accounts for about 80% of all interpersonal workplace conflict. Passive–aggressive behavior is exhibited verbally, nonverbally, and through physical noncompliance (but not physically assaultive). When processing passive–aggressive behavior, dialogue is generally effective for maintaining emotional stability and may be useful at the early stages of directly aggressive behavior. Moreover, the LEARNS Deescalating Communication System is effective for processing passive–aggressive behaviors.

Passive–aggressive behavior includes:

■ Verbal uncooperativeness and low-level verbal abuse.
■ Resistance to requests or demands by procrastinating.
■ Expressed sullenness and stubbornness.
■ Entrenchment.

Passive–aggressive behavior may manifest itself in several different ways. For example, a person might repeatedly make excuses to avoid certain actions as a way of expressing their dislike or hidden anger toward individuals or authority.

Verbal passive–aggressive examples:

■ "I'm not going to take my medicine!"
■ "I don't want to!"
■ "You can't make me!"

Nonverbal or physically noncompliant passive–aggressive examples:

■ Refusal to talk or answer questions, or respond sarcastically.
■ Refusal to move from a stationary position.
■ Body language indicating noncompliance.

Security officers need to be aware that passive–aggressive behavior has the potential to quickly escalate into directly aggressive behavior if they're not managed and deescalated.

Direct Aggression

Direct aggression is verbal and initially non-assaultive behavior that is often a prelude to violence, which is directed at people or property. Aggression is defined by psychologists as behavior that is meant to hurt others. It is generally divided into hostile aggression and instrumental aggression. Direct aggression is accompanied by strong emotions, particularly anger. It is associated with impulsive, unplanned, overt, or uncontrolled behaviors. The use of verbal assertiveness by security officers at the early stages of direct aggression may be effective, but communication alone is usually ineffective and inappropriate when processing personal threats of violence.

Often the primary difference between passive–aggressive and directly aggressive behavior is the intensity of verbal abuse. In contrast, passive–aggressive behavior doesn't involve threats directed at an individual or an object. However, it may include statements like, "I'm so pissed off I could scream!" But statements like, "I'm so pissed off I could punch you in the face!" cross the passive–aggressive behavior threshold into directly aggressive behavior. Once an individual directs a verbal threat at an individual (or themselves) or an object, they have crossed into the directly aggressive behavior phase. Directly aggressive behaviors may include verbal and physical threats of violence that haven't (yet) been acted on.

Directly aggressive behavior presents the most challenging workplace conflict dilemma because under some conditions, verbal assertiveness may be effective, but under most conditions, it won't keep an individual's behavior from escalating and the use of protective force may be needed.

Directly aggressive examples:

- "F-you" (and other variants)
- "I'll come over there and punch your face!"
- "I'm going to hurt myself!"
- "I'll take this chair and break it over that machine!"

Violent

Violent behaviors are actions that actively cause physical harm. At this BP, verbal strategies are ineffective (and probably inappropriate) and protective tactics and tools are the only acceptable methods for resolving and neutralizing violent behavior. Assaults could be directed at others or at the engaged individual (self-harm). Assaults can be accomplished with or without a weapon (armed or unarmed). When interacting with violent behaviors, multiple support personnel, such as additional security or law enforcement personnel, are necessary to neutralize the threat. Officers should attempt to deescalate the behavior and use crisis intervention techniques, if it's safe to do so, prior to the use of deadly force to neutralize a lethal threat.

Misdiagnosing and Classifying Behaviors

Some behaviors are easy to identify and don't require a great deal of training to identify or process. For example, cooperative behavior is easy to identify and usually takes very little input to maintain it. Similarly, violent behavior is easy to identify, but unlike cooperative behavior, it's much more challenging and dangerous to process and neutralize.

The two most common behavioral misdiagnoses are:

1. Classifying cooperative behavior as passive–aggressive; a higher level of resistance.
2. Classifying directly aggressive behavior as passive–aggressive; a lower level of resistance.

These misdiagnoses are responsible for two potentially disruptive and dangerous outcomes:

A. Misdiagnosing lower to higher level behaviors exacerbates interpersonal tension.
B. Misdiagnosing higher to lower levels behaviors increases personal risk.

When employees misdiagnose cooperative behavior as passive aggressiveness, a higher level of resistance, they exacerbate the interaction when they use verbal assertiveness to deescalate the interaction. On the other hand, when employees misdiagnose directly aggressive behavior as passive aggressiveness, a lower level of resistance, and use conflict management strategies instead of conflict resolution strategies to deescalate the interaction, they increase risk. In the former instance, the application of verbal assertiveness to cooperative behavior creates less satisfied customers. While in the latter situation, the misapplication of conflict management strategies creates a false sense of safety for the involved parties and may enable directly aggressive individuals to become physically violent. It's important that employees accurately distinguish between passive–aggressive behaviors, which generally require no physical force to process, and directly aggressive customer behaviors that require verbal assertiveness and the possible use of protective force to resolve.

Misdiagnosis: Potential Causes

1. A lack of standardized or universally agreed upon behavioral risk matrix (both organizationally and industry wide).
2. A lack of employee BA training and/or inconsistent training.
3. Unclear policies for processing workplace conflict.
4. Inconsistent employee discipline for intervening/failing to intervene to process conflict.
5. A misunderstanding of the natural limitations of communication to resolve high levels of individual resistance and the subsequent misapplication of communicative solutions.
6. A lack of personnel screening for qualifying employees responsible for processing conflict.

Inconsistent Evaluations

The use of varied criteria for assessing and classifying an individual's unsafe behaviors, even within the same organization, creates a significant challenge for processing workplace conflict. Varying classifications make it difficult for employees to properly align consumer behaviors with the most appropriate response. Inconsistent behavioral interpretations create employee and customer injuries, workers' compensation claims, and employee time off and increases in potential liabilities. Even within organizations that use the same workplace conflict management systems (e.g., CPI, MAB, Verbal Judo, or LEARNS, to name a few), there is still a high level of inconsistency in categorizing consumers' behaviors. These inconsistencies create the possibility that multiple employees (even those who have received the same conflict management training) who interact with the same individual may classify the individual's behavior significantly different, which requires differing and possibly contradictory (or unsafe) employee responses.

Additionally, when policies and procedures for processing workplace conflict are ill-defined (or nonexistent) employees tend toward two extremes: they do nothing or they use their own preferred solutions.

The inconsistent application of employee accountability, both negative and positive reinforcement, is another factor that may influence an employee's decision to avoid intervening to short-circuit escalating emotions and behaviors. If employees who regularly intervene in workplace conflict are disciplined for their decisions, even when their response falls within the range of organizationally acceptable actions, other employees will be discouraged from intervening. Likewise, employees who take decisive and appropriate action should be recognized and praised to create an organizational cultural bias toward action. Unfortunately, some organizations focus exclusively on identifying employees who act outside of official (or unofficial) workplace conflict policies, which create a disincentive for anyone to get involved.

Nonconsensual Physical Contact

Unlike law enforcement officers, non-sworn private security officers have narrower limits for making physical contact with unarrested subjects without their expressed consent. Physical contact with unarrested subjects should only be initiated for protective purposes. Under some circumstances, the individual's affiliation status may provide greater latitude for nonconsensual contact.[6] Generally, to justify making physical contact with an individual, including personal contact necessary for the application of protective tactics or tools, the person must be:

1. An immediate physical threat to the security officer, others or themselves.
2. An active physical threat to the security officer, others, or themselves.
3. Placed under arrest for a serious, non-property-related criminal violation (e.g., battery or sexual assault), when it's in the best of interest of the organization to control and restrain the subject and turn them over to a law enforcement agency for prosecution.

---

[6] As an example, a college student may sign a *standard of conduct* agreement that allows for nonconsensual searches.

Absent legal, ethical, and moral justification for making physical contact with an unarrested individual, security officers who make nonconsensual contact may create unnecessary civil liability.

Protective Force

To determine the quality and quantity of PA that's necessary and reasonable to prevent and respond to workplace violence and protect others, security officers must evaluate the totality of the circumstances known to them at the time of the subject interaction. The decision to use PA must be made through objective and reasonable means, and the strategies officers employ must be evaluated by its potential effectiveness in their unique circumstances.

As a reminder we define protective force as:

> Deliberate, nonpunitive, personal interaction, whether it's accomplished through the use of a protective tactic or with a protective tool used for the narrow purpose of protecting the involved individuals (including employees, consumers, or visitors) from immediate or active physical harm; or used to control a subject who is a danger to themselves or others or has committed an interpersonal crime, and is applied in a manner that balances employee safety with a resistant individual's legal/ civil rights.

Justifying Physical Contact

Although there's no exhaustive and authoritative set of circumstances that require the use of protective force beyond the subject being an intermediate or active physical threat, the following are useful criteria to assist security officers in determining the best choice in any given conflicted interaction: objective criteria, subject/security officer interaction factors, security officer/subject interaction factors, subject behavioral factors, environmental conditions, and situational factors.[7]

---

[7] We use the term *subject* to identify an individual who's behavior is physical threat.

Objective Criteria (Non-Exhaustive List)

- Amount and nature of the resistance observed or perceived.
- Immediacy and the probability of threats to life.
- Knowledge/history of the subject.
- Subject is armed or has access to weapons.
- Subject not submitting peacefully.
- The type and severity of the crime.

Subject/Security Officer Interaction Factors

- Individual's potential state of mind.
- Diminished mental or psychological capacity.
- Health or mental crisis.
- Housing challenged.
- Immature, infirm, or elderly.
- Physical size.
- Specialized training (e.g., trained fighter).
- Under the influence of drugs or alcohol.

Security Officer/Subject Interaction Factors

- Security officer's state of mind.
- Emotional stability.
- Experience.
- Knowledge.
- Physical condition/injury or exhaustion.
- Training.

Subject Behavioral Factors (Non-Exhaustive List)

- Stated verbal disagreement.
- Threats of physical attack.
- Profanities.
- Challenges to fight.
- Expressed refusal to follow verbal commands.
- Obscene gestures.
- Assuming an aggressive or fighting stance.
- Damaging physical property.

Environmental Conditions (Non-Exhaustive List)

■ Standing or footing. What's the terrain like—stairs, steps, porch, balcony, furniture, slick floors, curbs, gutters, parking bumpers, landscaping, sloping, uneven ground, gravel, sand, vehicle traffic, or ground affected by weather conditions such as rain, ice, or snow?

■ Number of subjects. Anyone in the immediate area, including bystanders, may also be friends of the subject.

■ Availability of assistance. Backup from other security officers or law enforcement officers.

■ Access to cover. The ability to reach the closest objects that can be used for suitable cover.

Other Officer Considerations

■ Knowledge, understanding, experience, and training in high-conflict situations.

■ Physical condition, strength, fitness level, self-defense or protective-force expertise, and confidence in the application of force.

Situational Factors (Non-Exhaustive List)

■ Severity of crime: Nonviolent misdemeanor, violent misdemeanor, nonviolent felony, or violent felony.

■ Timing of crime: In progress, immediate but post-assault, or stale.

■ Multiple subjects: More than one subject, active or passive subjects.

■ Individual's relative physical strength. An obviously physically fit subject.

■ Subject/security officer proximity. The physical distance between the parties; the closer the gap, the greater the possibility for potential injury.

■ Time/decision ratio. How urgent is the need to act? Compare the difference between a subject that's actively charging at a security individual versus a subject held up for hours in a hostage situation.

■ History/prior subject knowledge. The security officer has previous knowledge or previous contact with the subject.

- Proximity to physical weapons. An actual weapon, for example, knives or firearms; improvised weapon, for example, pipes, bats, broken glass, rocks.
- Security officer on the ground. Security officers and/or subjects are not standing up. This creates a much greater physical danger for officers.
- Physical environment: Hot, cold, wet, flat, uneven, hilly, obstacles, grass, gravel, cement, sunny, or dark.
- Social–political environment: Cultural, racial, ethnic, gender, or other considerations.
- Mobs/riots/protestors. Large out-of-control groups with a unifying goal or message.

Situational Protective Action Risk Continuum

To assist security personnel in processing workplace conflict and violence, we've developed the Situational Protective Action Risk Continuum chart or SPARC chart, a graphic visual representation of the PA decision-making matrix. As referenced by the chart (starting at the bottom), the officer begins the process by analyzing an individual's behavior and determining which BP to assign their behavior: cooperative, passive aggressive, directly aggressive, or violent. Each BP is correlated to the appropriate set of responses or RZs. The security officer simply aligns the BP with the corresponding RZ, and realigns it as behavior deescalates or escalates, and chooses the most appropriate communicative and/or protective tactics or tools, based on the totality of the circumstances (see Figure 12.1).

Response Zones

We've divided a security officer's potential responses into four zones correlated to the subject's level of cooperation/resistance. Within each of these four RZs, security officers have various protective options. Depending on the officer's tactical knowledge, the actual circumstances, the departmental policy, or the protective tool array that security officers carry, some options within a RZ may be unavailable, ineffective, or unacceptable.

For instance, in RZ three there are five protective force options: Baton, CRT, CEW, OC/Pepper Spray, and PPM. Security officers need to justify their reasoning for choosing a specific protective option within a RZ as opposed to another choice. An organization's protective force

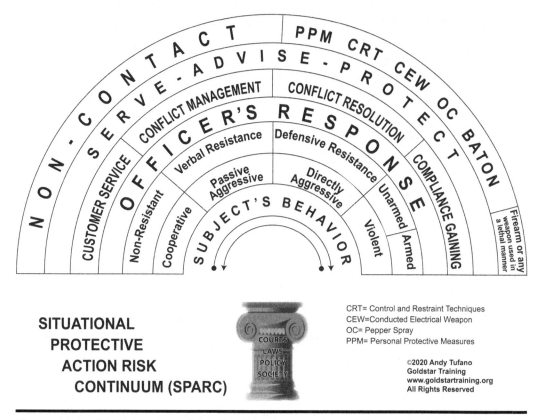

SITUATIONAL PROTECTIVE ACTION RISK CONTINUUM (SPARC)

CRT= Control and Restraint Techniques
CEW=Conducted Electrical Weapon
OC= Pepper Spray
PPM= Personal Protective Measures

©2020 Andy Tufano
Goldstar Training
www.goldstartraining.org
All Rights Reserved

Figure 12.1   SPARC is a graphic visual representation of the PA decision-making matrix.

policies may dictate that security officers prioritize their protective force options within each of these RZs.

Response Zone One: Customer Service

RZ One is a noncontact area and the use of effective communication is a key to maintaining positive relations with consumers.

Response Zone Two: Conflict Management

In RZ Two, the behavior is/has become resistant but not physical. RZ Two is also a noncontact zone. Collaborative communication is usually effective at deescalating passive–aggressive behaviors. But as behaviors escalate, a more forceful communicative approach may be required to keep behaviors from escalating.

Response Zone Three: Conflict Resolution

In RZ Three, the behavior is/has become directly aggressive and is an immediate risk and security officers must intervene and can use protective tactics and less lethal tools. Protective tactics include:

1. Personal Protective Measures (PPM).
2. Control and Restraint Techniques (CRT).

While, the use of protective (less lethal) tools includes:

1. OC/Pepper Spray.
2. Defensive Baton.
3. CEW or Taser®.

Long ago, the defensive baton was adopted by security departments as a carryover from the law enforcement community. In California, as in many States, the baton is classified as a dangerous weapon under the law and it's unlawful to possess one without appropriate training, licensing, and a legitimate legal purpose. The baton could be an effective protective device, but its use also has the potential to create unnecessary liability. However, we think that a Taser is a more useful and effective protective tool and creates less potential liability and is a better option than a baton. We recommend security departments consider replacing the baton with a Taser.

Tasers or a Conducted Electrical Weapon (CEW) is used to control and restrain assaultive subjects. CEWs are the most effective protective device available to private security officers. One of the many advantages of carrying and using a CEW is that it can be used in three protective modes to influence behavior: verbal reference, display, or actual use. It's the only tool that protects officers, resistant subjects, and organizations, without creating any long-lasting physical injuries. We support and highly encourage organizations to train and equip their security officers to carry and use CEWs because doing so supports their organization's protective mission. If security officers could only carry one protective tool, we would recommend a Taser.[8]

---

[8] TASER is an acronym for Thomas A. Swift's Electric Rifle and is a trademark of Axon Enterprise, Inc.

Response Zone Four: Compliance Gaining

In RZ Four, the behavior is/has become violent and security officers must neutralize the behavior and are authorized to use both protective tactics and tools to *protect* themselves and others against serious bodily injury or life-threatening physical assaults. However, since most private security officers don't typically carry firearms, they should not proactively engage with armed, violent behaviors, and if possible, should wait for an armed response (typically a law enforcement officer). Moreover, it's important for security officers to understand the limitations of their tactics and tools and how they may be used lethally when resisting a life-threatening attack. The reality is that if someone is trying to kill a security officer, the officer can use *any* protective tactic, tool, or any object to protect themselves.[9]

Firearms

A firearm is a lethal tool used to protect against life-threatening physical assaults. Although most private security officers don't carry firearms, there are some private, free-market organizations that authorize their security personnel to carry them.[10] However, if an organization authorizes its security officers to carry a firearm, the officers should meet a minimum health and wellness standard and pass a psychological screening. When a private security officer carries a firearm, the greatest threat to an organization is not from an individual officer making a bad decision using it; rather it's from the injuries and liabilities associated with a suspect taking the firearm away from the security officer and using it to assault innocent victims. I am a strong advocate for arming more private security officers when the level of risk warrants it and they are required to meet and maintain a minimum health and wellness standard (in addition to other requirements).

Summary

The use of protective tactics and tools are necessary for preventing and responding to workplace violence and protecting people. Security officers need to be trained and authorized to use the full spectrum of protective

---

[9] Officers should attempt to deescalate the behavior and use crisis intervention techniques, if it's safe to do so, prior to the use of deadly force to neutralize a lethal threat.

[10] California, City of Hope (Hospital) and California Baptist University employ private security officers that carry firearms.

tactics and tools to process conflict. Although most workplace conflicts can be managed using effective communication, there are times when it's necessary for security personnel to use protective force.

Recommendations

1. Conduct an operational risk assessment to determine the range of protective tactics and tools necessary to protect employees, consumers, visitors, others, and security officers.
2. Assure that security officers are proficient at evaluating behavioral risk.
3. Train and equip security officers in a full range of protective tactics and tools.
4. Train security officers to use the SPARC chart decision matrix.
5. Require human resources personnel, corporate attorneys, and organizational risk managers to share organizational power and partner with the senior security director/manager to gain a better understanding of the risks associated with preventing and responding to workplace violence.

Chapter 13

Security Officer Accountability

Problem

Organizations don't have a reliable accountability system in place for evaluating their security officer's decision to use protective force.

Introduction

Accountability plays an important role in creating a successful workplace violence prevention plan that involves occasionally using force to protect people. Responsible and effective policies and procedures and supervisory controls are needed to hold security officers accountable for the decision to either use or refrain from using protective force to resolve workplace conflict and protect people. Since the decision to use protective force in protecting individuals could create potential liability for an organization, security officers need to understand their legal and ethical justifications for its use. Although most people think of accountability in the negative, justifying an action that was made, a decision *not to act* also needs accounting. The choice to use protective force needs to be accountable to the organization, the security department, other vested organizational stakeholders, and community members.

Today more than ever, communities are sensitive to and focused on ensuring that individuals who interact with an organization's security officers are treated fairly, even when the resistant subject's behavior is criminal. The only way to ensure that people are treated fairly while guaranteeing the effectiveness of an organization's approved conflict resolution strategies is to hold security officers and supervisors accountable.

Process

Today, the decision to use protective action in a private setting to resolve conflict is a sensitive matter. However, an organization's or community's sensitivities should not be justification for avoiding the use of protective action if it's necessary and appropriate for a given situation. Whenever security officers use physical protective action, or fail to use it, when it's necessary, the decision needs to be accountable to the organization's protective force policy.[1]

Documentation

Professionalism dictates that security officers justify their protective-action decisions both verbally and in writing. Incidents involving force are some of the most scrutinized actions, and the reports are used by various internal and external stakeholders to protect the organization or to attack it. A legal or civil action against an organization could take years to surface, and the report may be the only remaining evidence of the incident. When protective force has been employed, the security officers' written report must include the critical interaction information needed to ensure the chronology and the details of the events, including a full accounting of the involved parties' actions. Failure to accurately detail a resistant subject's physical actions and the security officer's decision to use physical force may result in an inaccurate interpretation of the interaction.

When security officers follow their organization's protective force policy and they're characterized by responsible decision-making, they shouldn't be concerned about being scrutinized for their decisions. Any security officer employed for any length of time can recall numerous examples in which security officers were unfairly disciplined or fired for using physical force

---

[1] Too many organizations don't have a protective force policy, and if they do, they're often weak and ineffective.

to protect people. Whether these stories are accurate, anecdotal, or purely perceptual, there is universal skepticism among security officers about any system of accountability.

Unfortunately, many security officers have difficulty documenting their decision-making processes and their actions in a professionally written report. It's extremely important for security officers to accurately describe (in fine detail) the subject's specific acts in their full context and their own responsive use of protective force. Even when security officers are justified in their actions, they often create unwarranted criticism for their protective-action choices because they're unable to clearly justify their actions in an acceptable written format.[2]

Supervisory Controls

Responsible supervisory controls are necessary to maintain a team of professional security officers who are authorized to use protective force to protect employees, consumers, visitors, and others. Supervisors need to monitor their subordinates' performance to ensure they're adhering to the organization's protective force policies and procedures, maintaining the department's minimum productivity levels, demonstrating respect for community members, and not creating unnecessary liability. Supervisors need to identify officers who continually demonstrate an inability to successfully manage or resolve conflict and determine if they can be rehabilitated, retrained, or needed to be disciplined or discharged. Ideally, supervisors should be conflict resolution experts and be exemplary role models for their subordinates to emulate.

Staff Accountability

If security officers exceed their limited legal authority, or use undue influence, and use inappropriate protective force when trying to protect themselves or others, they can be criminally prosecuted, sued civilly, lose their employment, or create negative public perceptions and dissension in their communities.

---

[2] As a college professor, I can attest that this is not unique to security officers; it's also a challenge for many of my students.

Inappropriate use of protective force can lead to security officers being civilly sued for behavior that falls short of criminal culpability but is still inappropriate. Through vicarious civil liability, the security officer's employer or other corporate personnel can also be drawn into a civil action created by the security individual's inappropriate actions. The consequences of a civil action are personal financial judgments and a possible financial judgment against a security officer's employer. The application of inappropriate protective force can lead to security officers being disciplined, up to and including loss of employment.

Interpersonal cooperation plays an important role in the creation and maintenance of violence-free organizations. To be effective, security officers need to gain the cooperation of the communities they serve. The inappropriate use of protective force can create community dissension. If community members feel mistreated, security officers lose their moral and ethical standing and subsequently the community's trust. It's impossible to maintain high levels of protection for employees, consumers, visitors, or others, when large segments of the organization and community perceive security officers as their adversaries. When security officers are confronted by uncooperative subjects, the best way to avoid alienating organizational and community members and protect people is to follow the organization's policies and procedures.[3]

Peer Intervention

To hold security officers accountable for their protective-action decisions, other security officers may need to intervene if an officer becomes emotionally unstable and loses self-control. (In truth, even the most composed security officer can become emotionally unstable given the right set of triggering circumstances.) Since community members expect to be treated fairly, they also expect other security officers and other nonsecurity stakeholders to intervene if an officer is acting inappropriately.

Peer intervention prevents or stops inappropriate or unlawful physical contact or assaultive behavior against resistant subjects. Peer intervention

---

[3] In too many instances the organization's written, and oral, policies and procedures are vague, incongruent, and unenforced, which provide easy justification for security officers to create their own.

affords officers an opportunity to maintain or restore their composure and professionalism. Although there's no exhaustive list of behaviors that may require security officers to intervene, some of those behaviors include:

▪ Inappropriate or unlawful application of force.
▪ Or, other unethical/inappropriate behavior.

The failure of security officers to intervene may lead to decreases in officer safety, professionalism, and credibility. Peer intervention protects officers from:

▪ Civil liability.
▪ Criminal action.
▪ Creating negative attitudes about their organization, their personnel or the security industry.
▪ Customer service complaints.
▪ Disciplinary action up to the loss of employment.
▪ Loss of personal integrity.
▪ Loss of professionalism.
▪ Physical injury.

Appropriate peer intervention involves various (and sensitive) techniques for protecting community members and restoring or maintaining professional behavior during attempts to process interpersonal workplace conflict. Depending on the specific circumstances of each interaction, it may be necessary to intervene immediately; in other instances, it may be wise to wait until after the interaction. When someone is verbally assaulted or witnesses someone being physically attacked, it's normal to experience strong emotions and empathy for victims.

These strong emotions may influence security officers as they attempt to conduct behavior analysis in an emotionally unstable manner, increasing the possibility of acting inappropriately without the officer even realizing it. Security officers need to immediately intervene under these conditions in order to protect all parties. In some instances, departmental policy may dictate that peer interventions be reported to supervisors.[4] Under certain circumstances, it may be appropriate to immediately intervene verbally or by physical touch or physical restraint. If security officers become agitated

---

[4] We encourage organizations to enact policies that *require* intervention and reporting.

or angry or appear to be losing professional objectivity with a resistant individual, a peer can tell the offending security officer that they'll take charge of the interaction. For instance, if a security officer is engaged in a heated verbal confrontation with a subject and starts to become increasingly agitated, a peer could lightly touch the security officer and offer a tactful reminder that their behavior is becoming unstable or offer to take responsibility for the interaction.

If security officers use unlawful or clearly unreasonable force, a peer may be *required* to physically intervene and control the offending security officer and physically separate them from the subject.

In situations that have already taken place, it may be necessary to implement a delayed peer intervention technique. Some delayed peer interventions include discussion, admonishment, or offering training advice. If a security officer is verbally condescending to a subject, a peer can casually discuss the inappropriateness of the behavior when the officer has regained emotional homeostasis. If security officers use inappropriate, demeaning language, or profanity while interacting with organizational or community members, a peer could inform the offending security officer that his/her behavior is unacceptable, and that it may end up exacerbating the situation.

Factors Affecting Peer Intervention

Although security officers are ethically, morally, and possibly, through departmental policy, obligated to intervene when they observe inappropriate behavior by a peer, personal and emotional circumstances may prevent security officers from intervening.[5] Officers may fail to act when a peer is behaving inappropriately because of several factors, including:

- Anger,
- Conflict avoidance,
- Diffusion of responsibility ("It's not my fault!"),
- Evaluation apprehension,
- Fear of being ostracized,
- Fear of physical harm,
- Incompetence,

---

[5] Much of the information in this section is drawn from the CA. POST LD 20:6 on Intervention.

- Misplaced loyalty,
- Peer pressure, and
- Situational ignorance.

If security officers witness a peer resorting to or on the verge of behaving inappropriately, the officer should intervene to protect both the officer and the resistant subject. This requires making a rational decision about the offending officer's inability at that moment to act appropriately. Intervention also demonstrates personal integrity, enhances personnel and organizational safety, preserves professionalism, protects the organization's reputation, and reduces personal and corporate civil liability.

Post-Incident Review and Reporting Process

A post-incident review and reporting process is necessary for creating the type of transparency that's necessary for developing organizational and community partnerships and demonstrating an organizational commitment to treating all community members, including resistant subjects, fairly.

An effective and responsible use of protective force policy must include a fair and thorough post-incident review process. The organization, community members, and security officers depend on a fair and accountable post-incident review process. The post-incident review process achieves the following:

- Affords organizations an opportunity to determine whether their policies and procedures are effective at creating violence-free organizations while minimizing potential financial exposure.
- Allows organizational and community members to feel confident that security officers are treating all people with dignity.
- Assures security officers that their protective-action decisions will be fairly evaluated.

Using Metrics as an Element of Accountability

One of the most challenging components of creating a fair and reliable protective force review process is determining an appropriate standard against which to measure its use. Two standards are generally used to evaluate protective action decision-making: hindsight and situational metrics. Unfortunately, the inevitability, unavoidability, and unpredictability of interpersonal workplace conflict create social, political, and financial pressures that often interfere with a fair evaluation process. These pressures often create a disincentive for senior stakeholders to defend their security officer's use of protective force (especially when they involve physical injuries). If security officers don't have faith in their organization's evaluation process, they become unproductive, consciously avoiding any interaction that may involve conflict, leading to decreases in personal and organizational safety.

In *Graham v. Connor* the courts codified what law enforcement officers knew for years preceding the decision: A hindsight use-of-force standard is unfair. Although the court's decision doesn't directly apply to private security officers, the courts' rationale should. The court ruled what seems obvious to anyone employed in any protective vocation that interacts with uncooperative, dangerous, and violent individuals: Field decision-making is much more complicated than office decision–making. The truth is that policies and procedures that guide behaviors for interacting with potentially violent individuals cannot be completely or perfectly defined and must allow officers to make choices based on the particular set of circumstances they face. Therefore, it's unfair to apply a hindsight standard to a security officer's protective-force choices.

From a business perspective, it's understandable that organizations would be reluctant to implement both situational use-of-protective force policies and a situational after-action review process. On one hand, a *situational* approach may seem to place employers in an impossible position for holding security officers accountable for their protective actions. On the other hand, it's unethical for organizations to create unrealistic standards against which to measure their security officer's actions. No matter how challenging it may be for organizations to find the proper balance between productivity and liability protection, organizations need to hold their security officers accountable using a fair evaluation process.

The Role of Review Boards in Accountability

Depending on the type and kind of subject interaction, it may be appropriate to utilize a protective-action review board to conduct an inquiry into the incident. Security officers who use protective force must justify and document its use, and their actions need to be subject to a review process. This process should be a thorough assessment of the circumstances and outcome of the officer's protective force decisions. This process should not be punitive or a *witch hunt*. This after-action evaluation also affords organizations an opportunity to access the effectiveness of their supervisory controls and their security officers' training.

Summary

Security officer accountability plays an important role in the success of an organization's workplace violence prevention program. To create violence-free workplaces, security officers will need to use protective tactics and tools to protect employees, consumers, visitors, and themselves. Systems of accountability need to include effective policies, training, supervisory controls, and a fair after-action review and reporting process. These processes ensure that the people who interact with an organization's security officers are treated fairly and provide a high level of confidence for security officers who may need to use protective action.

Recommendations

1. Create a culture of officer accountability.
2. Create a fair standard to evaluate a security officer's protective force choices.
3. Enact supervisory controls to monitor and enforce the organization's approved protective-force policies.
4. Require security officers to provide a full accounting, both verbally and in writing, whenever they're involved in incidents involving the use of protective force to resolve workplace conflict or to gain an individual's compliance.
5. Utilize a review board to ensure quality control for evaluating an officer's use of protective force.

Index

Printed in the United States
By Bookmasters